COLLINS GEM
CATS

COLLINS GEM
Chinese
ASTROLOGY

牛鼠
兔

COLLINS GEM
Classic
BOOKS

COLLINS GEM
Classic
FILMS

COLLINS
HORSES
& PONIES

D0727095

COLLINS GEM
MUSHROOMS
& TOADSTOOLS

COLLINS GEM
SNAKES

COLLINS GEM
SPIDERS

COLLINS GEM
STRESS
Survival Guide

COLLINS GEM
TAROT

COLLINS GEM
WINE
Guide

COLLINS GEM
WORLD
atlas

COLLINS GEM
YOGA

COLLINS GEM
ZODIAC
Types

COLLINS GEM
WINE
Dictionary

David Rowe

REFERENCE

WORCESTER COLLEGE
OF TECHNOLOGY

0103000

Acknowledgements

The author wishes to thank the following for reading
the manuscript of this revised and updated edition,
and for their many useful comments and suggestions:
Kathy Buckley, Harold Heckle, Stephen Hobley,
David Kingsbury, Roger Voss.

HarperCollins Publishers
PO Box, Glasgow G4 0NB

First published 1991
This edition published 1999

Reprint 10 9 8 7 6 5 4 3

© David Rowe 1991, 1999

ISBN 0 00 472202-7

Printed in Italy by Amadeus S.p.A.

Contents

Introduction

The *Gem Wine Dictionary* provides an extensive and easy-to-use introduction to the world's wines. The compact, pocket-size format makes it easy to consult at the supermarket or wine merchant, in a restaurant, or on holiday in wine-producing regions.

The bulk of the book consists of an A–Z section, which gives definitions for many of the terms found on wine labels. The entries are designed to help the newcomer to wine, faced with an unfamiliar bottle, to find out more about it – which grapes it is made from and what it is going to taste like. The introduction also explains how to store and serve wine, and which wines to drink with various foods.

The entries are thoroughly cross-referenced (cross-references appear in bold lettering), so it is possible to start with any term on a wine label. The label on a bottle of Rioja, from Spain, for instance, might say Rioja Reserva Denominación de Origen, Cosecha 1990, Produce of Spain. By looking up Rioja, the entry will give information on the wines of that region, how they are made, from which grape varieties, and what they taste like. Equally, the reader could start with *reserva, denominación de origen, cosecha,* or even Spain, and be led to the same information via the cross-references.

There has not been room to cover every possible wine-label term. If there is no entry for the first term chosen, try starting elsewhere on the label. This dictionary does not cover the names of individual wine-producing companies, or their trademarks.

The A–Z section also explains unfamiliar words used by wine writers in newspapers and the specialist wine press. Wine writers have their own vocabulary for describing wines, with many common words used in a special context. There are separate entries for the most commonly used tasting terms. There are also definitions of many of the specialist terms used by winemakers to describe special techniques and equipment.

A DEFINITION OF WINE

Wine is the fermented juice of the grape – a simple definition, because wine is the simplest and most natural of alcoholic drinks. With the presence of wild yeasts on the skin, and the sugar-rich juice of the grape, it only requires for the skin to be broken and to wait. However, within that simple definition there are seemingly infinite variations. The fascination and enjoyment of wine has endured through the centuries because no two wines are ever the same. All that is written and spoken about wine derives from the analysis of the factors that make one wine different from another.

Nearly all wine is made from the grapes of the *Vitis vinifera* species of vine, native to Europe and central Asia, but now widely planted throughout the world. Within this species, there are thousands of different grape varieties (or, more correctly, vine varieties), each producing wines with distinctively different tastes and characteristics. The choice of grape, either a single variety or a blend of several, has a profound effect on the taste of the wine produced. However, there are also many other factors at work.

The Pinot Noir grape variety, for instance, is planted in Burgundy, California and Romania (to name just three areas); and the wine produced in each region tastes appreciably different. Further, a wine made from grapes grown on a particular slope in Burgundy can be distinguished from one that has its origins only a few hundred yards away. Thus natural factors, such as regional climate, soil type, drainage and exposure of the vineyard to the sun, all have an effect on the taste of wine, as does the local climate (microclimate) of an individual vineyard site.

In most regions, the climate during the grape growing season is not identical from year to year, and so the vintage can also have an effect on the taste of wine produced.

Then there is the effect of the methods of production used by the wine-producer. Growers can allow each vine to produce as many grapes as possible, in which case the wine will taste relatively thin, or dilute. Alternatively, they can restrict the yield from each vine, so that the flavour and the nutrients from the soil are concentrated in fewer bunches of grapes, thereby producing a more flavourful and concentrated wine.

Once the grapes are harvested, winemakers can exert the most profound influence on the taste of the wine while it is in the winemaking cellar. They can make indiscriminate use of all the grapes available, or they can select only the ripest and most healthy. They can squeeze every last drop of juice out of the grapes, or use only the best-quality juice from a light pressing. Growers may allow yeasts that occur naturally on the grape skins to do their work, or alternatively use yeasts cultivated in a laboratory. They can also control the temperature of the fermentation. In some regions where grapes are deficient in natural sugar, more sugar may be added to achieve a satisfactory alcohol content.

Once the wine is made, the winemaker has the option of making a blend of wine from different grape varieties, or different parts of the vineyard.

HOW WINE IS MADE

The juice of nearly all grapes is white (the colour of red wine derives largely from the skins of red grapes rather than the juice). In making white wine, the first step is normally to crush and press the grapes and extract the colourless juice, which is then kept separate from the skins. The unfermented grape juice is then sometimes clarified to remove unwanted solids, either by cold settling, or by using a centrifuge or filter. Yeast can then be added to the juice, to begin its work of converting the sugar in the grape juice into alcohol. The two major by-products are carbon dioxide gas and heat.

Carbon dioxide is normally allowed to escape into the atmosphere. The heat produced during fermentation can be a problem. If uncontrolled it can mar the taste of the wine produced. Winemakers often go to great lengths to keep the fermenting juice cool. Various methods may be used, from leaving the cellar door open, to more sophisticated methods involving stainless-steel tanks with computer-controlled cooling systems.

Gradually, the sugar is converted into alcohol, and the juice becomes wine. In the case of dry wines, all the sugar is converted. In the production of sweet wines, the fermentation is stopped before all the sugar is fermented out, either naturally (once the alcohol content reaches a certain level), or by human intervention, such as chilling, filtering, or, to produce a fortified wine, by adding brandy.

After the first, alcoholic, fermentation is complete, the wine may undergo another transformation, called the malolactic fermentation. In this complex process, tart malic acid is converted into the smoother, softer lactic acid. Winemakers may encourage the malolactic fermentation, by warming the cellar, or they may avoid it altogether, depending on the style of wine desired.

Before it is bottled, the wine may undergo some period of maturation. This can range from storing the wine in huge stainless-steel vats, to ageing it in small oak barrels. All wine is aged to some extent, although the duration can vary from a few days in bottle (e.g. Beaujolais Nouveau), to decades in oak casks (e.g. Tawny Port). Ageing in oak barrels results in a controlled oxidation of the wine. If the barrels are small, and relatively new, the ageing process can also impart flavours and tannins to the wine, improving its potential to age further in bottle.

To make red and rosé wine, the unfermented grape juice
must be kept in contact with the skins. The grapes are
just lightly crushed, and the mixture of skins and juice is
placed in a fermentation vat. The length of skin contact,
or maceration, varies widely: it may be short – only a few
hours in the case of pale pink wines – or several weeks in
the case of a full-flavoured red. As well as colour, the
juice also picks up tannin from the skins and pips, an
essential component of a well-balanced red wine. If
some or all of the stalks are also included in the
fermentation vat, the wine will pick up more tannin and
bitterness.

When the winemaker has achieved the desired degree of
maceration, the skins are separated from the fermenting
juice and pressed. Some or all of the wine extracted from
this pressing, which is usually more bitter and tannic,
may be added back into the vat, or it may be disposed of
separately. Once the alcoholic fermentation is complete,
red wines usually undergo malolactic fermentation. A
period of ageing is then usual, more so than with whites,
before the red wine is bottled.

Sparkling wines are usually made by inducing a second
fermentation in still wine. This occurs in a closed vessel
so that the carbon dioxide gas produced cannot escape.
In the case of Champagne, and other quality sparkling
wines, the process is achieved by adding sugar and yeast
to a still wine in bottle, and then securing it with a tight-
fitting closure. The yeast turns the added sugar into
alcohol and carbon dioxide, but the gas cannot escape
this time; it is retained in the wine as bubbles. Once the

second fermentation is complete, a deposit of dead yeast cells forms in the bottle. This is removed by slowly shaking and turning the bottle over a period of weeks, while gradually moving it to a vertical, upside-down position in a specially designed rack. The yeast cells gather in the neck of the bottle. This is then plunged, still upside-down, into freezing brine, and a plug of wine and sediment freezes in the neck of the bottle. The cork is then removed, and the plug flies out under pressure, leaving a clear sparkling wine. After topping up, the bottle is re-stoppered, with a secure wired cork.

Alternatively, the second fermentation can take place in bulk, in a sealed vat, and the sparkling wine is bottled under pressure.

BOTTLE AGEING

Even after a wine is bottled, it is still developing and changing. Indeed, one of the hallmarks of a fine wine is that it has the potential to improve as it grows older.

Bottle ageing is a complex process, not fully understood. In the case of a red wine, the simple tannins of a young, purple red join together to form progressively longer chains, and the colour changes through shades of red and orange, eventually to brown. At the same time, the flavours soften and blend to produce a harmonious taste. After reaching its peak, which it may maintain for several years, a wine will go into irreversible decline if it is allowed to age further.

It is impossible to generalise about the correct length of

time to age a wine. Full-bodied reds which are often
found to improve with bottle age include the top wines
of Bordeaux, Burgundy, Barolo, Brunello di Montalcino,
New World Cabernets and Vintage Ports. The best
Champagnes often benefit from a year or two in bottle,
and Sauternes and sweet whites from the Loire and
Germany can benefit from prolonged ageing.

At a less grand level, even humble table wines, especially
reds, can benefit from a few months' ageing to soften
them. However, beware of losing the freshness of crisp,
light white wines, which is their very attraction.

STORING WINE

Most people buy wine as and when it is needed; a couple
of bottles for a dinner party the same day, or simply to
drink while enjoying a relaxing evening at home. Storage
is not really an important factor.

Once people get really interested in wine, however, they
soon start to build up a 'cellar', often without even re-
alising it at first. You may start by buying two bottles,
one to drink straight away, another to keep in reserve.
Or you may decide to save a bit of money by buying a
case of your favourite wine from the local wine
merchant or wine warehouse, instead of buying by the
bottle. And if you want to enjoy wines such as mature
Vintage Port and fine Claret, you may have to buy them
young and lay them down for years if you are to enjoy
them at their peak. Before you know it, your stocks will
outgrow the wine rack in the kitchen, or in the cupboard
under the stairs.

If you are going to keep wine for any length of time –
more than a few months – storage conditions become
important. If you have a basement or cellar, this is a
great asset. You can fit it out with wine racks from a
DIY store, or improvise using wooden pallets, or old
bookcases. The important thing is to keep the wine in an
environment where the temperature is at least stable,
and preferably cool. A cellar is ideal, because the
temperature is probably cool and fairly constant.
Humidity may be a problem: too dry, and the corks will
shrink; too damp, and all your labels may fall off
(although this will not affect the condition of the wine).

Most modern houses do not have cellars, so it is
necessary to look for alternatives. A spiral cellar can be
built into the living-room floor, but this is an expensive
option, and is only suitable for those who are sure that
they are not going to move house in the foreseeable
future. Instead use somewhere in the house – a broom-
cupboard, or a spare room, for instance – where your
wine can be left undisturbed, away from central heating
and bright lights. Certainly, wine should never be stored
near radiators; there is nothing it dislikes more than
being regularly heated up and cooled down. For the
same reason the loft, although it may seem an attractively
large and under-used space, is also a danger.

If your wine collection does outgrow the house, then the
only option may be to entrust it to a commercial cellar or
wine merchant – of course you will have to pay for this
privilege. In this case, make sure that your wine is
insured, at the full replacement cost, and that each case

is clearly labelled as belonging to you.

Wherever you store your wine, make sure that the
bottles are lying flat, because this will help to stop the
cork from drying out and letting oxygen into the bottle,
or letting wine leak out.

SERVING WINE

The first essential when it comes to serving wine is
temperature. Most people have at least a vague idea that
white wine should be served cold, and red wine at room
temperature. The full enjoyment of wine – in restaurants
as well as private homes – is often marred by serving it at
the wrong temperature.

For most white wines, one hour in the fridge is quite
sufficient, although the same effect can be achieved in
under 15 minutes in an ice bucket. If using an ice
bucket, be sure to fill it with a mixture of ice and water
as this will chill the wine far more efficiently than ice
alone. Less expensive wine often tastes better when it is
very cold, while good-quality wine can lose some of its
complexity if it is over chilled.

Tradition has it that red wine should be served *chambré,*
or at room temperature. However, rooms in most houses
are warmer now than they used to be, and red wine is
usually served too warm rather than too cold. If you
store your wine in a cool area, then bring it into a warm
room about one hour before serving. Never plunge it in
boiling water, microwave it, or put it by the fire. If
anything, err on the side of serving red wine too cool.

It will soon warm up in the glass; cooling it down in the glass is more difficult.

Some red wines, such as light Beaujolais and Loire reds, can taste better if lightly chilled; maybe 20 minutes or half an hour in the fridge. The same goes for Tawny Port.

Much nonsense is written and spoken about decanting. The main reason for decanting a wine is to separate it from any sediment that may have developed – which mainly affects red wines that have been in bottle for a considerable time. Some people decant wine 'to let it breathe', but it will aerate much more efficiently once it is poured into glasses.

Generally only Vintage Port and mature Claret, or similar old reds, really need to be decanted. Let the bottle stand upright for 24 hours. Take the cork out without moving the bottle more than is necessary. Then gently pour the contents into a decanter or carafe, always keeping an eye on the sediment gathering in the shoulder of the bottle. Only stop pouring when there seems to be a danger of some sediment coming out. If you wish, it is possible to filter the sediment using coffee-machine filter paper in a clean plastic or glass funnel.

The choice of glass is all too often neglected. For Champagne, use a flute, not a saucer-shaped glass. For chilled fino Sherry use the traditional Spanish *copita*. The appreciation of both reds and whites will be enhanced if you can see and smell the wine as well as taste it. So avoid decorative cut glass, and choose a plain, generously sized glass, preferably tapering inwards towards the top, to concentrate the aroma, and do not fill it right up to the brim. Needless to say, the glass should be clean. However, any residual traces of detergent will kill the fizz in any sparkling wine, so use as little as possible, and rinse the glass thoroughly.

WINE WITH FOOD

The hard and fast rule about matching wine with food is that there is no hard and fast rule. The great thing is to experiment. Do not be afraid to drink red wine with fish – it can be delicious. On the other hand, avoid making it too difficult for a fine wine by matching it with a vindaloo curry.

Apart from such obvious pitfalls as a curry, some apparently innocuous foods can pose problems. Eggs, for example, deaden the palate and spoil the appreciation of the subtleties of a fine wine. Certain green vegetables, such as artichokes, sorrel and spinach, can prove difficult to match. Their flavours react with the wine, producing an undesirable, metallic taste. Vinegar in large amounts will kill the taste of any good wine, causing the wine itself to taste vinegary. If a salad is to be served dress it with oil and wine, or prepare a vinaigrette with a sparing measure of mellow balsamic vinegar. Similarly, citrus fruit should also be avoided if a wine is to be fully appreciated.

An aperitif should freshen the palate, and start the gastric juices running. Champagne, or another sparkling wine, is a good bet, as is fino Sherry – or you can serve any bone-dry, light white wine.

In matching wine with food, there are two schools of thought: matching like with like (a rich pâté of foie gras with a rich, sweet Gewürztraminer or Sauternes); and providing contrast (rich, fatty meat, cut by the acidity of a lean, bone-dry, fruity white). Both can be successful, and you can use both within the same meal. Avoid overwhelming delicate dishes with powerful wines, and vice versa.

Light soups, or consommés, can be partnered by fresh, light whites, or dry Sherry or Madeira, and the latter can cope with really strong and spicy tastes. Seafood needs crisp whites with plenty of acidity: Muscadet and oysters is a great combination. Delicate fish calls for delicate wine: a dry, gently flavoured Riesling, for example. Stronger tasting fish can cope with fuller whites, or even light reds.

With poultry, the choice of wine depends partly on the method of cooking. Chicken poached in white wine can be enjoyed with the same wine as was used for cooking (never cook with a wine you would not drink). With poultry cooked in red wine, on the other hand, you could try a red Burgundy, or a Pinot Noir from the New World. Red Burgundy and Claret also go well with roast birds, particularly turkey, and with well-hung game.

Pork, like veal, provides an accommodating background for both reds and whites. The acidity of a light, fresh red, with plenty of zest, or a fruity white, such as German

Riesling or Loire Chenin Blanc, will help offset any
fattiness.

Red meat dishes are generally well-matched by smooth
red Burgundy, which has the necessary power to cut
through any creamy sauce. The firmer, more tannic reds
of Bordeaux marry better with the direct flavours of a
plain roast. Game or casseroles are best with an equally
warming, robust red, such as a Rhône or Italy's Barolo.
The permutations are endless, but the basic object is to
match wine and food of compatible weight and intensity
of flavour.

Cheese can be a great friend and a great enemy. There is
a saying in the wine trade, 'Buy on apples, sell on
cheese', meaning that tasting a wine after having eaten a
tart, green apple exaggerates its faults; tasting the same
wine after having eaten a lump of cheese hides them. In
general, all but the mildest cheeses will overwhelm a fine
red wine. Sweet whites, such as Sauternes and sweet
Loire whites made from the Chenin Blanc grape, can
make a perfect match for salty, strong cheeses, like
Roquefort. And the combination of Port with fine
Stilton or Cheddar is a marriage made in heaven.

Puddings are a great danger. The term 'dessert wine' for
sweet whites is a bit of a misnomer, because they are
rarely a match for sweet food. And if there is chocolate
around, it is difficult to find any wine to match.

List of maps

abboccato Term found on Italian labels meaning 'medium-sweet'. It is used particularly for **Orvieto** wines, which may be **secco** (dry) or *abboccato*. See also **amabile**; **dolce**.

abocado Term found on Spanish labels meaning 'medium-sweet'. See also **dulce**; **seco**.

Abruzzo Wild and mountainous wine region in the east of central **Italy**. The region's best red is the deep, fruity **Montepulciano** d'Abruzzo (not to be confused with **Vino Nobile di Montepulciano**). The white wine of the region, **Trebbiano d'Abruzzo** (made from a local **clone** of the **Trebbiano** grape known as **Bombino**), is usually no better than a good, if rather neutral, quaffing wine.

AC (*appellation contrôlée*, also called **AOC**) Part of the French system that guarantees the origin of a wine from a demarcated area; its specific purpose is to guarantee authenticity, though it protects the producer more than the consumer. French wines are placed into three main categories, of which AC is the highest, followed by **VDQS**, and **vin de table** (see also **vin de pays**). Within regions there can be a hierarchy of *appellations*; in **Bordeaux**, for instance, there are generic ACs (e.g. AC **Bordeaux**), subregional ACs (e.g. AC **Médoc**), and, at the top, village ACs (e.g. AC **Pauillac**). In general, the laws of any AC control the following: the area entitled to the name; permitted grape varieties; density of vine plants; minimum **alcohol** levels; **yields**. The wine must be analysed and tasted before the **AC** is granted.

acetaldehyde (also called ethanal) Chemical substance formed in wine by the **oxidation** of **alcohol**. It is desirable in **Fino Sherry**, and other **flor** wines, but undesirable, if it can be tasted, in **table wines**. Acetaldehyde can be further **oxidized** to **acetic acid**.

acetic Tasting term used to describe a wine that is sharp, sour and tastes of vinegar. See also **acetic acid**.

acetic acid (also called ethanoic acid) Chemical substance formed in wine by the **oxidation** of **alcohol**. It is present in all wines in trace quantities, and is sometimes referred to as the **volatile acidity**. Too much acetic acid is a fault, and gives the wine an unpleasant, **acetic** taste.

acidity Integral component of a wine, which greatly affects its taste. The total acidity of a wine is the sum of its **volatile acidity** and fixed acidity. Volatile acidity refers to the presence of **acetic acid** (undesirable in excess), and fixed acidity is mainly composed of tartaric and malic acid (and small quantities of citric acid); see **acids**.

It is also used as a complimentary tasting term, particularly used to describe a dry white wine with a refreshing crispness on the **palate**. It is also desirable as a foil to the sweetness in dessert wines. See also **flabby**.

acids Essential components in all wines. The 'fixed' acids, such as tartaric, malic and citric, come largely from the grape. Malic acid is transformed into the softer lactic acid during the **malolactic fermentation** that occurs in many wines after the alcoholic **fermentation**. These acids give a wine crispness and bite and can aid cellaring potential. See also **acetic acid**.

adega Portuguese term for a wine-making **cellar**, similar to the Spanish **bodega**.

Adelaide Hills Cool-climate wine-growing region in **South Australia** producing good quality red and white **varietals**.

aftertaste Tasting term that describes the sensation, pleasant or otherwise, that is left in the mouth after the wine has been swallowed (or spat out). The intensity and duration of the aftertaste is described as the **length**. A long and pleasant aftertaste is one of the hallmarks of a great wine.

ageing All wine is 'aged' to some extent, although the duration can vary from a few days in bottle, e.g. **Beaujolais** Nouveau, to decades in **oak** casks, e.g. **Tawny Port**. Ageing in oak barrels results in a controlled **oxidation** of the wine. If the barrels are relatively new, the ageing process can also impart flavours and tannins to the wine, improving its potential to age further in bottle.

Bottle ageing is a more complicated process. In the case of a red wine, the simple **tannin** molecules of a young, purple red join together to form progressively longer chains, and the colour changes through shades of red and orange, eventually to brown. At the same time the flavours soften and meld to produce a harmonious taste. The tannins and colouring matter eventually precipitate in the form of sediment. After reaching its peak a wine will go into irreversible decline with further ageing.

It is impossible to generalize about the correct length of time to age a wine. Full-bodied reds that are often found to improve with **bottle age** include the top wines of **Bordeaux**, **Burgundy**, **Barolo**, **Brunello di Montalcino**, New World Cabernets and Vintage **Ports**. The best **Champagnes** often benefit from a year or two in bottle, and **Sauternes** and sweet whites from the **Loire** can also benefit from prolonged ageing.

Agiorgitiko (St George) Greek grape variety producing smooth, softly fruity reds, particularly in Nemea.

aggressive Tasting term, usually pejorative, that describes the effect of excessive **tannin** or **acidity** on the **palate**. However, a red wine that is aggressive in its youth may become more mellow with age. Aggressive young white wines, e.g. **Loire**, **Champagne** or German, may also soften and improve with age.

Aglianico Top-quality red grape variety of southern **Italy**, used to make deep-coloured, intensely flavoured wines such as **Taurasi** in **Campania**, and **Aglianico del Vulture** in **Basilicata**.

Aglianico del Vulture Full-bodied, red Italian **DOC** wine made from the **Aglianico** grape in the hills surrounding the Monte Vulture, **Basilicata**. The wine can be excellent but unfortunately rarely is.

aguardente Neutral grape spirit (usually 77% **alcohol**) used to fortify **Port**. *Aguardiente*, with an 'i', is the Spanish equivalent.

Ahr Small wine region, or **Anbaugebiet**, in Northern **Germany**. Two-thirds of its production is of light, red wines, which may be dry or sweet, made from the **Spätburgunder** (the best) and **Portugieser** grapes. The remainder is largely white from **Riesling** and **Müller-Thurgau**. There is one **Bereich** and one **Grosslage**, Klosterberg, covering the region.

Airén Most widely planted grape variety of **Spain**. It is found particularly in **La Mancha** and **Valdepeñas**, where it is used to produce vast quantities of rather ordinary white wine, some distilled to make Spanish Brandy. It was also traditionally blended with local reds. With the use of modern winemaking techniques it can make fresh, fruity, gently **aromatic** whites.

Aix-en-Provence See **Coteaux d'Aix-en-Provence**.

Ajaccio AC wine of **Corsica** that may be red, rosé, or occasionally white. The reds are based on the **Sciacarello** grape, and the whites on **Malvoisie** de Corse.

Alameda Wine-producing county in **California** to the east of San Francisco, whose most important **AVA** is the Livermore Valley. It produces mainly good-quality white **varietals**, such as **Sauvignon Blanc** and **Sémillon**.

Alba Town in **Piedmont**, **Italy**, and the region where

Barolo, **Barbaresco**, **Nebbiolo d'Alba**, **Barbera** d'Alba and **Dolcetto** d'Alba are produced.

Albalonga White German grape variety that is a **cross** of **Silvaner** and **Riesling**. It is grown mainly in the **Rheinhessen**, where it produces fruity, zesty white wines.

Albana Italian grape variety grown mainly in **Emilia-Romagna**, where it is used to produce the white **DOCG** wine **Albana di Romagna**.

Albana di Romagna White Italian **DOCG** wine, produced in **Emilia-Romagna**. It can be dry, medium, or sweet, still or sparkling. At its best the dry version is creamy and nutty, if rather neutral. The sweet Albana shows more potential. Quality is variable, and the granting of the DOCG in 1986 – the first for a white wine – was controversial.

Albania European wine-producing country bordering on **Greece** and the former Yugoslavia. Relatively small volumes of wine are produced from Cabernet, **Welschriesling**, and **Mavrud**, little of it of acceptable quality for export markets.

Albariño White Spanish grape variety grown in **Galicia**, producing fresh, crisp, sometimes peachy whites. See also **Alvarinho**.

albariza Finest of the three soil types of the **Sherry** region around the town of Jerez de la Frontera, near Càdiz in **Spain**. The white colour of this chalky soil helps the grapes to ripen by reflecting sunlight, and the chalk has good water-retention properties. Also found in parts of **Penedès**.

alberello Italian term meaning **bush vine**.

Albillo Spanish grape variety producing neutral white wine.

Alcamo (also called Bianco d'Alcamo) A dry white Italian **DOC** wine produced in western **Sicily** around the town of Alcamo, from the **Catarratto** grape.

alcohol (also called **ethanol**) Colourless, inflammable liquid. It is naturally present in all wine, and is produced by the action of **yeast** on sugar from the grapes (**fermentation**). Although alcohol is colourless and odourless, it does have a slightly sweet taste in its pure form. But the main tasting sensation from alcohol is a warm, even hot, feeling in the mouth.

alcohol content Amount of **alcohol** present in a wine, usually expressed as a percentage by volume. '12% Vol' means that 12% of the volume of the wine is pure alcohol. A glass of **Port**, at 20% alcohol by volume, will have twice the intoxicating effect of the same sized glass of **table wine**, at 10%. For comparison, the most common spirits are 40% or 43%.

aldehydes Class of organic chemical compounds sometimes found in wine, of which the most common is **acetaldehyde**.

Aleatico Native Italian red grape variety used to make dark, rich, sometimes sweet wines in **Latium** (e.g. Aleatico di Gradoli) and **Apulia** (e.g. Aleatico di Puglia). It is also found on the island of **Elba**, around the villages of Portoferraio and Lacona. Outside **Italy**, it is also planted in **Chile**, **Australia**, and **California**.

Alella DO wine from north of Barcelona in Catalonia, **Spain**. Mainly white wine is produced, but some red and rosé is also made. The whites come largely from **Xarel-lo** and **Garnacha** Blanca grapes, together with some varieties new to the region, including **Chenin Blanc** and **Chardonnay**. The whites may be dry (**seco**) or medium-sweet (**semi-seco**), and still or sparkling (**Cava**). Much of the former vineyard area has been built on, and the wines are rarely better than dull.

Alentejo Vast demarcated wine region in southern **Portugal**. It produces strong white wines, from the Roupeiro grape, and full-bodied reds, mainly from **Periquita**, Aragonez, and Moreto. The quality of the wines, particularly of the reds, is increasing fast. The region is also an important source of **cork**.

Alexander Valley AVA of **Sonoma** county, **California**.

Alezio Small **DOC** region around Gallípoli in **Apulia**, **Italy**. It produces mainly red and some **rosato** wines from the **Negroamaro** and **Malvasia** Nera grapes. The *rosato* can rank along with the best rosé wines of Italy, and overall quality is improving rapidly.

Algarve Southernmost, coastal wine region of **Portugal**. It produces mainly low-quality, high-**alcohol**

reds from **Tinta Negra Mole**, Trincadeira and **Periquita** grapes, and undistinguished fortified whites.

Algeria North Africa's major wine-producing country. Under French occupation Algeria made vast quantities of full-bodied, red wine, some of it ending up in French bottles. Today, with the French gone, the vineyard area has been reduced and some former wine-producing vineyards have been given over to table grape production. However, what is left can produce acceptable reds made from **Cinsault**, **Grenache**, **Mourvèdre**, **Syrah**, **Carignan**, **Alicante Bouschet** and **Cabernet Sauvignon**. The whites, from **Ugni Blanc** and **Clairette**, are undistinguished. The main wine regions are in Alger ('Aïn Bessem-Bouira, Medea and Coteaux du Zaccar) and Oran (Mostagenem, Coteaux de Mascara, Haut-Dahra, Monts du Tessalah and Coteaux du Tlemcen).

Alicante DO region on the Mediterranean coast of **Spain**. The DO includes the town of Alicante, although most of the vineyards are just inland, in the Upper Vinalopo hills. Most of the wine produced is deep-coloured, high-**alcohol** red from the **Monastrell** grape, which is better used for blending than drinking on its own. Sweet white wine is produced from the **Moscatel** grape, and undistinguished dry white from **Merseguera** and **Airén**.

Alicante Bouschet **Teinturier**, red-fleshed grape, a **cross** of **Grenache** and Petit Bouschet (itself a crossing of **Aramon** and Teinturier du Cher). It is widely planted in the **Languedoc-Roussillon**, **France**, as well as in North Africa and **California**, and good results have been obtained in the **Alentejo**, **Portugal**. In France it is mainly used to add colour to pale reds made from the **Aramon** grape and to boost colour in certain **AC** wines in difficult years.

Aligoté White grape variety of **Burgundy**, playing second fiddle to **Chardonnay**. It produces fresh, lemony, often sharply acidic wines, traditionally used in **kir**, and is usually planted on the poorer sites in Burgundy and sold as **AC Bourgogne** Aligoté. The best examples come from **Bouzeron**, the northernmost village of the **Côte Chalonnaise** which has its own *appellation*, and from the villages of Saint-Bris-le-Vineux and Chitry-le-Fort near **Chablis**. Aligoté is also grown to produce **varietal** wines in **Bulgaria**, **Moldova**, **Russia**, and **Chile**.

Allier Forested department in central **France** where some of the best **oak** is grown for making wine barrels. The oak's dense, narrow-grained wood has a high phenol content, which imparts a straw flavour; it has a particular affinity with **Cabernet Sauvignon**. See also **Limousin**; **Nevers**.

almacenista Small-scale maturer of **Sherry**, who buys wine from small producers, ages it, and then sells it, usually to a larger **bodega**, for blending.

Almansa DO region of southeast **Spain**, near **Jumilla** and **Yecla**, that produces mainly full-bodied, high-alcohol red wine from **Garnacha** Tintorera (a red-juiced **teinturier** variety) and **Monastrell** grapes. Its white wines, from the **Merseguera** grape, are of low quality.

almond Tasting term that can be complimentary when referring to a pleasant almond-paste smell in white wine, or pejorative when the smell is of bitter almonds, which usually indicates a winemaking fault.

almude Unit of measurement in the **Port** trade, equal to 25.4 litres. One **pipe** is equivalent to 21 *almudes*, and there are about 12 **canadas** (of 2.1 litres) in one *almude*. The origin of these strange measures is said to have been that an ox-cart could pull a *pipe*, an *almude* could be carried on a man's head and a *canada* was the right amount for a man to drink.

Aloxe-Corton Village and *appellation* at the northern end of the **Côte de Beaune**, **Burgundy**. It produces mainly red wine from **Pinot Noir** and some white from **Chardonnay**. It can produce among the finest of red Burgundies, although the very best wines do not bear the name Aloxe-Corton.

The two **grands crus** are **Corton** (mainly red) and **Corton-Charlemagne** (white), both producing rich, top-quality, long-lived wines. These *grands crus* are shared with the neighbouring villages of **Pernand-Vergelesses** and **Ladoix-Serrigny**, and the latter also includes some vineyards classified as Aloxe-Corton *cru*. The **premiers crus** are not of the same depth and richness as the *grands crus*, but they can be fine and elegant, while the communal wines, sold as **AC** Aloxe-Corton, have less style.

Alsace Region in northeast **France**, between the Vosges mountains and the Rhine, which was once part of

Germany. It produces mainly white wines from single grape varieties. The best are **Riesling** and **Gewürztraminer**, followed by **Pinot Blanc**, **Pinot Gris**, **Muscat**, **Sylvaner**, and **Chasselas**. The reds, usually light, are made from **Pinot Noir**. The whites range from dry, scented wines to rich, intense **vendanges tardives**, made from late-harvested grapes, and **Sélection de Grains Nobles**, made from grapes affected by **botrytis**.

Most Alsace wines are plain **AC** Alsace, though there is a classification of **grands crus**, specially selected and supposedly superior sites. **Edelzwicker** is a blend of several of the lesser white-wine grape varieties. **Crémant d'Alsace** is the region's sparkling wine. Quality can be sublimely good for the top Rieslings and Gewürztraminers, and it is rare to find a poor bottle of any Alsace wine on export markets. There is, however, a large volume of cheap, inferior Alsatian wine on sale on the domestic market.

Alsheim Village between Worms and **Oppenheim**, in the **Rheinhessen**, **Germany**. It produces high-quality white wines from the **Riesling** grape. The best, sloping vineyard sites are in the **Grosslage** Rheinblick, and its best-known **Einzellage** is Fühmesse. The flatter land is in the Krötenbrunnen *Grosslage*.

Altenbamberg Village in the Burgweg **Grosslage** of the **Nahe**, **Germany**, on the River Alsenz (a tributary of the Nahe). It produces excellent white wines from the **Riesling** grape.

Altesse (also called Roussette) Grape variety found mainly in Savoie, **France**, which produces dry, full-bodied, spicy, **aromatic** whites. It is the basis of the still and sparkling **AC Seyssel** wines. It is entitled to the Roussette de Savoie *appellation*, under which it may be blended with other varieties including **Chardonnay**. Altesse is also grown in **Bugey**.

Alto Adige (also called Südtirol) Most northern wine region of **Italy**. It was formerly part of **Austria**, and is known to its German-speaking population as Südtirol (South Tyrol). More than half the wine produced is red, much of it from the native **Schiava** (Vernatsch) grape, which gives light, scented wines with a soft fruity taste. French red grapes are also important here, particularly the **Cabernets** and **Merlot**, which produce herbaceous reds with **ageing** potential, and Pinot Nero which is increasingly successful and fashionable here.

The crisp, fruity dry whites of Alto Adige are made from French and German varieties, including Pinot Grigio (**Rülander**), **Chardonnay**, Pinot Bianco (**Weissburgunder**), **Riesling Renano** (**Rhine Riesling**), **Silvaner**, **Müller-Thurgau**, and **Traminer**. For the other DOCs of the region see **Colli di Bolzano**; Lago di **Caldaro**; **Santa Maddalena**; **Terlano**; **Valle Isarco**.

Alvarinho Portuguese white grape variety, probably the best of the **Vinho Verde** region. It is grown in and around Monção, near the Spanish border in the north of the region, where it produces the Vinho Verde's only single-variety wine, fresh, crisp, and sometimes peachy. See also **Albariño**.

amabile Term found on Italian labels. It indicates a sweet wine, sweeter and fuller-bodied than **abboccato**.

Amador County Wine area in the **Sierra Foothills** region of eastern **California**. It produces mainly rich, heady red wines from the **Zinfandel** grape, together with smaller quantities of **Cabernet Sauvignon**, **Sauvignon Blanc**, **Chardonnay** and **Chenin Blanc**. **AVAs** include **Fiddletown** and Shenandoah Valley.

Amarone Unusual bitter-sweet, raisiny **DOC** red wine made by the **passito** method in **Valpolicella**, **Italy**. About 10 days before the normal vintage, carefully selected grapes (of the usual Valpolicella varieties), are laid out on straw mats, in a dry, airy room. They are allowed to dry until January, when the shrivelled grapes are crushed and fermented slowly in wooden barrels. Some barrels stop fermenting at around 13% **alcohol** with some **residual sugar**, and become **Recioto della Valpolicella**. Others continue to ferment to dryness, reaching around 15-16% alcohol, producing the strong, bitter-sweet Amarone. The wines are produced in limited quantities; their quality can be stunningly good, with a long **ageing** potential. Amarone has seen a boom in recent years, leading to a dearth of plain Valpolicella.

American oak Species of **oak** used in barrel manufacture, cheaper than French oak. See **oak**.

amontillado Name given to a completely dry, nutty **Sherry**, with an amber colour. It results when a **fino** is allowed to mature without being refreshed with younger wines. Less-expensive, medium-sweet Sherries are often described as *amontillado*, but in fact these are sweetened blends containing only a small amount of true *amontillado*.

ampelography Science of studying and identifying grape varieties, usually from leaf, berry, or bunch characteristics.

Ampurdán-Costa Brava DO region of Catalonia, in northeastern **Spain**. It produces very ordinary **rosado** wine from the **Cariñena** and **Garnacha** grapes, mainly for consumption by holiday-makers on the Costa Brava. Sweet, fortified red wines are also produced, together with heavy reds and semi-sparkling and sparkling whites.

Amtliche Prüfungsnummer See **AP Nr**.

Anbaugebiet Term used in German wine law to indicate the 13 major quality regions: **Ahr**, **Baden**, **Franken**, **Hessische Bergstrasse**, **Mittelrhein**, **Mosel-Saar-Ruwer**, **Nahe**, **Rheingau**, **Rheinhessen**, **Pfalz**, **Saale-Unstrut**, Sachsen, and **Württemberg**. The name of the *Anbaugebiet* must appear on the label of a quality wine. Each can be further subdivided into **Bereich**, **Grosslage** (or **Ursprungslage**) and **Einzellage**. See **QbA**.

Andalucía (Andalusia) Southern region of **Spain**, where **Sherry**, **Montilla-Moriles**, **Málaga**, and Condado de Huelva are produced.

Anderson Valley Cool wine region of **Mendocino** County, **California**, that is well-suited to growing **Pinot Noir**, **Chardonnay**, **Gewürztraminer**, and **Riesling**. It is rapidly gaining a reputation as a good area for sparkling wine produced from Pinot Noir and Chardonnay.

Anjou-Saumur Region of the **Loire** valley, **France**, centred on the town of Angers. Most of the production is of rosé wine, from **Grolleau** (e.g. **AC Rosé d'Anjou**) or, much better, from **Cabernet Franc** grapes (e.g. AC **Cabernet d'Anjou**). There are also large quantities of red and white AC Anjou made from **Gamay** or **Cabernet Franc** (reds) or **Chenin Blanc** (whites).

The Anjou-Villages *appellation* applies to 46 villages in Anjou. They produce red wines made from **Cabernet Franc** and **Cabernet Sauvignon**, and the quality is generally better than straight AC Anjou **Rouge**. The greatest wines of the region are, however, dry whites (e.g. **Savennières**), sweet whites (e.g. **Coteaux du Layon**, **Quarts de Chaume**, and **Bonnezeaux**) made from **Chenin Blanc**, and fine reds from **Cabernet Franc** in the **Saumur-Champigny** *appellation*.

The production of the **Loire**'s finest **méthode traditionnelle** white wine, **Saumur** – made chiefly from **Chenin Blanc** but increasingly featuring **Chardonnay** – is centred on the town of Saumur.

annata Italian for year

AOC (*Appellation d'Origine Contrôlée*) See **AC**.

Aosta See **Valle d'Aosta**.

AP Nr (Amptliche Prüfungsnummer) Number given to quality German wines to indicate that they have undergone an official blind tasting and chemical analysis. Although all quality wines must undergo the AP test, it is very rare for any to fail, so it is of limited use as a system of quality control.

appellation contrôlée See **AC**.

apple Tasting term used to indicate the smell or taste of apples. It may describe the tartness of green apples, as in an immature wine, or the old-apple smell of some mature whites (often due to the presence of malic **acid**).

Approved Viticultural Area See **AVA**.

Apremont Named **cru** of the **Vin de Savoie** appellation. The wines are mainly dry, biting whites, made from **Jacquère** and **Chardonnay** grapes.

Aprilia DOC region south of Rome, in **Latium**, **Italy**. It produces reasonable-quality, soft reds from the **Merlot** grape, dull reds from **Sangiovese**, and dull, dry whites from **Trebbiano**.

Apulia (also called Puglia) Region in southern **Italy**, which produces a vast quantity of **table wine**, and only 2% **DOC** wine. In the Salento peninsula, in the south of the region, the main grapes are **Negroamaro** and **Malvasia** Nera, which are used to make red and rosé DOC wines and **vino da tavola**. The DOCs based on these two grapes include **Alezio**, **Brindisi**, **Copertino**, **Leverano** (which are also whites), Matino, **Salice**

Salentino and **Squinzano**.

In the north, the **Uva di Troia** grape is the most important for reds, often blended with **Sangiovese** and **Bombino** Nero. The best DOCs are **Castel del Monte** (red, white and rosé) and Rosso di Cerignola (red). Cacc'e Mmitte di Lucera, **Rosso Barletta** and **Rosso Canosa** are rarely good.

The **Primitivo** grape is used to make **Primitivo di Manduria**, a big, deep red which may be dry or sweet and may be fortified. A curious red dessert wine, which may or may not be fortified, is made throughout Apulia from the **Aleatico** grape. The best white DOC of the region is **Locorotondo**, made from the Verdeca and **Bianco d'Alessano** grapes. These wines are dry and fruity, and can be still or sparkling. DOC **Martina Franca** is similar, and the white DOC wine Gravina is based on the Verdeca grape. Some adventurous producers have made successful wines from French grapes, particularly **Chardonnay**, **Cabernet Franc**, **Pinot Noir** and **Pinot Blanc**.

Apulia is an increasingly important source of reliable quaffing wines for supermarkets, often under the new **IGT** category.

Aquileia DOC region of **Friuli-Venezia Giulia** in **Italy**. It produces fruity, soft, good-quality reds from the native **Refosco** grape, and light, but less-successful reds from **Merlot**, **Cabernet Franc**, and **Cabernet Sauvignon**. Fairly ordinary whites are made from Pinot Grigio, Pinot Bianco and **Riesling Renano**, as well as delicate, light whites from the native varieties **Tocai Friulano**,

Traminer, and **Verduzzo Friulano**. A light, dry **rosato** is also produced, mainly from the Merlot grape.

Aramon Very high-yielding red grape, still extensively grown in the **Midi**, **France**, but declining in popularity. When yields are high, it produces a very thin, pale wine, which must be blended with deeply-coloured **teinturier** varieties such as **Alicante Bouschet**.

Arbin Named **cru** of the **Vin de Savoie** *appellation*. The **Mondeuse Noire** grape can produce good quality, smoky, beefy reds.

Arbois 1. **AC** wine of the **Jura** region of **France**. It may be red, white, or rosé, still or sparkling. The most important grape variety for the reds is **Trousseau**, which produces distinctive, flavourful wines of a good quality. Also used are **Pinot Noir** and **Poulsard**, which produce more delicate reds. **Savagnin** is the local white variety, occasionally softened with **Chardonnay**, which makes distinctive, nutty sweet-sour whites. See also **vin jaune**. 2. White grape variety (also known as Menu Pineau) grown in the **Loire** valley, France, where it is used to make the white wines of **Valençay** and as part of the blend in **Cheverny**.

are Unit of area, equal to 100 m². There are 100 ares in 1 **hectare** (2.47 acres).

Argentina Highest-volume wine-producing country of South America. Most of the wine has been consumed on the home market, though exports are increasingly important. The potential to produce wines as fine as those of **Chile** is now being realized. Most of the vineyards are situated in the foothills of the Andes, mainly in **Mendoza** (sub-divided into the main region, around Mendoza city; Tupungato; and San Rafael). Other important regions are Salta, La Rioja, Rio Negro, and San Juan.

The country's wine industry had its origins in the 16th century, when the Jesuits planted **Vitis vinifera** vine varieties. The country's most widely planted grapes today, **Criolla** and **Cereza**, are thought to be descended from these vines, and Criolla may be the same as Chile's **País**. It yields basic, ordinary **table wine**. **Torrontés** is also widely planted, and produces **aromatic** whites. Among the reds, **Bonarda** is widely planted, producing soft, fruity reds, as is the **Tempranillo** of **Spain** (here called *Tempranilla*).

'Foreign' varieties are increasingly important. **Malbec** produces better wines here than in its home in **Bordeaux**, deeply coloured, fruity, and well-structured. **Cabernet Sauvignon**, **Chardonnay**, **Chenin Blanc**, **Merlot**, and **Pinot Noir** are all grown successfully.

Arinto White-wine grape variety of **Portugal**, and the main component of **Bucelas**. It yields wines of high **acidity** and little flavour when young, although complexity can develop with age.

Armenia Minor wine-producing country on **Turkey**'s north east border. Most vineyards are planted on the Ararat plain, producing mainly strong white wines and brandy from local grape varieties such as **Rkatsiteli**.

Arneis White grape variety grown in **Piedmont**, **Italy**. It produces dry, nutty, full-bodied white wines of increasingly good quality, which are best drunk young. It makes a **DOC** wine in Arneis del **Roero**.

aroma Tasting term used loosely to mean the smell of the wine, and more correctly to describe the smells deriving from the grape and from the **fermentation** process. See also **bouquet**.

aromatic Tasting term used to indicate a fragrant-smelling wine, particularly one made from grapes such as **Muscat** or **Gewürztraminer**.

arrope Spanish term for a dark-coloured, caramelized grape concentrate, made by boiling grape juice. It is mixed with more **must** and then fermented to make **vino de color**, which is the colouring agent in brown **Sherry** and **Málaga**.

Arroyo Grande Valley AVA in the **San Luis Obispo** area of **California**. It is important for the production of sparkling wines from **Chardonnay**, **Pinot Noir** and **Pinot Blanc**.

Arroyo Seco AVA in Monterey county, **California**, stretching from Soledad south to Greenfield. The soil, containing large, grapefruit-sized stones, produces some of the county's finest **Chardonnay** and **Riesling**. **Cabernet Sauvignon** and **Sauvignon Blanc** are also planted, and the region is also a source of grapes for making sparkling wine.

Arvine White grape of the Valais district of **Switzerland**, best suited to producing sweet wines.

ascorbic acid (vitamin C) Anti-oxidant, used in winemaking as a useful adjunct to **sulphur dioxide**.

Asprino (also called Asprinio) White grape used to make a dry, white, **frizzante** wine of the same name in **Basilicata** and **Campania**, southern **Italy**. The wine lacks character, and is mainly gulped down as a thirst-quencher in the bars of Naples.

assaggio Italian term for a wine tasting.

assemblage French term used to describe the process of blending wines. It is particularly used in **Bordeaux**, where vats of wine from different parts of the vineyard, and different grape varieties, are blended to 'assemble' the wine before **ageing** in **oak** barrels. The exclusion of inferior vats from the assemblage, or 'selection', is one of the keys to producing great red **Bordeaux**.

Assmannshausen Wine village in the **Rheingau**, **Germany**, situated in the **Grosslage** of Steil. It is famous for its red wines produced from **Spätburgunder** (**Pinot Noir**), which may be dry or sweet.

Assyrtiko Good-quality, high-acid, white grape variety from **Greece**. It is grown on the island of **Santorini**, where it is one of the main ingredients in the island's white wine. The high **acidity** is sometimes exploited by blending Assyrtiko with the low-**acidity** Savatiano.

Asti (formerly Asti Spumante) Sweet sparkling white **DOCG** wine of **Piedmont**, **Italy** (much the largest DOCG in volume terms). It is made from the **Moscato** grape, grown in the Langhe and Alto Monferrato hills. The grape juice is allowed to ferment to 4–5% **alcohol** and then chilled to stop **fermentation**. The fermentation is re-started in sealed stainless-steel tanks, so that the bubbles of **carbon dioxide** produced are trapped in the wine, and it is then bottled under pressure. The resulting wine is low in alcohol (7.5–9%), delicately sweet, **aromatic**, grapey and thirst-quenching. It is ideal for drinking outdoors on a summer day.

astringent Tasting term for a dry, mouth-puckering feeling on the **palate**. It is caused by excess **tannin** or **acidity**, usually encountered in young red wines. A young wine may become less astringent as it matures.

Aszú Hungarian term for grapes affected by **botrytis**, and used specifically in the production of Tokaji *Aszú* (see **Tokaji**).

Attica Wine region around Athens, **Greece**, which is the source of the best **Retsina**, made from the Savatiano grape.

Aube Southernmost region of **Champagne**. Its vineyards are planted mainly with **Pinot Noir** and **Chardonnay** grapes. The resulting rich and fruity wine is often considered inferior to that obtained from the Marne, further north. Much of it is sold by growers to the Champagne houses for blending, although some Aube growers bottle their own Champagne.

Ausbruch Rich and raisiny white wine category peculiar to **Austria**, with a **must weight** of 138 **Oechsle** (between **Beerenauslese** and **Trockenbeerenauslese**). The rich grapes, which are affected with **botrytis**, are moistened with **Spätlese** juice before pressing.

Auslese German and Austrian quality white wine category, meaning 'selected harvest'. Individual bunches of very ripe grapes (which may be affected by **botrytis**) are selected at least a week after the **Spätlese** harvest. Unripe or diseased grapes must be removed from the bunches. Minimum **must weights** are laid down according to region and grape variety. At their best, particularly when made from **Riesling**, the wines are rich, sweet and honeyed, although **trocken** (dry) Auslesen do exist. See also **QmP**.

austere Tasting term, not necessarily uncomplimentary, which describes a tough, severe or reserved taste on the **palate**.

Australia Important wine-producing country, with a relatively recent reputation for good-quality **varietal** wines and blends made from varieties including **Chardonnay**, **Cabernet Sauvignon**, **Sauvignon Blanc**, **Shiraz**, **Sémillon**, **Rhine Riesling**, **Muscat** and **Marsanne**.

The first **Vitis vinifera** grapes were planted towards the end of the 18th century, but until the 1960s wine production concentrated on **fortified wines** and inferior reds. Then there was a winemaking revolution, with the introduction of new varieties, techniques and

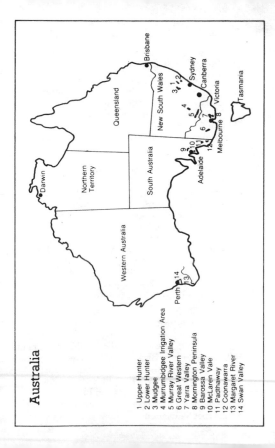

Australia

1 Upper Hunter
2 Lower Hunter
3 Mudgee
4 Murrumbidgee Irrigation Area
5 Murray River Valley
6 Great Western
7 Yarra Valley
8 Mornington Peninsula
9 Barossa Valley
10 McLaren Vale
11 Padthaway
12 Coonawarra
13 Margaret River
14 Swan Valley

equipment, so that today Australian winemakers are considered among the most technically advanced in the world.

The main wine-producing regions are concentrated in the southeastern part of the continent, in **New South Wales**, **Victoria** and **South Australia**, and around Perth in **Western Australia**. There are also vineyards in **Queensland** and **Tasmania**. See individual entries for each state and region.

Austria Central European country that produces mainly white wine of increasingly good quality. The vineyards are found in the eastern part of the country, north and south of Vienna and along the Hungarian, Czech, Slovak and Slovenian borders. The major regions are Weinviertel (dry whites and sparkling whites); Kremstal, Kamptal, and Donauland (good dry whites from **Grüner Veltliner**); Wachau (good dry **Riesling** and Grüner Veltliner); **Burgenland** (sweet whites and the best reds), **Niederösterreich** (predominantly dry whites), Steiermark (reds and very dry whites) and Wien (mainly the white wine Heurige).

Grüner Veltliner is the most important white grape variety planted. It produces largely dry whites, high in **acidity**, which are good as an accompaniment to fatty Austrian food. Other white grapes are **Müller-Thurgau**, **Welschriesling**, **Pinot Blanc** (Klevner), **Neuburger**, and Muskat-Ottonel (see **Muscat**). There are also small plantings of **Chardonnay**. The light-bodied red wines of Austria are produced mainly from **Blauer Portugieser**. Some producers are now experimenting with **Cabernet Sauvignon**.

The quality designations are similar to those used in **Germany**, though stricter, with **Tafelwein**, **Landwein**, Qualitätswein, **Kabinett**, **Spätlese**, **Auslese**, **Beerenauslese**, **Eiswein** and **Trockenbeerenauslese**. In addition, Austria operates the **Ausbruch** category, which comes between *Beerenauslese* and *Trockenbeeren-auslese* in must weight.

autolysis Process whereby flavour and **aroma** compounds are leached from dead **yeast** cells. Also used as a tasting term to describe the bready smell derived from dead yeast cells, particularly in sparkling wines.

autovinificator **Fermentation** vat sometimes used in the production of **Port**. The pressure of **carbon dioxide** produced during fermentation is used to force the **must** to circulate, to extract the maximum colour and **tannin** from the grape skins. This is otherwise achieved by treading the grapes by foot in a stone vat. Some producers still use the traditional method, though only for a limited part of their production. The autovinificator was also commonly used in **Australia** for red wine production in the 1970s and 1980s, though it has now largely been replaced with rotary fermenters.

Auxerrois 1. Low- to medium-quality white grape variety grown in **Alsace**, **France**, where it is mainly blended with other varieties to make **Edelzwicker**. 2. Local name for the **Malbec** grape in **Cahors**, **France**. 3. Term for the area of vineyards around Auxerre and **Chablis** in **Burgundy**, particularly the villages of **Irancy**, Saint-Bris-le-Vineux, Chitry-le-Fort and **Epineuil**.

Auxey-Duresses Village and *appellation* of the **Côte de Beaune**, **Burgundy**. Two-thirds of the wine it produces is red, made from the **Pinot Noir** grape, and one-third white, from **Chardonnay**. The best reds are pleasant, fairly light, good-value, cherry-scented wines, while the premiers crus, which include Les Duresses, La Chapelle and Clos du Val, have more body. The whites are more variable in quality. The best have a biscuity flavour reminiscent of nearby **Meursault**. All should be drunk young.

AVA (Approved Viticultural Area) US term roughly equivalent to, though less strict than, the French **AC** system, used to define winemaking areas. Boundaries are drawn up according to natural features, soil type, and climate. There are currently 150 AVAs in 27 states, and just over half are in the state of **California**. Some AVAs cross state boundaries. The regions vary widely in size, though there is a trend towards smaller, sometimes single vineyard, appel-lations.

Avelsbach Village in the **Grosslage** of Römerlay near **Trier** in the **Mosel-Saar-Ruwer** region of **Germany**. Its vineyards are planted with a very high proportion of **Riesling**. The best **Einzellage** sites are Altenberg, Herrenberg and Hammerstein.

Azerbaijan Minor wine-producing country of the **CIS**, producing mainly inferior whites (**Rkatsiteli**, **Pinot Blanc**, **Aligoté**) and brandy. Most wine is shipped to **Russia**.

azienda agricola Italian term for a wine estate producing wine from its own grapes. An azienda vinicola may produce wines from bought-in grapes.

B

Bacchus German white grape variety. It is a **cross** between **Müller-Thurgau** and **Silvaner-Riesling**, another cross. This early ripening variety is widely planted in the **Rheinhessen**, and produces a full-bodied wine low in **acidity** which is often blended into **Liebfraumilch**. It is also a popular variety in the vineyards of **England**.

Bacharach Town and **Bereich** in the **Mittelrhein**, **Germany**. It produces steely white wines of a reasonable quality from the **Riesling** grape.

Baco Blanc (Baco 22A) **Hybrid** grape variety planted in Gascony, **France**, where the wine it produces is distilled to produce the brandy Armagnac. However, it is considered inferior to **Ugni Blanc (Trebbiano)** for Armagnac production and is gradually disappearing.

Baco Noir **Hybrid** grape variety, a crossing of **Folle Blanche** with *Vitis riparia*. It is grown in the eastern **United States** and produces fruity red wines, often described as **foxy**.

Bad Dürkheim Spa town in the **Pfalz**, **Germany**. It produces good-quality white wines from **Riesling** and other white grape varieties, as well as some less-distinguished reds. The vineyards are in three **Grosslagen**: Feuerberg, Hochmess and Schenkenböhl. The wines do not have 'Bad' in their names, so a wine would be labelled, for example, 'Dürkheimer Feuerberg'.

Baden Most southerly **Anbaugebiet** in **Germany**. It produces mainly white wine, as well as some red and rosé. The majority of the whites are made from the **Müller-Thurgau**, **Ruländer** and Gutedel grapes, and are more full-bodied than the wines of other regions. The reds are made mainly from the **Spätburgunder** grape, as is the rosé **Weissherbst**. The rosé **Badisch Rotgold** is made by mixing **Spätburgunder** and **Ruländer**.

The **co-operative cellars** in the region account for the majority of the wine production. There are eight **Bereiche**, including **Bodensee**, Kaiserstuhl, Tuniberg, Markgräflerland and **Ortenau**.

Bad Kreuznach Spa and main city of the **Nahe** region of **Germany**. Some of the finest whites of the **Nahe** are produced in the **Grosslage** of Kronenberg, and these are labelled 'Kreuznacher Kronenberg'.

Badisch Rotgold Rosé wine from **Baden**, **Germany**, which is made by mixing **Spätburgunder** and **Ruländer** grapes.

Baga Most widely planted red grape variety of **Portugal**, and the dominant variety used to produce red **Bairrada**. It can produce rich fruity wines, but traditionally it is fermented with the stalks, leading to an **astringent** wine.

Bairrada DOC wine of **Portugal**, usually red but occasionally white, or sparkling. The reds, which are made mainly from the **Baga** grape, are traditionally full and fruity, but with an **astringent** taste. Modern winemaking techniques have produced softer, smoother wines, which rank among the best of Portugal's red **table wines**. The whites are made largely from the Maria Gomes grape.

balanced Tasting term to indicate that the component parts of a wine (i.e. fruit, **acid**, **tannin**, sugars and **alcohol**) are present in the right proportions.

balthazar Large **Champagne** bottle of 12 litres capacity, equivalent to 16 bottles of the normal size (75 cl).

Bandol AC wine from the vineyards around the town of Bandol in **Provence**, **France**. It may be red, white, or rosé, but the finest – and the largest quantity produced – is red. The main grape for the red is **Mourvèdre** (at least 50%), supported by **Grenache**, **Cinsault** and **Syrah**. The red wine must be aged at least 18 months in barrel, and at its best is long-lived, rich and fragrant, although quality is extremely variable. The rosés, based on **Mourvèdre**, can be extremely fine, but the dry whites, made from **Clairette**, **Ugni Blanc**, **Sauvignon Blanc**, and **Bourboulenc**, are usually bland and expensive.

Banyuls Sweet, fortified **AC** wine from the foothills of the Pyrenees, in the **Midi**, **France**. It may be red or tawny in colour. Banyuls is based on **Grenache** (at least 50%), and is similar, but inferior, to **Port**. Banyuls **Grand Cru** has a higher proportion of Grenache (75%), and is matured in wooden barrels for 30 months. Banyuls that is allowed to age for longer acquires a **rancio**, **oxidized** flavour and a tawny colour.

Barbaresco Red **DOCG** wine from **Piedmont**, **Italy**. It is grown around the villages of Barbaresco, Neive and Treiso, to the north of **Alba**. It is made exclusively from the **Nebbiolo** grape. The wine is aged for at least two years (one year in cask) before release; some producers age Barbaresco in small **oak barriques**. As in **Barolo**, some labels bear a single vineyard, or **cru** name, but these are not officially regulated. The wines can be tough and **tannic** in their youth, with a good **ageing** potential, often developing a complex, exquisite, truffly **aroma**. Quality is variable, but the best Barbarescos rank among the great Italian reds.

Barbarossa Rare red grape variety grown exclusively on the Fattoria Paradiso estate in **Emilia-Romagna**, **Italy**. It yields a fine, deep, red wine, **tannic** in its youth, but capable of developing great complexity with age.

Barbera Red grape variety planted widely in **Italy**, particularly in **Piedmont**, **Oltrepò Pavese** and **Emilia-Romagna**. It is an up-and-coming variety, particularly in Piedmont, where it has been discovered to have an attractive affinity with new **oak**, sometimes in a blend with **Nebbiolo**. The best wines are the DOCs Barbera d'Alba and Barbera d'Asti, which are capable of **ageing**. **DOC** Barbera del Monferrato is made to be drunk young and frizzantino, with a slight sparkle. They are all a deep, purply red, with spicy, leathery fruit and a high **acidity**, which can make them a good match for food.

Bardolino Popular dry red or rosé **DOC** wine, made around the village of Bardolino on Lake Garda in the **Veneto**, **Italy**. It is made from **Corvina**, **Rondinella**, **Molinara** and **Negrara** grapes. The red is light and grapey, with a slight bitterness in the background, and has the potential to age three or four years. The rosé, or **chiaretto**, is cherry pink and light-bodied. It provides Italy's most successful **carbonic maceration** vino novello.

Barolo Red **DOCG** wine of **Piedmont**, **Italy**, that ranks among the finest red wines of the world. It is made in the Langhe hills southeast of **Alba**, exclusively from the **Nebbiolo** grape. The wine must be aged for at least three years in barrel before release, and has a reputation for being **austere** and **tannic** in its youth. It develops great complexity and depth with age, developing an exquisite **aroma** of truffles and a rich, full-bodied taste. Some producers now age Barolo in small **oak barriques,** to make it more approachable in its youth, much to the annoyance of traditionalists.

As in **Barbaresco**, many labels now bear the name of a vineyard, or **cru**, but these are not yet officially regulated. Fine Barolo from a good vintage needs long **ageing** in bottle before it reaches its peak.

Barolo Chinato Curious red drink, based on **Barolo** wine flavoured with quinine.

Baroque White grape, used particularly to make the white wine **Tursan** (which must contain 90% Baroque). It was also once found in the rare white wines of **Béarn**.

Baroque produces strong, flavourful wines with fine **aroma**.

Barossa Valley District in **South Australia**, northeast of Adelaide, and source of much of the best Australian wine. The region was first settled and developed by German immigrants in the 19th century and originally produced mainly fortified and dessert wines. Today, however, it produces some fine **varietal** wines from grapes including **Shiraz**, **Grenache**, **Cabernet Sauvignon**, **Rhine Riesling**, and **Chardonnay**. Original plantations were on flat land, but excellent results have been achieved from cooler, high-altitude vineyards.

barrel Cylindrical container, usually made of wood, used to store and mature wine. Traditionally barrels were made from several different types of wood, but today most are made of oak. A new barrel imparts **tannin** and a vanilla flavour to wine, and the smaller the barrel, the more marked is this effect. An old barrel, if it is clean, will impart no flavour but it will allow a slow, controlled oxidization of the wine. See also **ageing**; **barrique**; **oak**.

barrique An **oak barrel** of 225 litres capacity, originally used in **Bordeaux**, and now found in many wine regions throughout the world.

Barsac One of the five communes of the **AC Sauternes** in **Bordeaux**, **France**. It produces sweet, white wines of high quality and complexity. Barsac also has its own **AC**, although its wines may be labelled Sauternes, or Sauternes-Barsac. The wine is produced from the

Sémillon, Sauvignon Blanc and Muscadelle grapes. Its distinctively rich balance between fruit and **acidity** derives from the action of **botrytis** on the grapes.

Basilicata Wine region of southern **Italy**, which produces only one **DOC** wine, **Aglianico del Vulture**. Other wines from the region include the fizzy white **Asprino**, dry or sweet white wines from the **Malvasia** grape, sweet golden whites from **Moscato** and red **table wines** from the **Montepulciano** grape.

Bastardo Red grape variety of **Portugal**, once frequently used in the production of **Port** and **Madeira**, but now mainly used in the red **table wines** of **Dão** and **Bairrada**. Also found in **Australia** and **California**. See also **Trousseau**.

Bâtard-Montrachet **Grand cru** vineyard in the villages of **Puligny-Montrachet** and **Chassagne-Montrachet** in the **Côte de Beaune** region of **Burgundy**. It produces rich, mouth-filling white wines of classy **bouquet** and flavour from the **Chardonnay** grape. However, it is generally reckoned to be inferior to the neighbouring *grands crus* of Le **Montrachet** and **Chevalier-Montrachet**.

Baumé Widely used French scale for measuring the concentration of sugar in grape **must** (1° *Baumé* equals 17–18 grams of sugar in 1 litre of water). A reading of, for example, 12° *Baumé* indicates that the must would yield a wine of approximately 12% **alcohol** by volume, if it were fermented to complete dryness. See also **Brix**; **Oechsle**.

Bay of Plenty Tiny wine-growing region on the North Island of **New Zealand**. It is planted mainly with **Chardonnay** and **Sauvignon Blanc** grapes.

Béarn AC wine from three separate areas of southwest **France**, east of Biarritz. It includes the ACs of **Madiran** and **Jurançon**, and the towns of Bellocq and Salies-de-Béarn. The majority of the wine produced is firm, **tannic** red and made from **Tannat**, **Cabernet Franc** and **Cabernet Sauvignon** grapes. A light fruity rosé is made from either the pure Tannat grape or Cabernet Franc. A white is also produced, but only in tiny quantities and from many permitted grape varieties, including Raffiat de Moncade, Manseng and **Courbu**.

The producers of AC Jurançon can also label their red wine as AC Béarn, and in AC Madiran rosé wines use the Béarn *appellation*.

Beaujolais AC wine and a region of **Burgundy**, producing mainly fruity, jammy, easy-drinking red wines from the **Gamay** grape, and some whites from **Chardonnay**. **Beaujolais Nouveau** is designed for early drinking (possibly chilled) in the year of the vintage. Most of the wine is labelled Beaujolais or Beaujolais-Villages, and is a simple, fruity, easy-drinking wine. The best wines of the regions are **cru** wines from 10 specified areas: **Brouilly**, **Chénas**, **Chiroubles**, **Côte de Brouilly**, **Fleurie**, **Juliénas**, **Morgon**, **Moulin-à-Vent**, **Régnié** and **Saint-Amour**, the names of which appear on labels. Each wine has its own special character, and all have more complexity and **ageing** potential than the ordinary Beaujolais.

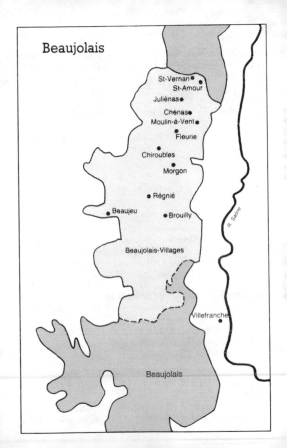

Beaujolais

St-Vernan
St-Amour
Juliénas
Chénas
Moulin-à-Vent
Fleurie
Chiroubles
Morgon
Régnié
Beaujeu
Brouilly
Beaujolais-Villages
Villefranche
R. Saône
Beaujolais

Beaujolais Nouveau (also called Beaujolais Primeur)
Light, easy-drinking red **AC** wine of **Burgundy** made
from the **Gamay** grape. It is marketed on the third
Thursday of November after the **vintage**. It never has
the complexity of the **cru** wines of Beaujolais, but it is
not intended to. Its success has been as a marketing
tool, to create public interest in Beaujolais, and to
improve cash-flow for growers. The drawback has been
the early-drinking, quaffing-wine image that has
resulted, to the detriment of serious, *cru* Beaujolais
producers. The concept has been widely imitated in
other regions and countries.

Beaumes-de-Venise Village in the **Côtes du Rhône,
France**, which is entitled to its own **AC** Côtes du
Rhône-Villages for its red wines. It is, however, more
famous for its **Muscat de Beaumes-de-Venise**, a **vin
doux naturel**, a white, **fortified wine** made from the
Muscat grape. Sweet, fragrant and easy to drink, it has
almost universal appeal.

Beaune Town and an **AC** wine in the **Côte d'Or** region
of **Burgundy**. It gives its name to the **Côte de Beaune**,
the southern section of the Côte d'Or, as well as to the
wines of its own vineyards. Mainly red wines are
produced from the **Pinot Noir** grape, as well as some
whites from the **Chardonnay**.

The best Beaune wines, from the **premier cru** vineyards
of Les Marconnets, Teurons and Grèves (to name but a
few), can be of a high quality, with a great **ageing**
potential. The straight Beaune reds are less
complicated and can be enjoyed within five years of the

vintage, and the whites, too, are generally best drunk young. The town of Beaune is home to many of Burgundy's **négociants**.

Beauroy A **premier cru** vineyard of **Chablis**.

Beerenauslese German and Austrian quality white wine category, literally meaning 'selected grapes'. Individually selected overripe grapes, probably affected by **botrytis**, are cut from the bunches and carefully pressed. The minimum **must weight** is generally in the range 110-128° **Oechsle**. The wines are yellow gold in their youth, turning to deep amber with age. They are exceedingly rare, luscious and quite sweet, but with a balancing **acidity**. The most successful are made from the **Riesling** grape. See also **QmP**.

beery Tasting term used to describe an undesirable malty or yeasty smell in wine.

Bellet AC of **Provence**, **France**, which produces small quantities of good quality red, white and rosé wine. The white is made mainly from the **Chardonnay** and **Rolle** grapes, and is quite full-bodied and flavourful. The red is made mainly from the Folle Noire and Braquet grapes, and occasionally **Cinsault**. It is light and elegant, but is capable of **ageing** well. Most of the production is consumed locally by holiday-makers on the Riviera.

bentonite Clay used to treat most white wines to improve protein stability and thereby ensure a perfectly clear wine in bottle. See also **fining**.

Bereich German wine law term used to describe a wine-growing district. The larger **Anbaugebiet** regions are divided into *Bereich* districts. Each *Bereich* is a combination of sites in neighbouring villages, which, theoretically, produce wines of similar character. The *Bereich* usually takes its name from the most famous village, for example *Bereich* **Bernkastel**. A *Bereich* may be further subdivided into several **Grosslagen**, combinations of vineyards.

Bergerac AC wine and a region in the southwest of **France**, to the east of **Bordeaux** on the Dordogne River. AC Bergerac may be red or white; the red is produced (like Bordeaux) from the **Cabernet Sauvignon**, **Cabernet Franc** and **Merlot** grapes; the white, which is labelled Bergerac Sec, is made from **Sauvignon Blanc**, **Sémillon** and **Muscadelle**. The reds are similar to red Bordeaux in taste, and they can be of a good quality, although they never reach the heights of the great wines of the **Médoc**. The whites are clean and fruity and should be drunk young. A small amount of rosé is also produced.

The Bergerac region includes the ACs **Monbazillac**, **Montravel**, **Pécharmant** and **Rosette**.

Bernkastel Bereich in the **Mosel-Saar-Ruwer** region of **Germany**, covering the Mittelmosel area. Wines sold as *Bereich* Bernkastel, which are made from the **Müller-Thurgau** grape, should be crisp and fresh, and are best drunk young. Those made from the **Riesling** grape should be of a higher quality and more complex. The top wines of the area are sold under their own vineyard or **Einzellage** names.

Bernkastel-Kues Village on the banks of the Mosel river in the **Mosel-Saar-Ruwer** region of **Germany**. Many of the finest vineyards of the **Bereich Bernkastel** are concentrated around the village, in two **Grosslagen**, Badstube and Kurfürstlay. The Doktor vineyard is the most famous **Einzellage**; it produces some of Germany's top **Rieslings**.

bianco Italian for white.

Bianco d'Alcamo See **Alcamo**.

Bianco Capena See **Capena**.

Bianco d'Alessano White grape variety grown in the **Apulia** region of southern **Italy**. It is blended with Verdeca, to make the **DOC** wine **Locorotondo**.

Bianco dei Colli Maceratesi White **DOC** wine from the **Marches** region of **Italy**, made from the **Trebbiano** Toscano and Maceratino grapes. This delicate, dry white should be drunk young.

Bianco della Val d'Arbia White **DOC** wine from the Arbia valley between Radda and Montalcino in **Tuscany**, **Italy**, made from **Trebbiano** and **Malvasia** grapes. It is a dry, clean and, at its best, fruity wine which should be drunk young. **Vin Santo** is also made in this area.

Bianco della Valdinievole White wine from **Tuscany**, **Italy**, made from **Trebbiano** grapes grown around the towns of Montecatini Terme and Pescia.

It is light and dry, and is best drunk young. **Vin Santo** is also made in this area.

Bianco di Custoza White **DOC** wine from around Lake Garda in the **Veneto** region of **Italy**, made mainly from the **Trebbiano** Toscano, **Garganega** and **Tocai Friulano** grapes. It is a dry wine and, at its best, softly fruity, and more **aromatic** than its neighbour **Soave**. A **spumante** version also exists, which is made by the **Charmat method**.

Bianco di Gravina White **DOC** wine from around Gravina in the **Apulia** region, southern **Italy**, made from the Verdeca grape. A medium-weight, dry wine that should be drunk young.

Bianco di Pitigliano White **DOC** wine from southern **Tuscany**, **Italy**, made mainly from the **Trebbiano** and **Grechetto** grapes. A clean, fruity, if somewhat neutral wine that should be drunk young.

Bianco di Scandiano White **DOC** wine from around Scandiano in the **Emilia-Romagna** region of **Italy**, made from **Sauvignon**, **Malvasia** and **Trebbiano** grapes. This soft, sparkling white can be dry or medium-dry and **frizzante** or **spumante**.

Bianco Pisano San Torpè White **DOC** wine from **Tuscany**, **Italy**, southeast of Pisa, made from **Trebbiano**, **Canaiolo Bianco** and **Malvasia** grapes. It is a light, dry wine which should be drunk young.

Bianco Vergine della Valdichiana White **DOC** wine from the Chiana valley between Arezzo and

Chiusi, in **Tuscany**, **Italy**. It is made mainly from the **Trebbiano** grape together with **Malvasia** and **Grechetto**. A soft, dry and pleasantly fruity wine, better than many other Tuscan whites.

Bical White grape variety with good **acidity** and a fine fruit **aroma**, used for the production of white wines in the **Bairrada** and **Dão** regions of **Portugal**.

Bienvenues Bâtard-Montrachet **Grand cru** vineyard in the village of **Puligny-Montrachet** in the **Côte de Beaune** region of **Burgundy**. It produces rich, mouth-filling white wines of classy **bouquet** and flavour from the **Chardonnay** grape. The vineyard is virtually an enclave of **Bâtard-Montrachet** and its wines are similar in quality and taste.

Bierzo DO wine of north-west **Spain** producing increasingly good-quality wines from the native grape varieties Mencia (red) and Godello (whites).

Biferno DOC wine from the **Molise** region of **Italy**. It can be red or rosé, made from the **Montepulciano** grape, or white, made from **Trebbiano**.

big Tasting term which can be used to describe a wine's intensity of colour, smell, taste or finish.

Bingen Town in the **Rheinhessen** area of **Germany**, which also gives its name to one of the Rheinhessen's three **Bereiche**. The vineyards around Bingen come under the Sankt Rochuskapelle **Grosslage** and produce some of the region's finest **Rieslings**. The best-known **Einzellage** is Binger Scharlachberg.

Binnissalem Red and white **DO** wine from the Spanish island of Majorca. The wines, made from Prensal, Manto Negro, and Negra Moll, have improved in recent years, since the introduction of modern winemaking techniques to the island.

bite Tasting term used to describe the attack of **acidity** (and sometimes **tannin**) on the **palate**. Desirable in a young wine destined for **ageing**, it can mellow with time.

bitter Tasting term, usually pejorative, which describes a sharp taste on the **palate** or **finish**. A slight bitterness on the finish of some light red wines can be attractive.

blackcurrant Tasting term that describes the smell and taste of blackcurrant fruit, which is often a characteristic of the **Cabernet Sauvignon** grape. Some tasters use the French equivalent, **cassis**.

Blagny Village and **AC** wine between **Puligny-Montrachet** and **Meursault** in the **Côte de Beaune**, **Burgundy**. The AC is given for the reds only. They are earthy, gamey wines made from the **Pinot Noir** grape. The whites from the Blagny vineyards are entitled to the Puligny-Montrachet **Premier cru** or Meursault Premier cru ACs.

blanc French for white.

blanc de blancs Term used on labels, mainly in **France**, to indicate a white wine made from white grapes. Thus nearly all white wines could be described

as *blanc de blancs*. The term is only truly relevant in
Champagne; most white Champagne is made from
both red (**Pinot Noir** and **Pinot Meunier**) and white
(**Chardonnay**) grapes, but *blanc de blancs* Champagne
is pure Chardonnay.

Blanc de Morgex et de la Salle Dry white **table
wine** made in the **Valle d'Aosta** region of **Italy**, to the
southeast of Mont Blanc. It is clean and delicately
flavoured, made from the Blanc de Valdigne grape and
grown at an altitude of 1000 m. A sparkling **méthode
traditionnelle** version is also produced. Both wines are
best drunk young.

blanc de noirs Term used on labels, mainly in **France**,
to indicate a white wine made from 'black' grapes.
Nearly all grapes yield white juice when pressed and it
is the grape skin that gives the colour of red wines. The
term is used mainly in **Champagne**, where it usually
means a white Champagne made exclusively from the
black **Pinot Noir** and **Pinot Meunier** grapes (without
any **Chardonnay**).

Blanc Fumé de Pouilly See **Pouilly-Fumé**.

Blanchots One of the seven **grand cru** vineyards of
Chablis.

blanco Spanish for white.

Blanquette de Limoux Méthode traditionnelle
sparkling white **AC** wine, produced around the town of
Limoux, southern **France**. The wine is made mainly

from the **Mauzac Blanc** grape (called Blanquette locally), together with limited amounts of **Chardonnay** and **Chenin Blanc**. It is dry and can be quite complex. Its quality can be good, but without reaching the heights of top **Champagne**. Similar wines, with a higher proportion of Chardonnay and Chenin, are produced under the AC **Crémant de Limoux**.

Blauburgunder German name for the **Pinot Noir** grape, also used in German-speaking parts of **Italy**. Also called **Spätburgunder**.

Blauer Portugieser (also called Portugieser) Grape variety that produces light red wines of a very ordinary quality. It is the most widely planted red variety in **Austria**, and is also found in **Germany**, **Croatia**, **Hungary** and (only rarely) **France**.

Blaufränkisch Grape variety that produces light-bodied, quite acidic red wines of decent quality. It is the second most widely planted red variety in **Austria**, and is also found in **Germany** (where it is called Blauer Limberger), **Bulgaria**, **Slovakia** (as **Frankovka**), Friuli in **Italy** (where it is called Franconia), and **Hungary** (where it is called **Kékfrankos**).

Blaye Town and **AC** of **Bordeaux**, found on the **Right Bank** of the Gironde estuary. A little red and white wine is made under the AC, but the better wines of the region are bottled as **Premières Côtes de Blaye** or **Côtes de Blaye**.

bleichert German term for a rosé wine.

blush Term used, mainly in the **United States**, to indicate a pale pink wine made from red grapes. **White Zinfandel** is, in fact, normally a pale pink, or 'blush'. Lesser quality blush wines have been made by blending red and white wine. See also **rosé**.

Bobal Red grape variety extensively planted in **Spain**, especially **Utiel-Requena**, as well as **Alicante** and **Cariñena**. It can produce good-quality wines with good **acidity**, and relatively low **alcohol**.

Boca Dry red **DOC** wine from the Novara Hills near Boca in the **Piedmont** region of **Italy**, made mainly from **Nebbiolo**, together with **Bonarda** and Vespolina. The wine can be of a fine quality, solid and tough in its youth and **ageing** well, but it is rarely seen outside Piedmont.

Bocksbeutel Squat, flagon-shaped bottle of green glass. It is used in **Germany** for the quality wines of **Franken** and some wines of north **Baden**. A similar shape is sometimes used in **Portugal** and **Chile**.

bodega Spanish for wine **cellar**. It is used to indicate any place where wine is made or matured, or, more loosely, a wine-producing company.

Bodensee German name for Lake Constance, and one of the **Bereiche** of the **Baden** region of **Germany**; some vineyards also lie within **Franken** and Württemburg. The wine produced is sometimes known as Seewein, because of the lake's warming influence on the climate. The main grapes are **Müller-Thurgau** and **Spätburgunder**. The latter is often made into the rosé **Weissherbst**.

body A tasting term used to describe the weight of a wine in the mouth. High **alcohol** content and high extract make for more body.

Bolgheri White and rosé **DOC** wine from Bolgheri in **Tuscany**, **Italy**. The **rosato** is made from **Sangiovese** and **Canaiolo** grapes, and can be of good quality. The white is made from **Trebbiano** and **Vermentino**.

Bolgheri Sassicaia Single-wine **DOC** for **Italy**'s most famous red wine, long produced as a **vino da tavola**.

Bolivia South American country whose wine industry is in its infancy. Most of the vines planted are **Muscat** of Alexandria, and most of the wine produced is distilled into brandy.

Bombino Red and white grape varieties, grown mainly in the **Apulia** region of **Italy**. Bombino Nero is used to make red and rosé **Castel del Monte**. Bombino Bianco is widely planted, and is used to make the white Castel del Monte and **San Severo** in Apulia. In **Abruzzo**, Bombino Bianco is known as **Trebbiano d'Abruzzo**.

Bommes One of the villages entitled to the **AC** of **Sauternes**.

Bonarda Red grape variety used to make blended and **varietal** wines in the **Oltrepò Pavese** region of **Italy**. It produces a dark-coloured, fruity wine, often quite **tannic**. See also **Bonarda Piemontese**. A different variety, also called Bonarda, is planted in **Argentina**, where it produces soft, fruity reds; it may be related to **Charbono** of **California**.

Bonarda Piemontese Red grape variety related to, but distinct from, **Bonarda**, which produces a lighter, more supple wine. As its name suggests, it is planted in **Piedmont**, **Italy**, particularly around Turin.

Bonnezeaux Sweet white **AC** wine in the **Coteaux du Layon** area of **Anjou-Saumur** in the **Loire** valley, **France**. The wines, made only from the **Chenin Blanc** grape, are of a very high quality, rich and luscious, with their sweetness balanced by **acidity**, and are very long-lived.

Bordeaux City and major wine region of **France**, perhaps the most famous and celebrated in the world. The greatest wines are from the **Médoc**, where some of the world's finest reds are produced from **Cabernet Sauvignon**, **Cabernet Franc**, **Merlot**, **Malbec** and **Petit Verdot** grapes. On the **Right Bank** of the Gironde estuary the emphasis is mainly on Merlot, and great red wines are made in **Saint-Emilion** and **Pomerol**, as well as slightly lesser wines in **Fronsac**, **Canon-Fronsac**, the **Côtes de Bourg** and the **Premières Côtes de Blaye**.

South of the Médoc, great reds and dry whites are made in the **Graves**, especially in the separate **AC** of **Pessac-Léognan**. Some of the most celebrated sweet white wines are made in **Sauternes** and **Barsac**, from **Sauvignon Blanc**, **Sémillon** and **Muscadelle** grapes affected by **botrytis**. Between the Garonne and Dordogne rivers, the vast **Entre-Deux-Mers** region produces increasingly good dry whites from the same

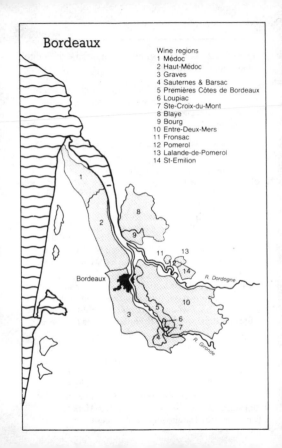

Bordeaux

Wine regions
1 Médoc
2 Haut-Médoc
3 Graves
4 Sauternes & Barsac
5 Premières Côtes de Bordeaux
6 Loupiac
7 Ste-Croix-du-Mont
8 Blaye
9 Bourg
10 Entre-Deux-Mers
11 Fronsac
12 Pomerol
13 Lalande-de-Pomerol
14 St-Emilion

Bordeaux

R. Dordogne

R. Gironde

varieties used in Sauternes, although occasionally from 100% Sauvignon Blanc. **Loupiac** and **Sainte-Croix-du-Mont** produce wines similar in style to Sauternes, but of normally lesser quality.

Bordeaux mixture Fungicide spray based on copper sulphate, used to treat vines against oidium, mildew, anthracnose and other diseases.

Bosnia Hercegovina Minor wine-producing country, formerly part of Yugoslavia. Acidic whites are made from the native Zilavka grape, and mediocre reds from Blatina.

botrytis (also called botrytis cinerea) Fungus respon sible for the creation of '**noble rot**' (Fr. **pourriture noble**) on grapes. This allows water to evaporate from the grape juice, leading to an increased concentration of sugar. The presence of this beneficial rot is the key to the production of the great sweet wines of **Sauternes**, **Monbazillac** and **Anjou-Saumur** in **France**, the **Beerenauslese** and **Trockenbeerenauslese** wines of **Germany** and **Austria**, **Tokaji** in **Hungary**, and some New World sweet wines. In most other regions, botrytis is undesirable and can lead to the development of grey rot, which causes the grapes to spoil. Botrytis is called **Edelfäule** in German.

botte Italian name for a large barrel, usually made of **oak** or chestnut, used to store and mature wine. See also **ageing**.

Botticino Dry red **DOC** wine from east of Brescia in the **Lombardy** region of **Italy**. It is made from the

Barbera, **Marzemino**, **Schiava** and **Sangiovese** grapes. It is usually bright red in colour, quite sturdy and develops well after three to four years in bottle.

bottle age Term attributed to wine that has spent some months or years in bottle, and the associated mature **bouquet** and flavour that it develops. See also **ageing**.

bottle fermented Term used to describe sparkling wine in which the secondary **fermentation** has taken place in bottle (e.g. **Champagne**).

bottle sickness (also called bottle shock) Term used to describe a temporary deterioration in a wine tasted shortly after it has been bottled.

bottle stink Smell of stale air, trapped in a wine bottle, which is sometimes detectable when the cork is drawn. It usually fades quickly.

Bouchet Alternative name for the **Cabernet Franc** grape, used in **Saint-Emilion**

Bougros One of the seven **grand cru** vineyards of **Chablis**.

bouquet Tasting term, used loosely to describe the smell of the wine, and more correctly to describe the characteristics of smell that develop as the wine matures in bottle.

Bourboulenc White grape variety, one of the 13 permitted in the red wine of **Châteauneuf-du-Pape** in the **Rhône** valley, **France**. On its own it produces a thin, neutral wine.

Bourg See **Côtes de Bourg**.

Bourgogne Basic **AC** wine of **Burgundy**. Its wines are red, made from the **Pinot Noir** grape(AC Bourgogne Rouge), or white from **Chardonnay** (AC Bourgogne Blanc) or **Aligoté** (AC Bourgogne Aligoté).

Bourgueil Red **AC** wine of the **Touraine** region of the **Loire** valley, **France**, made mainly from the **Cabernet Franc** grape (called Breton locally). It is one of the finest-quality red wines of the Loire, with a grassy, raspberry fruit flavour, and is capable of some **ageing**. **Saint-Nicolas-de-Bourgueil** is similar, but has its own AC.

Bouvier (also called Bouviertraube) White grape variety grown usually for eating, but cultivated for wine mainly in the **Burgenland** and Styria regions of **Austria**, former Yugoslavia (where it is known as Ranina) and **Hungary**. It produces wine of very ordinary quality, mostly used for blending with more characterful varieties, but it can have good **must weight**.

Bouzeron Village in the **Côte Chalonnaise** in **Burgundy**. It produces one of the best white wines from the **Aligoté** grape.

Bouzy Village of **Champagne**. Its vineyards, rated 100%, are planted with the **Pinot Noir** grape. Most of this is made into Champagne, but some still Bouzy

Rouge is bottled, and some is used to give blended pink Champagnes their colour.

Bozner Leiten German name for **Colli di Bolzano**.

Brachetto Red grape variety grown mainly in **Piedmont**, **Italy** and in **Bellet**, **Provence** (where it is known as Braquet). In Piedmont it makes medium-sweet to sweet sparkling wines, either **frizzante** or **spumante**, with a fruity strawberry flavour. The wine is **DOC** in Brachetto d'Acqui and Brachetto d'Asti.

Bramaterra Dry red **DOC** wine grown in the hills around the village of the same name in **Piedmont**, **Italy**. It is made mainly from the **Nebbiolo** grape, together with **Croatina**, **Bonarda Piemontese** and Vespolina. It is a fairly full-bodied, robust red with a good **ageing** potential.

branco Portuguese for white.

Brauneberg Small village within the **Grosslage** of Kurfürstlay, in the **Mosel-Saar-Ruwer** region of **Germany**. Its vineyards are planted with a high proportion of **Riesling** grapes, which can produce fine-quality, rich, full-bodied wines. The best **Einzellage** is Juffer.

Brazil Large wine-producing country in South America. Most of the vines are not **Vitis vinifera**, and so are unsuitable for quality wine production. This is slowly changing and *vinifera* varieties planted now include **Sauvignon Blanc**, **Cabernet Sauvignon**, **Chardonnay**,

Johannisberg Riesling, **Merlot**, **Pinot Noir**, **Sémillon** and **Trebbiano**. These are planted mainly in the vineyards of Santana do Livramento in the southern state of Rio Grande do Sul, which borders **Uruguay**, and Frontera on the Argentinian border.

Breganze DOC wine from the **Veneto** region of **Italy**, north of Vicenza. It comes in seven versions: **Bianco**, a dry, delicate white from the **Tocai Friulano** grape; Rosso, a pleasant, grapey red based on **Merlot**; Cabernet, an excellent dry red of high quality made mainly from **Cabernet Franc**; Pinot Bianco and Pinot Grigio, both fresh and smooth dry whites; Pinot Nero, which is light but fruity; and Vespaiolo, which is a dry white with a citrus flavour.

Breisgau One of the **Bereiche** of the **Baden** region of **Germany**.

Breton Alternative name for **Cabernet Franc**, used in the **Loire** valley, **France**.

Brindisi DOC wine grown inland from the port of the same name in the **Apulia** region of **Italy**. Dry red and rosé versions are produced, both based on the **Negroamaro** grape. The red can achieve quite a good quality and has a good **ageing** potential.

British wine Beverage prepared in the UK from imported grape concentrates. It is not to be confused with **English wine**, which is made from grapes grown out of doors in **England**.

Brix Scale used for measuring the amount of sugar in grape juice. 1° Brix represents 1% sugar in solution. See also **Baumé**; **Oechsle**.

Brouilly **Cru** of **Beaujolais** with the largest area of vineyards. The wines are among the finest of Beaujolais, fruity, supple and full of flavour.

Brunello di Montalcino DOCG wine of **Tuscany**, **Italy**, made only from the Brunello grape, a superior **clone** of **Sangiovese**. This dry red wine is among Italy's finest. It is deep-coloured, powerful, structured, **tannic** and very long-lived.

brut French term meaning 'very dry', usually found on the labels of **Champagne** and other sparkling wines, not necessarily from **France**. Extra brut is drier, and *Ultra brut* or *Zero brut* contains virtually no sugar at all.

Bual Grape variety grown on the island of **Madeira**, where it gives its name to a category of wine. It is sweet, full and smoky, and can rank among the best of all Madeiras.

Bucelas White wine of **Portugal**, made chiefly from the **Arinto** grape, plus Cercial, Esgana Cão, and Rabo d'Ovelha. Dry, but rich, it is one of the few Portuguese whites that can improve with age, and it is currently undergoing a renaissance.

Bugey VDQS wine region between Savoie and Lyon, **France**. It produces light red, white and rosé wines, which may be still, semi-sparkling, or sparkling.

The reds are made mainly from the **Pinot Noir**, **Gamay** and **Mondeuse Noire** grape varieties. The whites are made from **Altesse** (also called Roussette) and, increasingly, **Chardonnay**.

Bulgaria Important eastern European wine-producing country, and the one that has most successfully tailored its winemaking to international tastes. Traditionally, the vineyards were planted with native varieties. Since World War II, noble west-European varieties have taken over, principally **Cabernet Sauvignon**, **Merlot** and **Pinot Noir** among the reds, and **Chardonnay**, **Aligoté**, **Sauvignon Blanc**, **Riesling**, **Gewürztraminer** and **Pinot Gris** among the whites.

The top-quality wines come from defined **Controliran** areas. 'Reserve' wines are aged in **oak**, two years for whites and three for reds. The wines tend to lack any great complexity, but they are good value.

Burgenland Region of **Austria**, in the east of the country near the Hungarian border. It produces mainly sweet white wines. There are four subregions: **Neusiedlersee**, Neusiedlersee-Hügelland, Mittelburgenland and Südburgenland.

Burgundy Region of **France** and one of the most famous wine areas of the world, producing some of the finest white and red wines in relatively small quantities. From north to south, it includes the subregions of **Chablis**, the **Côte de Nuits** and **Côte de Beaune** (which together form the **Côte d'Or**), **Côte Chalonnaise**, the **Mâconnais** and **Beaujolais**. The dominant grape

Burgundy

Wine regions
1 Chablis
2 Côte de Nuits ⎫
3 Côte de Beaune ⎭ Côte D'Or
4 Côte Chalonnaise
5 Mâconnais
6 Beaujolais

varieties are **Chardonnay** for the whites and **Pinot Noir** for the reds, with **Aligoté** and **Gamay** playing important secondary roles.

bush vine New World term for **gobelet** system vines, in which the plant resembles a low bush.

butt Barrel used for **ageing Sherry**, with a capacity of 600-650 litres or 500 litres (shipping butt).

buttery Tasting term describing the smell and taste of butter, often found in mature, **oak**-aged white wines, especially those made from the **Chardonnay** grape.

Buzet AC area of south-west **France**, which produces mainly red wines, similar in style to those of **Bordeaux**. The reds are made from the **Cabernet Sauvignon**, **Cabernet Franc** and **Merlot** grapes, and the few whites are mainly from **Sémillon**. Quality is good, and the wines usually represent good value for money.

C

Cabardès Recently promoted **AC** wine produced near the town of Carcassonne in south-west **France**. The wine can be red or rosé, and is made mainly from **Cabernet Sauvignon**, **Merlot** and **Malbec**, along with usually smaller proportions of **Carignan**, **Cinsault**, **Grenache**, **Mourvèdre** and **Syrah**. The reds are increasingly good, well-structured with ripe fruit flavours.

Cabernet d'Anjou Rosé **AC** wine produced in **Anjou-Saumur** in the **Loire** valley. It is similar to **Rosé d'Anjou**, but better in that it is made from the **Cabernet Franc** grape with fresh, grassy, fruit flavours.

Cabernet de Saumur Rosé **AC** wine produced in **Saumur** in the **Loire** valley. It is similar to **Cabernet d'Anjou**, but usually slightly off-dry. It is made mainly from the **Cabernet Franc** grape, with occasionally some **Cabernet Sauvignon** added.

Cabernet Franc Red grape variety planted in **Bordeaux** and the **Loire** valley, **France**, and in the **Friuli-Venezia Giulia**, **Trentino-Alto Adige** and **Veneto** regions of northeast **Italy**.

In Bordeaux, Cabernet Franc is very much in the shadow of **Cabernet Sauvignon**, and in most regions it contributes only a minor part to the blend. However, **Saint-Emilion** and **Pomerol** are exceptions, where

Cabernet Franc (here known as **Bouchet**) plays a more important role, along with **Merlot**.

In the Loire, Cabernet Franc (alias Breton) has a chance to shine, in the great red wines of **Bourgueil**, **Saint-Nicolas-de-Bourgueil**, **Chinon** and **Saumur-Champigny**, and the pleasant rosé wines **Cabernet d'Anjou** and **Cabernet de Saumur**.

In northeast Italy, Cabernet Franc is **DOC** in many zones, either as a **varietal** or as a blend with Cabernet Sauvignon. Some Cabernet Franc is also planted in **California**, mainly in **Napa Valley** and **Sonoma**. It is mainly used for Bordeaux-style blends with Cabernet Sauvignon and Merlot. In **Chile**, it is sometimes vinified along with Cabernet Sauvignon. Also found in **Argentina**.

Cabernet Sauvignon Red grape variety, one of the most important and distinctive. It is planted widely throughout the wine-producing world. It is the most important ingredient in nearly every red wine from **Bordeaux** (with notable exceptions in **Saint-Emilion** and **Pomerol**), usually blended with **Cabernet Franc** and **Merlot**. Cabernet Sauvignon is also widely planted in other French regions, especially the **Loire** valley, **Languedoc-Roussillon** and Bordeaux's satellites.

In terms of quality, it is the most important red variety of most New World wine-producing countries; in **California**, **Australia** and **New Zealand** it makes fine **varietal** wines, as well as blends (notably with Cabernet Franc and Merlot in California, and with **Shiraz** in Australia). It is also notably planted in **Chile** and **South**

Africa, and **Bulgaria** (where it founded the modern wine industry, with sales of varietal Cabernet Sauvignon to the West).

In northeast **Italy**, in **Friuli-Venezia Giulia**, **Trentino-Alto Adige** and the **Veneto**, Cabernet Sauvignon is **DOC** in many zones, either as a varietal, or blended with Cabernet Franc. In **Tuscany**, Cabernet is found in **Carmignano**, and can play a minor role in the blend for **Chianti**. There are also many fine **vini da tavola** made from pure Cabernet, or a blend of Cabernet and **Sangiovese**.

Cabernet Sauvignon wines have a distinctive blackcurrant **aroma** and taste, capable of developing great complexity with age. Mint and eucalyptus flavours can also be discerned in some wines, particularly those from the New World. Cabernet Sauvignon marries beautifully with **oak** flavours derived from **ageing** in **barrique**, though unoaked Cabernets can also be very fine.

Cadillac White **AC** wine of **Bordeaux**, produced at the southern end of the **Premières Côtes de Bordeaux** area, from the **Sémillon**, **Sauvignon Blanc** and **Muscadelle** grape varieties. The wine is good value, light and sweet, but without any of the richness, elegance and concentration of **Sauternes** or **Barsac**.

Cahors Red **AC** wine of south-west **France**, produced on the banks of the river Lot, around the town of Cahors, from the **Malbec** (known locally as **Cot**, or sometimes **Auxerrois**), **Merlot** and **Tannat** grape varieties. It is a deep-coloured wine, with plummy richness and blackcurrant flavours, capable of long **ageing**. Quality can be very good.

Cairanne See **Côtes du Rhône**.

Calabrese Alternative name used, confusingly, for the **Canaiolo** Nero, Nero d'Avola and **Sangiovese** grape varieties. In **Sicily**, the names Calabrese and Nero d'Avola are interchangeable for the island's finest red variety, which makes robust, good-quality wines on its own, and is also useful in blends. In dialect, it is known as Calavrisi.

Calabria Region of southern **Italy**, at the 'toe' of the peninsula. Pale, light red wines are produced in the mountainous west, mainly from the **Gaglioppo** grape variety (see **Donnici** and **Pollino**). The most famous wines are **Cirò**, white, red and **rosato**, and the white Greco di Bianco (see **Greco**). **Melissa** is similar to Cirò, but generally of lower quality. See also **Mantonico di Bianco**.

Calatayud Red and white **DO** wine region of **Spain**. The strong red is made from **Garnacha** or, increasingly, **Tempranillo**; the crisp, fruity white from Viura.

Caldaro (also called Kaltern; Kalterersee; Lago di Caldaro) Red **DOC** wine of the **Alto Adige** region of northeast **Italy**, produced around the lake of the same name, from the **Schiava** grape variety. An easy-drinking, slightly bitter, pale red wine, it is best drunk young and fresh.

California Most important wine-producing state of the **United States**, with a wide variety of climatic conditions. It produces high-quality **varietal** wines from grape varieties as diverse as **Cabernet Sauvignon**, **Chardonnay**, **Chenin Blanc**, **Gewürztraminer**, **Merlot**, Petite Sirah, **Pinot Noir**, **Riesling**, **Sauvignon Blanc** and **Zinfandel**, among others, as well as large quantities of medium-quality '**jug**' wine, usually from unspecified grape varieties. California is also a source of high-quality **méthode traditionnelle** sparkling wines. The most important regions are **Napa Valley** and **Sonoma**. See **Amador County**; **Edna Valley**; **Fiddletown**; **Lake County**; **Madera**; **Mendocino**; **Paso Robles**; **Russian River Valley**; **San Luis Obispo**; **York Mountain**.

Caluso See **Erbaluce di Caluso**.

Calvi See **Vin de Corse**.

Campania Region of southern **Italy**, centred on the town of Naples. Good Campanian wines are few and far between, with very few quality winemakers. The best wine is probably the red **Taurasi**, produced in the hills surrounding the village of the same name, mainly from the **Aglianico** grape variety. It has deep colour and good **ageing** potential, although **austere** tannins can mask the fruit flavours when young. **Asprino** is a fairly characterless, fizzy white thirst-quencher, while the red **Falerno** bears the same name as ancient Rome's favourite wine and in its modern incarnation is fruity and full-bodied, and better than the white version.

Aglianico del Taburno is an up-and-coming red wine

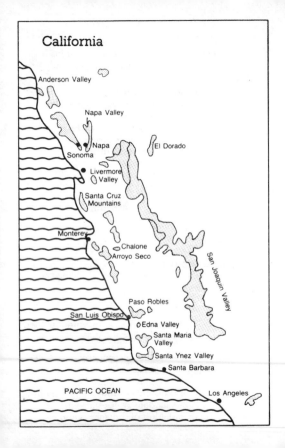

California

Anderson Valley

Napa Valley

El Dorado

● Napa
Sonoma

● Livermore
○ Valley

Santa Cruz
Mountains

Monterey ●

○ Chalone
Arroyo Seco

San Joaquin Valley

Paso Robles

San Luis Obispo ○
● Edna Valley
Santa Maria
Valley
Santa Ynez Valley
● Santa Barbara

PACIFIC OCEAN

● Los Angeles

from the Aglianico grape variety and Falanghina is both a grape variety and a wine that have recently been rediscovered with some success.

The white **Fiano di Avellino** can have a pleasant nuts and pears **aroma** at its best, but quality varies enormously. The white Greco di Tufo (see **Greco**) can have a good fruity and crisp flavour, and the island of **Ischia** produces fine white **vini da tavola** and less interesting **DOC** wines. Lacryma Christi del Vesuvio, which can be dry red, **rosato**, or white, still or sparkling, is rarely as interesting as its name.

Campidano di Terralba Dry red **DOC** wine produced on the Italian island of **Sardinia**, mainly from the Bovale and **Monica** grape varieties. It is a medium, deep red, but lacks depth and body, best drunk when young and fresh.

Campo de Borja **DO** wine produced in a region to the south of **Rioja** and **Navarra**, in northeast **Spain**. The wine can be red or **rosado**, based mainly on the **Garnacha** grape variety, plus a little **Macabeo**. Traditionally it has been very high in **alcohol** and lacking in **acidity**, but there are signs of a move towards lighter, more approachable reds.

Canada Minor wine-producing country of north America, traditionally a producer of wines from native, non-**Vitis vinifera** vines. In recent decades there has been a move towards planting **hybrids** and true *vinifera* varieties (especially **Chardonnay**, **Riesling** and **Cabernet Sauvignon**). Most of the vineyards are in

British Columbia and Ontario, and the Niagara Peninsula area looks particularly promising. The best wines are probably 'icewines', made in the model of **Eiswein**.

canada Unit of measurement in the **Port** trade, equal to 2.1 litres. One **pipe** is equivalent to 21 **almudes**, and there are about 12 *canadas* in one *almude*. A *canada* was traditionally thought to be the right amount of Port for a man to drink.

Canaiolo Red grape variety of **Italy**, and a minor part of the blend for **Chianti**, to which it adds colour. It is also planted in **Umbria**, **Latium** and the **Marches** regions.

Canary Islands Wine-producing islands situated off the coast of Morocco and belonging to **Spain**. Tenerife produces light, **astringent** reds; Lanzarote produces dry and medium-sweet white wines from the **Malvasia** grape. The winemaking techniques are rustic, and quality is often poor.

Cannellino Unusual type of medium-sweet **Frascati**, made from very dry grapes, preferably affected by **botrytis**.

Cannonau Version of the **Garnacha** grape variety grown in **Sardinia**. It is **DOC** in Cannonau di Sardegna, which can be red or **rosato**, dry or **amabile**, and also **fortified**. All are quite high in **alcohol** (reds, minimum of 13.5% vol.), and the best and most popular are the dry reds.

Canon-Fronsac AC wine of **Bordeaux**, made in the
heart of the **Fronsac** region, producing chunky, deep
red-coloured wines, which are well-flavoured and
tannic, requiring more **bottle age** than plain Fronsac.
The main grape varieties are **Cabernet Franc**, **Cabernet
Sauvignon**, **Merlot** and **Malbec**. Quality is improving
and the wines are deservedly becoming better known.

Canterbury Cool-climate wine-producing region of
New Zealand's South Island. The climate is best suited
to white **varietal** wines, made from **Chardonnay**,
Gewürztraminer and **Riesling** grapes. A little red wine
is also made, from **Pinot Noir**.

cantina Italian term for a **cellar** or winery.

cantina sociale Italian term for a **co-operative** winery.

Cape Riesling White grape variety (no relation to
Riesling) grown widely in **South Africa**, where it makes
dry, rather neutral, gently **aromatic**, easy-drinking
wines. Its true name is **Crouchen Blanc**.

Capena (also called **Bianco** Capena) White **DOC** wine
produced in the hills north of Rome, in the **Latium**
region of **Italy**, from the **Malvasia**, **Trebbiano** and
Bombino grape varieties. A pleasant, easy-drinking dry,
or off-dry white.

Capriano del Colle DOC wine produced in the
Lombardy region, northwest **Italy**. Most of the
production is of a lively, easy drinking red, made from
the **Sangiovese**, **Marzemino** and **Barbera** grape

varieties. There is also a small production of varietally labelled, crisp dry white wine from the **Trebbiano** grape.

caratello Small barrel, of approximately 50 litres capacity, traditionally used for **ageing Vin Santo**.

carato Italian term for a barrel, of a similar capacity to the **barrique**.

carbon dioxide (or CO_2) Colourless, odourless and incombustible gas. In winemaking it is produced during **fermentation**, when grape sugar is converted into **alcohol**. Normally carbon dioxide is lost to the atmosphere. When fermentation takes place in a closed vessel (either a pressurized tank or during secondary fermentation in bottle), the carbon dioxide is trapped in the wine, until it is released as bubbles when the bottle is opened. Modern winemakers make much use of added carbon dioxide to protect grape juice and wine (particularly white) from **oxidation**.

carbonic maceration Technique sometimes used in **fermentation** of **Beaujolais** and other red wines intended for early drinking. Uncrushed grapes are fermented in vat under a blanket of inert **carbon dioxide**. The process of fermentation within the cells of the whole grape berries promotes **bouquet** and fruit flavours (ideal for the **Gamay** grape), and minimizes the extraction of **tannin**.

Carema Red **DOC** wine made in tiny quantities in the northern **Piedmont** region of **Italy**, from the **Nebbiolo**

grape variety. A light, lean and elegant dry red, the quality of which can be very good.

Carignan (also called **Cariñena**) Red grape variety widely planted in **France**, in **Languedoc-Roussillon** and **Provence**, and as an ingredient for much **vin de table** and inexpensive **vin de pays**. In **Spain** it is known as Cariñena, and contributes to the blend for the **DO** wine of that name as well as for many other DO wines of the northeast. In **Rioja** it surfaces as Mazuelo, a minor blending ingredient. Carignan is sometimes bottled as a **varietal**, but is chiefly valued for the deep colour and structure it can give to a blend.

Cariñena DO wine of northeast **Spain**. Most of the production is of red wine, the best of it full and soft, made mainly from the **Garnacha** and **Tempranillo** grape varieties, plus a little **Carignan** (which originally comes from this region), **Bobal** and **Monastrell**. White and **rosado** wines are also made.

Carmignano Fine red **DOCG** wine of **Tuscany**, similar to **Chianti** in that it is made from **Sangiovese** and **Canaiolo**, but differing in that it must also contain between 6 and 10% of **Cabernet Sauvignon** and/or **Cabernet Franc**. Some **rosato** is also produced, based on the same grape varieties.

Carneros (officially Los Carneros) **AVA** wine-producing region of **California**, shared by the **Napa Valley** and **Sonoma** regions. The relatively cool climate makes for fine **varietal** wines, especially from **Pinot Noir** as well as **Chardonnay**. Carneros also has a rapidly growing reputation for fine **méthode traditionnelle** sparkling wines.

Carso DOC wine of the **Friuli-Venezia Giulia** region of northeast **Italy**. Carso and Terrano del Carso are assertive, sturdy dry reds, both based on the native Terrano grape (a variety of **Refosco**, or **Mondeuse Noire**). **Malvasia** del Carso is a dry, vibrant white, sometimes with a honeyed, almond note. All are intended for drinking young.

Cassis AC wine of **Provence**, produced around the port of the same name. The fruity, fresh white is one of the most celebrated of the region, produced from the **Ugni Blanc**, **Clairette** and **Marsanne** grape varieties (plus sometimes **Sauvignon Blanc**). Red and rosé are both made, from **Grenache**, **Cinsault** and **Mour-vèdre**, but are rarely as good as the white version.

cassis French for blackcurrant, sometimes used as a tasting term even by non-French speakers.

Castel del Monte DOC wine of the **Apulia** region of southern **Italy**, produced in rocky, hilly vineyards in the centre of the region. The **bianco** is a neutral, inoffensive dry white, based on the Pampanuto grape variety. The dry **rosato** is more characterful, based on the **Bombino** Nero. Best of all is the **rosso**, made from Uva di Troia plus **Sangiovese**, **Montepulciano**, **Aglianico** and Pinot Nero, deep in colour and flavour and with good **ageing** potential.

Casteller Red **DOC** wine produced throughout the **Trentino** region of northern **Italy**, based on the **Schiava**

grape variety. Most of it is light, easy drinking, dry red, best drunk young. There is also an **amabile** version.

cat's pee (also called piss) Tasting term, used to describe the pungent, yet fruity, **aroma** which some connoisseurs look for in wine made from the **Sauvignon Blanc** grape.

Catarratto White grape variety native to **Sicily**, where it goes to make the **DOC** wines of **Alcamo** and **Etna**, as well as contributing to the blends for many of the island's **vini da tavola**. It is among the grapes used for the **fortified wine Marsala**.

Catawba Hybrid grape variety widely planted in the eastern **United States**, producing cheap white and rosé wines, often sparkling.

Cava Sparkling **DO** wine of **Spain**, produced mainly in the **Penedès** region by the **méthode traditionnelle**, from the **Macabeo**, **Parellada** and **Xarel-lo** grape varieties, plus, increasingly, **Chardonnay**. For **rosado** Cavas, **Garnacha** and **Monastrell** add the colour. Quality can be very good and, from some producers, is steadily getting better, especially where some Chardonnay is used to add class and fruit and improve the **ageing** potential.

cave French term for a place where wine is made or stored (whether or not it happens to be underground).

cave coopérative French term for a **co-operative** winemaking cellar. Growers, often without their own winemaking equipment, and without the capacity to bottle and market their own production, send their grapes to a central **vinification** centre. Here their grapes are usually lost in a blend that is sold under the co-op's label, but some co-ops produce special cuvées from individual members' vineyards. See also **cantina sociale**.

cedar Tasting term, used to indicate the cedar-wood **aroma** often found in fine, mature red **Bordeaux**, a characteristic of the **Cabernet Sauvignon** grape variety.

cellar Term used loosely to refer to any place where wine is made or stored (whether or not it happens to be underground).

Cellatica Red **DOC** wine produced in the **Lombardy** region of northwest **Italy**, from the **Schiava**, **Barbera** and **Marzemino** grape varieties. A dry, light red, with a characteristic bitter finish, it is best drunk young.

Cencibel Alternative name, used in **La Mancha**, for the **Tempranillo** grape.

Central Valley Large wine region of **California**, the source of much of the state's **jug wine**.

cépage French term for grape variety.

Cerasuolo di Vittoria Dry red **DOC** wine of **Sicily**, produced from the **Calabrese**, Frappato and **Nerello** Mascalese grape varieties. Cherry red in colour, hence its name, it is surprisingly full bodied and full flavoured. Best drunk young.

Cereza Grape variety still widely planted in **Argentina**, where it produces red, white and rosé wines of generally poor quality.

Cérons Sweet white **AC** wine produced in the communes of Cérons and Illats, within the **Graves** region of **Bordeaux**. The same varieties are used as for **Sauternes**: **Sémillon**, **Sauvignon Blanc** and **Muscadelle**. But the wines, soft and fairly sweet, never have the same richness and depth as Sauternes. Most producers now make dry white wine, which they can sell as AC Graves.

Cerveteri **DOC** wine produced in the north of the **Latium** region of **Italy**. The fairly bland, dry white version is made from a wide variety of grape varieties, including **Trebbiano** and **Malvasia**. The red is better, based on the **Sangiovese** and **Montepulciano** grape varieties.

Cesanese Red grape variety of the **Latium** region of **Italy**. In the Ciociaria hills, it is **DOC** in three wines: Cesanese di Olevano Romano, Cesanese di Affile and Cesanese del Piglio. Traditionally they were sweet, sparkling red wines; today, thankfully, they are warm, fleshy, dry red wines.

Chablais See **Switzerland**.

Chablis White **AC** wine of northern **Burgundy**, produced in vineyards around the town of Chablis from the **Chardonnay** grape variety. Chablis has a bone dry, steely taste, which distinguishes it from the more opulent Chardonnays from farther south in Burgundy. With **bottle age**, it can develop wonderful complexity of **aroma** and flavour, especially if it is from one of the **premier cru** or **grand cru** vineyard sites. Some producers age or ferment Chablis in new **oak** barrels, especially for *premier cru* and *grand cru* wines. Other producers maintain that the true taste of Chablis is masked by oak flavours, and use only stainless steel. Superb wines are to be found in both styles. The name Chablis has previously been usurped by producers outside Europe, who have used it as a generic term for dry white wine.

Chacolí de Guetaria Tiny red and white **DO** wine of the northern coast of **Spain**, also called Txakoli. The thin, sharp white is best enjoyed in the local fish restaurants. The red version is rarely seen.

chai French term, used particularly in **Bordeaux**, for an 'overground **cellar**', usually used for storing wine in barrel.

Chalk Hill Zone of **Sonoma** county, **California**. Its chalk soil is especially suited to production of **varietal** wines from **Chardonnay**.

Chalone Zone of Monterey County, **California**. Its high-altitude vineyards produce some fine **varietal** wines, particularly from **Chardonnay** and **Pinot Noir**.

Chambertin Grand cru vineyard – arguably the best – of **Gevrey-Chambertin** in the **Côte de Nuits** area of

Burgundy. It produces some of the greatest red Burgundies, combining finesse and elegance with power and depth of flavour.

Chambertin-Clos de Bèze Grand cru vineyard of **Gevrey-Chambertin** in the **Côte de Nuits** area of **Burgundy**. It produces some of the best red Burgundies, of very similar quality to **Chambertin**.

Chambolle-Musigny Red **AC** wine of the **Côte de Nuits** region of **Burgundy**, made from the **Pinot Noir** grape variety. At its best, the wine is light, classy and delicately perfumed, particularly from the **grand cru** vineyards of Bonnes Mares and **Musigny**.

chambré French term used to indicate a wine that has been brought to room temperature. When houses were kept at 15-17° C, this was indeed the ideal temperature for service of many red wines. Today most houses are kept warmer, and reds are frequently served too warm.

Champagne Sparkling **AC** wine of northeast **France**, produced around the towns of **Reims**, Epernay and Chalons-sur-Marne, from the **Chardonnay**, **Pinot Noir** and **Pinot Meunier** grapes. Champagne is certainly the world's finest and most highly prized sparkling wine. It is made by the *méthode champenoise*, which involves a second, bubble-forming **fermentation** in bottle, followed by **ageing** on the **lees**, then **remuage** and **disgorgement**.

The most important vineyard areas are the **Côte des Blancs**, planted mainly with Chardonnay; the **Montagne de Reims**, mainly Pinot Noir; and the **Vallée**

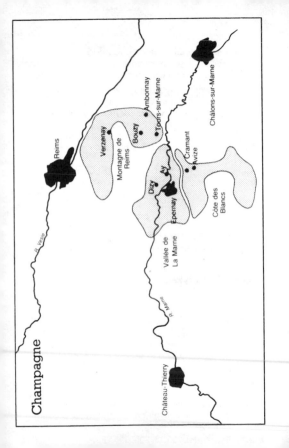

Champagne

Reims

R. Vesle

Montagne de Reims

Verzenay

Bouzy

Ambonnay

Tours-sur-Marne

Dizy

Épernay

Vallée de La Marne

Cramant

Avize

Côte des Blancs

Châlons-sur-Marne

Château-Thierry

R. Marne

de la Marne, mainly Pinot Noir and Pinot Meunier. The **Aube** is the southernmost outpost, planted mainly with Pinot Noir and Chardonnay.

Champagne is nearly always a blend of different grape varieties from different areas, and in the case of non-vintage from different years. **Blanc de blancs** is made entirely from Chardonnay, however, and **Blanc de noirs** is white Champagne made from the red grapes Pinot Noir and Pinot Meunier. **Vintage** Champagne is wine from a single year, but it is not necessarily superior to non-vintage. Pink, or rosé, Champagne is made either by allowing a short, controlled **maceration** of the fermenting wine on the skins of the Pinot Noir; or by adding a little still red wine, often from **Bouzy**, to the white before the second fermentation.

Chapelle-Chambertin **Grand cru** vineyard of **Gevrey-Chambertin** in the **Côte de Nuits** area of **Burgundy**.

chaptalization Practice of adding sugar to grape juice or **must** during **fermentation**, in order to increase the final **alcohol** content. It is permitted in many European regions where grapes do not always have a sufficient level of natural sugar. The amount of sugar that can be added is controlled by law, though the law is widely flouted in many regions.

Charbono Red grape variety still found occasionally in **California**. May be related to Argentinian **Bonarda**.

Chardonnay White grape variety, one of the most important and widely planted in the world.

Chardonnay is planted in almost every wine-producing country, producing a wide variety of styles from steely, bone dry, lemony, through to lush, buttery, fat wines.

In **France**, it produces some of the world's finest white wines in **Burgundy**, particularly in **Chablis** and the **Côte d'Or**. It is an important part of the blend in the world's greatest sparkling wine, **Champagne** (where it is usually blended with **Pinot Noir** and **Pinot Meunier**, but is sometimes vinified alone to make a **blanc de blancs**).

Chardonnay produces fine **varietal** wines in **California**, **Australia** and **New Zealand**. In **Italy** it is **DOC** in most areas, and also contributes to the blend for many sparkling wines. In **Spain** it is increasingly important as part of the blend for the sparkling wine **Cava**, and for the still wines of **Penedès**.

Chardonnay and **oak** is a marriage made in heaven, and it is probably the white grape variety most suited to oak **ageing**, although both oaked and unoaked Chardonnays have their fans.

Charmat method (also called *cuve close*) Method of producing sparkling wines in bulk by second **fermentation** in tank. A still base wine is produced in the normal way. Sugar and **yeast** are then added to the base wine in a sealed tank. A second fermentation takes place and the added sugar is converted into **alcohol** and **carbon dioxide**. Because the tank is sealed, the carbon dioxide cannot escape, and is dissolved in the wine. The sparkling wine can then be bottled under pressure. This is a less expensive and less time-consuming method than the *méthode champenoise* (**méthode traditionnelle**), in which the second **fermentation** takes place in bottle, but it undoubtedly results in wines of lesser quality.

Charmes-Chambertin **Grand cru** vineyard of **Gevrey-Chambertin** in the **Côte de Nuits** area of **Burgundy**.

Chasan White grape variety widely planted in the Languedoc, a crossing of Listan and **Chardonnay**. Well made, it can be difficult to distinguish from **Chardonnay**, while it has the advantage of earlier ripening and higher **yield**.

Chassagne-Montrachet AC wine of the **Côte de Beaune** region of **Burgundy**. Good quality white wine is produced from the **Chardonnay** grape variety, ranging from superb, from the **grand cru** sites of **Le Montrachet**, **Bâtard-Montrachet** (both shared with **Puligny-Montrachet**) and Criots-**Bâtard-Montrachet**, to very good from the **premier cru** sites. The red wine, made from **Pinot Noir**, is rarely as good as the white.

Chasselas White grape variety of **Switzerland**, also planted to a limited extent in **Germany**, **Alsace** and elsewhere. In general, it produces rather light, neutral wine; at its best, in the Valais and Vaud regions of Switzerland and **Baden** in Germany, it can produce a wine with a flinty, smoky **aroma**. In Switzerland it is sometimes known as Fendant and in Germany as Gutedel.

château French word for castle. In **Bordeaux** the term is used to indicate a wine estate, whether or not it possesses a castle or mansion.

Château-Chalon AC wine of the **Jura** region. Only **vin jaune** is produced, from the **Savagnin** grape variety, with its distinctive dry, assertive, nutty flavour.

Château-Grillet White AC wine produced in a tiny vineyard in the northern **Rhône**, from the **Viognier** grape variety. The wine has a delicious and distinctive apricot-and-cream **aroma** and taste. It is rare and consequently expensive.

Châteauneuf-du-Pape Red (and occasionally white) AC wine of the southern **Rhône**, produced in vineyards around the town of the same name. Although 13 grape varieties are permitted (eight red and five white), most producers use fewer. The majority of the production is of red wine, based on **Grenache**, **Syrah** and **Mourvèdre**. At its best it is a deep, plummy, spicy wine, packed with red fruit flavours, and capable of long **ageing**.

White Châteauneuf-du-Pape is much less common. Based on Grenache Blanc, **Clairette** and **Bourboulenc**, it can be highly **aromatic** in its youth, with fresh, spicy fruit balanced by a refreshing cut of **acidity**.

Châtillon-en-Diois AC wine of the **Rhône**. Very small quantities of white are produced, from the **Aligoté** and **Chardonnay** grape varieties, and red and rosé from **Gamay**, **Syrah** and **Pinot Noir**.

Chénas Red **AC** wine, the smallest of the 10 **crus** of the **Beaujolais** region of **Burgundy**, made from the **Gamay** grape. The wine is rich and chocolatey, similar to that of **Moulin-à-Vent**. Quality can be very good; among the best, if perhaps the least characteristic, of all Beaujolais.

Chenin Blanc White grape variety planted especially in the **Anjou-Saumur** and **Touraine** areas of the **Loire** valley. Chenin is highly versatile. It can make high-quality, bone-dry wines in **Savennières** and **Jasnières**, and luscious sweet, dessert wines in **Coteaux du Layon**, **Bonnezeaux** and **Quarts de Chaume**. In **Vouvray** and **Montlouis**, it can be dry, medium dry, or sweet and still, **pétillant**, or fully sparkling. In **Saumur**, Chenin is the base for **méthode traditionnelle** spark-ling wines. It has been adopted by many other winemaking countries, including **South Africa** (where it is known as **Steen**), **Australia**, **California** and **Argentina** (where it makes **varietal** wines for drinking young).

Chevalier-Montrachet Grand cru vineyard of **Puligny-Montrachet** in the **Côte de Beaune** area of **Burgundy**. It produces white wine of superb quality and richness from the **Chardonnay** grape variety, perhaps second only to Le **Montrachet**. Its colour begins as a greenish yellow, deepening to gold with age, as the dry but honeyed taste and **aromas** develop. The wine is rich and mouth-filling, and needs at least 10 years to reach peak maturity.

Cheverny AC wine produced in **Touraine** in the **Loire** valley. A harsh, unpleasant white called Cour Cheverny is based on the Romarantin grape variety; fresh, crisp, fruity whites from **Arbois**, **Chardonnay**, **Chenin Blanc** and especially **Sauvignon Blanc** are much better. The light, somewhat **astringent** reds of Cheverny are based on **Cabernet Franc**, **Cabernet Sauvignon**, **Gamay** and **Pinot Noir**. The same varieties are used to make light, attractive rosé, all best drunk young.

Chianti Red **DOCG** wine of **Tuscany**, produced mainly from the **Sangiovese** grape, with the option to add **Canaiolo**, **Trebbiano**, **Malvasia**, and certain other varieties including **Cabernet Sauvignon**. There is a separate DOCG for Chianti **Classico** and there are six subregions within the DOCG: Rufina (with good **ageing** potential), plus Colli Aretini, Colli Fiorentini, Colli Senesi, Colline Pisane and Montalbano. Quality varies enormously, from very ordinary to superb (especially in Classico and Rufina, which produce some of **Italy**'s finest red wines). In the past Chianti has suffered from overproduction, blending with wines from other regions, over-prolonged wood ageing and the use of inferior clonal material in the vineyard. Now Classico and Rufina in particular have addressed these problems, and overall quality is constantly improving.

Chianti is a versatile wine. The basic *non-riserva*, or *normale*, is a limpid, purple red, with delicious cherry flavoured fruit. **Riserva**, aged for three years before bottling, can be much deeper and more concentrated, with a full, fruity flavour supported by a **tannic** backbone. Most of the ageing is done in large **oak** or chestnut **botti**, but some producers make limited use of small oak **barriques**. The use of Cabernet in the blend is controversial: some producers say it enhances the structure and ageing potential of Chianti; others hold that, even at 10%, it can begin to mask the attractive fruit flavour of Sangiovese. Only Chianti Classico is officially allowed to be 100% Sangiovese. See also **governo**.

chiaretto Italian term for a light, rosé style wine. See also **Bardolino**.

Chignin See **Vin de Savoie**.

Chile An important wine-producing country of South America. The vine was brought here by the Spanish, and for many years the main variety grown was **Pais**, a high-yielding vine producing thin, poor wines, both red and white, which were purely for domestic consumption. In recent years, producers have planted more noble varieties, particularly **Sémillon**, **Sauvignon Blanc**, **Chardonnay**, **Cabernet Sauvignon** and **Merlot**, to produce wines for export. Good results have already been obtained with reds made from Cabernet, and refreshing, fleshy Merlots for early drinking. Fine crisp, white Sauvignon is also beginning to appear as producers adopt more modern winemaking techniques, although much of what is sold as Sauvignon is in fact made from the Sauvignon Vert (**Tocai Friulano**) variety, so the wines lack some of the juicy fruit intensity of top Sauvignons from the **Loire** and **New Zealand**. Wines made from Sémillon have so far been undistinguished, largely owing to the extraordinarily high **yields** obtained. Chile's vineyards are mostly free from **phylloxera**, and so are planted with ungrafted vines.

China Country with a relatively new tradition of wine production from grapes. Most of the vineyards are planted in the north west, and north-east coastal regions. Along with many grape varieties unique to China, there are widespread plantings of **Welschriesling**, **Rkatsiteli**, and **Muscat** of Hamburg, and there are small plantations of premium varieties including **Chardonnay**. Joint ventures with European and Australian companies are beginning to reveal China's potential as a serious wine producer.

Chinon Red AC wine of the **Touraine** area of the **Loire** valley, produced from the **Cabernet Franc** grape variety. It is one of the finest-quality red wines of the Loire, with grassy, raspberry fruit flavours, and capable of long **ageing**. Rosé and white Chinons exist, but are extremely rare.

Chiroubles Red AC wine, one of the 10 **crus** of the **Beaujolais** region of **Burgundy**, made from the **Gamay** grape. The wine is light and delicate, with delicious strawberry-flavoured fruit, best drunk young.

chocolate Tasting term, used to describe a rich, sweet, thick, chocolate-like **aroma** and taste, found particularly in some wines made from the **Gamay** grape variety, such as **cru Beaujolais**.

Chorey-lès-Beaune AC wine of the **Côte de Beaune** region of **Burgundy**. Most of the wine is red, made from the **Pinot Noir** grape variety: soft, fruity, good value for money, and best drunk relatively young. Many producers use the alternative AC of **Côte de**

Beaune-Villages. An insignificant quantity of white wine is also made.

Chusclan See **Côtes du Rhône**.

Cigales Mainly rosé **DO** wine of northern **Spain**, made from **Tempranillo** and **Garnacha**.

Cinqueterre White **DOC** wine produced in the **Liguria** region of northwest **Italy**, from the Bosco, Albarola and **Vermentino** grape varieties. Dry, light and fragrant in their youth, the wines oxidize easily and are best drunk young. A mildly sweet version, Schiacchetrà, is made from dried grapes.

Cinsault (also called Cinsaut) Red grape variety, widely planted in the south of **France**. When harvested at low **yields**, it can produce moderately deep-coloured wine with a beefy, full flavour and high **acidity**. It is much used as an ingredient in **vin de table** and **AC** wines of **Languedoc-Roussillon**, in some of the red wines of **Provence**, and in the southern **Rhône** (it is one of the 13 permitted varieties in **Châteauneuf-du-Pape**). It produces small quantities of **varietal** wine in **South Africa**, where it is known as 'Hermitage', and is also found occasionally in **Australia** and eastern Europe.

Cirò DOC wine produced in the **Calabria** region of southern **Italy**. The dry **bianco** is made from the **Greco** Bianco grape, plus some **Trebbiano**. The strong, dry **rosso** and **rosato** are based on **Gaglioppo**. Quality rarely rises above the ordinary.

CIS (Confederation of Independent States) Confederation of most of the republics of the former Soviet Union. The most important republics for wine production are **Azerbaijan**, **Crimea**, Georgia, **Kazakhstan**, **Moldova**, **Russia**, **Ukraine**, and **Uzbekistan**. See entries for individual republics.

Clairet Light red **AC** wine of **Bordeaux**. It is technically a red, in that the wine is fermented on skins for about 24 hours, though it resembles a deep-coloured rosé in appearance and taste. Quality ranges from ordinary to very good.

Clairette White grape variety grown in southern France, as an ingredient for blended **vin de table**, in the AC wines of **Provence**, and in the southern **Rhône** (it is one of the permitted varieties for **Châteauneuf-du-Pape**). On its own, it produces rather dull AC wine in Clairette de Bellegarde and Clairette du Languedoc, both in **Languedoc-Roussillon**. Its finest expression is in the sparkling Rhône wine Clairette de Die: the **brut** version is pure Clairette, while 'Tradition' is a blend of **Muscat** and Clairette, a delicious, light, fresh, grapey sparkling wine, and very good value for money.

Clare Valley Fine wine-producing region of **South Australia**, near the **Barossa Valley**. Excellent **varietal** wines are produced, particularly white **Riesling**, and red **Cabernet Sauvignon** and **Shiraz** (plus good blends of the two varieties). **Malbec** also does well here, generally used as a blending component.

Claret English term for any red **Bordeaux**.

clarete Spanish term for pale red wine. See also **tinto**.

classed growth English translation of **cru classé**.

classese Italian term for **metodo classico** sparkling wine produced in **Oltrepò Pavese**.

classico Italian term, sometimes appended to **DOC** and **DOCG** wine names, to indicate that the wine comes from a designated subregion within the DOC, often the historical or central area of production.

climat French term, used particularly in **Burgundy**, to indicate an individual vineyard site.

clone Sort of subvariety, within the family of a single grape variety. The **Sangiovese** grape, for instance, has many clones, some producing better wines than others, some suited to particular soil types and local climates.

clos French term used to describe a vineyard that is (or was once) surrounded by a wall.

Clos de Vougeot Red **grand cru AC** wine of the **Côte de Nuits** area of **Burgundy**, produced from the **Pinot Noir** grape variety grown in the largest *grand cru* of the Côte d'Or. Because of its size, and the large number of growers who own a tiny slice of it, quality is variable, not always up to *grand cru* standard. At its best, it can be fleshy, rich and chocolatey, sometimes with smoke and liquorice flavours on the long finish.

CM (*coopérative-manipulant*) Letters found on **Champagne** labels, indicating that the wine comes from a **co-operative** cellar. The numbers following the letters identify the co-op. See also **NM**; **RM**.

co-operative Winemaking cellar owned by a group of growers. Co-operatives are common in most European wine-producing countries. See **cantina sociale**; **cave coopérative**.

Colares Tiny **DOC** wine produced on the central west coast of **Portugal**, from vines not affected by **phylloxera** grown in sand-dune vineyards on the coast, near Lisbon. Most of the wine made is red, from the **Ramisco** grape, and is very tough and **tannic** in its youth. It takes ten years to become drinkable. White Colares is made from **Malvasia**.

Colheita Port Tawny Port with a date of harvest. **Port** of a single year is aged in wood, sometimes for decades, before being bottled. The label must bear the year of bottling, as well as the harvest date. Quality can be extremely good. Not to be confused with Vintage Port.

Colli Albani White **DOC** wine produced in the **Latium** region of **Italy**, from the **Malvasia** and **Trebbiano** grape varieties. Similar to, but not as good as the best of, **Frascati**.

Colli Altotiberini **DOC** wine of the **Umbria** region of **Italy**. **Bianco** is made from **Trebbiano** and **Malvasia**; easy-drinking and best while fresh and young. **Rosso**, made from **Sangiovese** with a touch of **Merlot**, can be softly fruity, and the same grapes make a good, dry **rosato**.

Colli Aretini See **Chianti**.

Colli Bolognesi DOC wine of the **Emilia-Romagna** region of Italy. The **bianco** is a dry white (sometimes **amabile**) based on the **Albana** grape variety. The four **varietal** whites are Pignoletto, Pinot Bianco, **Riesling Italico** and **Sauvignon Blanc**. The three red varietals are **Barbera** (the best), **Cabernet Sauvignon** (also very good) and **Merlot**.

Colli del Trasimeno DOC wine produced in the **Umbria** region of **Italy**. The **bianco** is a dry, refreshing white, based on the **Trebbiano** grape variety. The **rosso**, supple, fresh and fruity, is based on **Sangiovese** and **Gamay**.

Colli di Bolzano (also called Bozner Leiten) Dry red **DOC** wine, produced in the hills around Bolzano, in the **Alto Adige** region of northern **Italy**. It is based on the **Schiava** grape variety, and is a simple, easy-drinking wine.

Colli di Luni DOC wine produced in the **Liguria** region of northwest Italy. **Bianco** is a blend of the **Vermentino** and **Trebbiano** grape varieties, and there is also a **varietal** Vermentino. **Rosso** is a blend based on **Sangiovese**.

Colli di Parma DOC wine of the **Emilia-Romagna** region of Italy. A dry **rosso** (sometimes **frizzante**) is based on the **Barbera** and **Bonarda** grape varieties. **Malvasia** is a dry or **amabile** white (sometimes **spumante**), a blend of Malvasia and **Moscato**. Sauvignon is a dry **varietal** white, sometimes frizzante.

Colli Euganei DOC wine of the **Veneto** region of Italy. The **bianco** is a blend based on **Garganega** and the **rosso** is a blend of **Merlot**, **Cabernet Sauvignon** and **Cabernet Franc**, plus some **Barbera**. Both can be dry or **amabile**, still or sparkling. In addition there are **varietal** whites from Tocai Italico and Pinot Bianco (both usually dry), and **Moscato** (sweet, and sometimes sparkling). The red **varietals** are Cabernet (Cabernet Sauvignon and/or Cabernet Franc) and Merlot.

Colli Fiorentini See Chianti.

Colli Lanuvini White **DOC** wine produced in the **Latium** region of **Italy**, from the **Malvasia** and **Trebbiano** grape varieties. Similar to, but not as good as the best of, **Frascati**.

Colli Martani DOC wine produced in the **Umbria** region of **Italy**. There are two **varietal** whites, **Grechetto** and **Trebbiano**, and one varietal red made from **Sangiovese**.

Colli Orientali del Friuli DOC wine produced in the **Friuli-Venezia Giulia** region of northeast **Italy**. Excellent light whites, and reds which can take moderate **ageing**, are produced in 20 different styles. The whites are **varietals** made from **Chardonnay**, **Malvasia**, Pinot Bianco, Pinot Grigio, **Ribolla**, **Riesling Renano**, Sauvignon, **Tocai Friulano**, Traminer Aromatico and **Verduzzo Friulano** (all dry), plus the sweet whites Ramandolo (made from Verduzzo) and **Picolit**. Red varietals are Cabernet (**Cabernet Sauvignon** and/or **Cabernet Franc**), **Merlot**, Pinot

Nero, Refosco dal Peduncolo Rosso (a **clone** of **Refosco**) and Schioppettino. Dry **rosato** is based mainly on Merlot.

Colli Perugini DOC wine produced in the **Umbria** region of **Italy**. The **bianco** is based on the **Trebbiano** grape variety, the **rosso** and **rosato** on **Sangiovese**. None is very exciting.

Colli Piacentini DOC wine produced in the **Emilia-Romagna** region of **Italy**. There are four sub-zones: Gutturnio (dry red, sometimes sweet, sometimes sparkling, made from **Barbera** and **Bonarda**); Monterosso Val d'Arda, Trebbiano Val Trebbia, and Val Nure (all three, dry or **amabile**, sometimes sparkling, based on **Malvasia** and **Trebbiano**). There are three **varietal** reds (Barbera, Bonarda and Pinot Nero) and four varietal whites (Malvasia, Ortrugo, Pinot Grigio and Sauvignon).

Colli Senesi See **Chianti**.

Colli Tortonesi DOC wine of the **Piedmont** region of northwest **Italy**. Red **varietal** wine, made from the **Barbera** grape variety, is dry and often lightly fizzy. Varietal white is made from **Cortese**, dry and often lightly sparkling, or fully **spumante**.

Colline Pisane See **Chianti**.

Collio (also called Collio Goriziano) **DOC** wine of the **Friuli-Venezia Giulia** region of northeast **Italy**. Excellent full-bodied whites, and reds that can take

moderate **ageing**, are produced in 11 different styles.
Collio Bianco is a white blend of the **Ribolla**, **Malvasia**
and **Tocai Friulano** grapes. Then there are seven white
varietals made from Malvasia, Pinot Bianco, Pinot
Grigio, **Riesling Italico**, Sauvignon, **Tocai Friulano** and
Traminer; and three red varietals, **Merlot**, Pinot Nero
and **Cabernet Franc**.

Collioure Red **AC** wine of the **Languedoc-Roussillon**
region of **France**, produced from the **Grenache**,
Mourvèdre, **Carignan** and **Cinsault** grape varieties.
Assertive and full-bodied in its youth, it is capable of
long **ageing**.

Colombard White grape variety, which was
traditionally grown for distillation into Armagnac.
Recently it has enjoyed a revival as a wine grape,
making good, ordinary quality **varietal** wines in
California and in the **Côtes de Gascogne** in **France**.
In **Australia** it is often blended with a little **Chardonnay**
to produce an inexpensive but attractive dry white.

Commandaria Deep-coloured dessert wine produced
in **Cyprus** from semi-dried grapes. The best, sold as
'100 years old', lives up to its legendary reputation;
much of the modern, commercial product does not.

complex Tasting term, used to indicate a wine with
many layers of **aroma** and flavour; one of the hallmarks
of a great wine.

Conca de Barberá Small **DO** region near **Penedès** in
north-east **Spain**. Much of the white wine produced

goes to make **Cava**, but there are good-quality, inexpensive still wines made from **Parellada** and **Macabeo**, and the **Chardonnay** can be excellent, especially when fermented in barrel. Among the reds, **Tempranillo** produces good, softly fruity wines, while **Cabernet Sauvignon** and **Merlot** can produce wines of great richness and concentration.

Concord Red, non-**Vitis vinifera**, grape variety native to America and widely grown in the east of the **United States**. It is used to make usually sweet, often sparkling red wine, with the curious **foxy** flavour of the *labrusca* vine. It is also grown in **Brazil**.

Condrieu White **AC** wine of the northern **Rhône**, produced from the **Viognier** grape variety in tiny quantities. The wine has a delicious and distinctive apricot-and-cream **aroma** and taste. It is rare, although by no means so rare as **Château-Grillet**, and is consequently somewhat less expensive.

consejo regulador Spanish regulatory body (there is one for each **DO** wine region), which enforces the DO regulations and monitors production and movement of wines within the region.

consorzio Italian term for a voluntary consortium of producers, within a given region, which can supervise its members' production, or help to promote and market their wines.

Controliran Bulgarian term to indicate superior wine from a specified region.

Coonawarra Important wine-producing region of **South Australia**, with distinctive red soil (**terra rossa**). It produces superb **varietal** and blended red wines, among **Australia**'s best and longest-lived, from **Cabernet Sauvignon**, **Shiraz** and **Merlot**. Good whites are also made, largely from **Chardonnay** and **Riesling**.

Copertino DOC wine produced in the **Apulia** region of southern **Italy**. Full-bodied red and dry **rosato** wines are made mainly from the **Negroamaro** grape variety.

copita Spanish term for the smallish, quite narrow, tapering glass in which **Sherry**, particularly chilled **fino**, should be served.

Corbières AC wine of the **Languedoc-Roussillon** region of southern **France**. Most of the production is of full-bodied, consistently good-value, meaty, spicy reds, based on the **Grenache**, **Cinsault** and **Carignan** grape varieties, plus limited quantities of **Syrah**. The small amount of white wine produced, mainly from **Bourboulenc** and **Clairette**, is less interesting, and is at best clean and refreshing.

Cori DOC wine produced in very small quantities in the **Latium** region of **Italy**. The **bianco** is based on the **Malvasia** and **Trebbiano** grape varieties, and the **rosso** is produced mainly from **Montepulciano** and **Cesanese**.

cork Substance traditionally used for keeping wine in the bottle, and the air out. Cork is made from the bark of the cork **oak** tree (Quercus suber), and **Portugal** is

the major centre of production. Problems with cork
taint from cheaper corks (see **corked**) have led
producers to experiment with synthetic corks and
initial results have been encouraging.

corked (also called corky) Tasting term used to describe
a wine that is 'off', with a stale, woody, mouldy smell
and taste, possibly accompanied by **oxidation**.

Cornas Red AC wine of the northern **Rhône**, **France**,
produced from the **Syrah** grape variety. It is deep-
coloured and **tannic** in its youth, developing a splendid
depth of flavour and complexity with age, with
delicious spicy, leathery red fruit.

Corsica French-owned wine-producing island in the
Mediterranean. **Nielluccio** is the most widely planted
native variety, followed by **Sciacarello**. Much of the
island is planted with **Cinsault**, **Grenache**, and
Carignan, recently supplemented by noble varieties
such as **Chardonnay**, **Cabernet Sauvignon**, **Syrah**, and
Viognier. These latter are generally labelled as **Vin de
pays** de l'Île de Beauté. See also **Ajaccio**; **Vin de Corse**.

Cortese White grape variety, grown mainly in
Piedmont, northwest **Italy**; it is also found in **Oltrepò
Pavese** and the **Veneto**. In Piedmont, it is DOC in
Cortese dell'Alto Monferrato (a fine dry white,
occasionally **frizzante** or **spumante**) and Gavi, or Gavi
di Gavi (from the heartland of the zone) one of Italy's
finest white wines, gently **aromatic**, fairly full, and with
a good cut of refreshing **acidity**. Cortese is also used in
Piedmont to produce white **Colli Tortonesi**.

Corton **Grand cru** vineyard of the **Côte de Beaune** region of **Burgundy**, shared by the villages of **Aloxe-Corton**, **Pernand-Vergelesses** and **Ladoix-Serrigny**. A rich, top-quality, long-lived red Burgundy of the highest quality. A very small quantity of white Corton is also produced.

Corton-Charlemagne **Grand cru** vineyard of the **Côte de Beaune** region of **Burgundy**, shared by the villages of **Aloxe-Corton**, **Pernand-Vergelesses**, and **Ladoix-Serrigny**. A rich, buttery, long-lived white Burgundy of the highest quality.

Corvina Red grape variety of the **Veneto** region of Italy. It is the best quality ingredient in the blends for **Valpolicella** and **Bardolino**, especially prized for the **recioto** and **Amarone** wines of Valpolicella.

cosecha Spanish term for vintage year.

Costers del Segre **DO** wine of northeast **Spain**, producing high quality red and white wines from a mixture of native varieties (including **Tempranillo**, **Garnacha**, **Parellada**, **Macabeo**, **Xarel-lo** and **Cariñena**) and imported varieties (mainly **Cabernet Sauvignon**, **Merlot**, **Pinot Noir** and **Chardonnay**).

Costières de Nîmes (formerly Costières du Gard) **AC** wine of the **Languedoc-Roussillon** region of southern **France**. Most of the wine produced is simple, beefy reds (and some fresh rosé) based on the **Carignan**, **Grenache** and **Syrah** grape varieties. A relatively small amount of fresh white wine, for early drinking, is based on **Bourboulenc**, **Clairette** and **Ugni Blanc**.

Cot Red grape variety of **France**, grown mainly in **Bordeaux** (where it is called **Malbec**, or **Pressac** in **Saint-Émilion**) where it is a very minor component in much of the red wine, particularly in the **Côtes de Bourg** and the **Premières Côtes de Blaye**. It is a more important ingredient in **Cahors** (where it is sometimes also known as **Auxerrois**), and for **Touraine** Tradition in the **Loire**. In **Spain** Cot is found in **Ribera del Duero**, and in **Italy**, in **Rosso Barletta** from **Apulia**. It really comes into its own in **Argentina**, where **varietal** Malbec is one of the finest and most distinctive reds produced.

côte French term for hill or slope, often extended to designate a region.

Côte Blonde See **Côte Rôtie**.

Côte Brune See **Côte Rôtie**.

Côte Chalonnaise Wine-producing region of **Burgundy** in **France**, producing white wine from the **Aligoté** and **Chardonnay** grape varieties, and red from **Pinot Noir** and **Gamay**. There are five **AC** wines. **Bouzeron** is one of the best white wines from the Aligoté grape. **Givry** makes mainly dry red wines from Pinot Noir, and a small amount of white from Chardonnay. **Mercurey**, produced around the village of the same name, is mostly red Pinot Noir plus a small amount of Chardonnay. **Montagny** produces good Chardonnay, especially with **oak ageing**. **Rully** produces soft, medium-bodied, nutty Chardonnay, sometimes with a touch of oak; reds, from Pinot Noir, are lighter bodied, and less successful.

Côte d'Or Heart of the **Burgundy** region, where some
of the world's finest red, from **Pinot Noir**, and white
wines, from **Chardonnay**, are produced. The Côte d'Or
('golden slope'), stretches in a thin band from
Marsannay in the north to **Santenay** in the south,
including the two subregions of the **Côte de Nuits** and
the **Côte de Beaune**.

Côte de Beaune Southern of the two subregions of
the **Côte d'Or** area of **Burgundy**. See **Aloxe-Corton**;
Auxey-Duresses; **Beaune**; **Blagny**; **Chassagne-
Montrachet**; **Chorey-lès-Beaune**; **Ladoix-Serrigny**; **Les
Maranges**; **Meursault**; **Monthélie**; **Pernand-
Vergelesses**; **Pommard**; **Saint-Aubin**; **Saint-Romain**;
Savigny-lès-Beaune.

Côte de Beaune-Villages AC wine from one or
more of 16 villages in the **Côte de Beaune**. Producers
can declassify from the more specific village *appellation*
if they want to blend wine from more than one village
AC, or for commercial reasons, for instance if the
village AC name is not well known.

Côte de Brouilly Red **AC** wine, one of the 10 **crus** of
the **Beaujolais** region of **Burgundy**, made from the
Gamay grape. The wine is full and perfumed, with
juicy, ripe sweetness, and strawberry flavours. The
quality is usually very good, among the best of all
Beaujolais.

Côte de Nuits Northern of the two subregions of the
Côte d'Or area of **Burgundy**. See **Fixin**; **Flagey-
Echézeaux**; **Gevrey-Chambertin**; **Marsannay**; **Morey-St-
Denis**; **Nuits-Saint-Georges**; **Vosne-Romanée**; **Vougeot**.

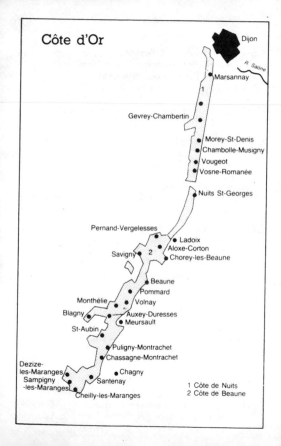

Côte d'Or

Dijon

R. Saône

Marsannay

1

Gevrey-Chambertin

Morey-St-Denis
Chambolle-Musigny
Vougeot
Vosne-Romanée

Nuits St-Georges

Pernand-Vergelesses

Ladoix
Aloxe-Corton

Savigny   2   Chorey-les-Beaune

Beaune
Pommard
Monthélie   Volnay
Blagny   Auxey-Duresses
Meursault
St-Aubin

Puligny-Montrachet
Chassagne-Montrachet

Dezize-
les-Maranges   Chagny
Sampigny
-les-Maranges   Santenay
Cheilly-les-Maranges

1 Côte de Nuits
2 Côte de Beaune

Côte de Nuits-Villages AC wine of the **Côte de Nuits** region of **Burgundy**, produced in the villages of Brochon, Corgoloin, Comblanchien, Prissey and **Fixin** (Fixin can also be sold under its own AC). Most of the wine produced is good-value, red Burgundy, from the **Pinot Noir** grape variety, and is best drunk fairly young.

Côte des Blancs Vineyard area in the **Champagne** region of **France**. It is planted almost entirely with the white grape variety **Chardonnay**, hence the name.

Côte Rôtie Red **AC** wine of the northern **Rhône**, produced mainly from the **Syrah** grape variety, with just a touch of the white **Viognier**. At its best, the wine is scented, fine and concentrated, with spicy, curranty fruit, capable of long **ageing**. The two best slopes are Côte Blonde and Côte Brune, occasionally vinified and bottled separately.

coteau French term for a slope or hillside.

Coteaux Champenois Still **AC** wine of the **Champagne** region. It can be white, made from the **Chardonnay** grape variety, or red, from **Pinot Noir** and **Pinot Meunier**. Both wines are usually rather thin, harsh and acidic. See also **Bouzy**.

Coteaux d'Aix-en-Provence AC wine of **Provence** in southern **France**. The best wines are reds, made from the **Grenache** and **Syrah** grape varieties and, increasingly, **Cabernet Sauvignon**, rich and fruity, and capable of moderate **ageing**. Good fresh rosé is made from the same grape varieties. Small quantities of fairly neutral dry white wine are also made, from varieties including **Ugni Blanc**, **Sauvignon Blanc** and **Sémillon**. The separate AC Coteaux des Baux-en-Provence makes some high-quality red wines, mainly from Cabernet Sauvignon, Grenache, and Syrah.

Coteaux d'Ancenis VDQS wine of the **Loire** valley, mainly light-bodied red and rosé from the **Gamay** and **Cabernet Franc** grape varieties, plus a little sharp white from **Chenin Blanc** and **Pinot Gris**.

Coteaux de l'Aubance White **AC** wine of the **Loire** valley, made from the **Chenin Blanc** grape. A delicate and medium-sweet wine, it is best drunk young.

Coteaux des Baux-en-Provence See **Coteaux d'Aix-en-Provence**.

Coteaux du Cap Corse See **Vin de Corse**.

Coteaux du Giennois VDQS wine of the **Loire** valley. Dry, fairly acidic white is made from the **Sauvignon Blanc** and **Chenin Blanc** grape varieties; ordinary red and quite decent rosé are made from **Gamay** and **Pinot Noir**.

Coteaux du Languedoc AC wine of the **Languedoc-Roussillon** region of southern **France**. The region produces good, fresh, fruity red and rosé wines, from the **Carignan**, **Cinsault**, **Grenache**, **Syrah** and **Mourvèdre** grape varieties, among others.

Coteaux du Layon Sweet white **AC** wine produced
in the **Anjou-Saumur** area of the **Loire** valley, made
from the **Chenin Blanc** grape variety. The wine is sweet
and fresh, and in exceptional years the grapes can be
affected by **botrytis**. However, Coteaux du Layon
seldom approaches the luscious richness of
Bonnezeaux and **Quarts de Chaume**. Seven villages in
Layon are entitled to the AC Côteaux du Layon-
Villages: Beaulieu sur Layon; Chaume; Faye d'Anjou;
Rablay sur Layon; Rochefort sur Loire; Saint Aubin de
Luigné; and Saint Lambert de Lattay. They are one
degree higher in **alcohol**, and have longer **ageing**
potential.

Coteaux du Lyonnais AC wine of **Burgundy**,
produced in vineyards south of Lyon. Mostly red is
produced – light, **Beaujolais**-like wine made from the
Gamay grape variety. A little rosé is also produced
from Gamay, plus a small amount of white, from
Chardonnay and **Aligoté**.

Coteaux du Tricastin AC wine of the southern
Rhône. Mostly red and rosé wines are produced, from
the **Grenache**, **Cinsault**, **Mourvèdre** and **Syrah** grape
varieties. They are light, fresh and fruity, for good-value
early drinking. Quality is steadily improving. A small
amount of white is made from **Bourboulenc** and
Marsanne.

Coteaux du Vendômois VDQS wine of the **Loire**
region, produced along the banks of the **Loir** tributary.
Dry, quite **austere** white is produced from the **Chenin
Blanc** and **Chardonnay** grape varieties. Light, dry reds

and rosés are based on **Pineau d'Aunis** and **Gamay**, with the possible addition of **Pinot Noir**, **Cabernet Sauvignon** and **Cabernet Franc** for the red.

Coteaux Varois VDQS wine produced in the **Provence** region of southern **France**. Light reds and fresh, dry rosés are produced from the **Grenache**, **Syrah**, **Mourvèdre** and **Cinsault** grape varieties and, increasingly, **Cabernet Sauvignon**.

Côtes d'Auvergne VDQS wine produced in vineyards near to Clermont-Ferrand, in the upper **Loire** valley. Most of the production is of red wine, light, fresh and **Beaujolais**-like, made from the **Gamay** and **Pinot Noir** grape varieties. Light, dry rosés are produced from the same grape varieties. A little white wine is produced from **Chardonnay**.

Côtes de Bergerac AC wine of the **Bergerac** region of southwest **France**. The red wines are simply a higher-**alcohol**, lower-**yield** version of red Bergerac. White Côtes de Bergerac is bigger and higher in alcohol than Bergerac Sec, and Côtes de Bergerac-Moelleux is the AC for the sweet whites of the region (see also **Monbazillac**).

Côtes de Blaye White **AC** wine of **Bordeaux**, produced on the east side of the Gironde estuary, facing the **Haut-Médoc**. The wine is light, softly fruity white, usually dry, made from the **Sauvignon Blanc** and **Sémillon** grape varieties, plus a touch of **Colombard**. Red **Blaye** comes under the AC of **Premières Côtes de Blaye**.

Côtes de Bourg AC wine of **Bordeaux**, produced on the east side of the Gironde estuary, just south of the **Premières Côtes de Blaye**. Nearly all of the production is of red wine, from the classic Bordeaux grape varieties, **Cabernet Sauvignon**, **Cabernet Franc** and **Merlot**, with the emphasis on Merlot. These are fresh, fruity, easy-to-drink wines, best drunk relatively early.

Côtes de Castillon AC wine of **Bordeaux**, produced in vineyards just to the east of **Saint-Emilion**. Nearly all of the production is red, from the classic Bordeaux grape varieties, **Cabernet Sauvignon**, **Cabernet Franc** and **Merlot**, with the emphasis on Merlot. These are fresh, fruity, easy-to-drink wines, best drunk relatively early. Quality is increasingly good.

Côtes de Duras AC wine of southwest **France**, just outside the **Bordeaux** area, and using much the same grape varieties. Good quality, fresh white wine is produced mainly from **Sauvignon Blanc**, plus some **Sémillon** and **Muscadelle**. Soft, fresh, good-value reds, best drunk young, are made from **Cabernet Sauvignon**, **Cabernet Franc** and **Merlot**.

Côtes de Francs Up-and-coming **AC** wine of **Bordeaux**, produced in vineyards just to the east of **Saint-Émilion**. Nearly all of the production is of red wine, from the classic Bordeaux grape varieties, **Cabernet Sauvignon**, **Cabernet Franc** and **Merlot**, with the emphasis on Merlot. These are excellent, good-value wines, deep, fruity, with a good **tannic** backbone to provide structure and **ageing** potential.

Côtes de Gascogne Vin de pays of southwest France, producing excellent, good-quality, good-value whites, particularly from the **Colombard** grape variety, as well as **Ugni Blanc** and **Sauvignon Blanc** whites. A small amount of rather thin red is also produced, from **Cabernet Sauvignon**, **Cabernet Franc**, **Merlot** and **Tannat**.

Côtes de Montravel Sweet, white **AC** wine produced in the west of the **Bergerac** region, from the **Sauvignon Blanc**, **Sémillon** and **Muscadelle** grape varieties. It lacks the richness of the great sweet wines of **Bordeaux**, and is declining in popularity, so production is switching to dry wines.

Côtes de Provence AC wine of **Provence** in southern **France**. Most of the production is of fresh, fruity, fairly full rosé wine, made mainly from the **Grenache** and **Cinsault** grape varieties, and fruity, herby reds based on **Mourvèdre**, **Syrah** and **Cabernet Sauvignon**, among others. Smaller quantities of rather dull white are made from **Sémillon**, **Rolle**, **Ugni Blanc** and **Clairette**.

Côtes de Saint-Mont VDQS wine of southwest France. Good, light and fruity red (and a little rosé) wine is produced from the **Cabernet Sauvignon**, **Cabernet Franc**, **Merlot** and **Tannat** grape varieties. Dry white is made from the two Manseng varieties, plus Arrufiac and Petit Courbu.

Côtes du Forez VDQS wine of the upper reaches of the **Loire** valley, not far from Lyon. Mainly red wine is

produced from the **Gamay** grape variety, similar to a
very pale version of **Beaujolais**.

Côtes du Frontonnais AC wine produced near the
town of Fronton in southwest **France**. Most of the
production is of medium-quality, fruity red wine, best
drunk young, based on the **Négrette** grape variety, plus
Cabernet Franc and **Cabernet Sauvignon**. A little rosé
is produced from the same grape varieties.

Côtes du Jura AC wine of the **Jura** region of eastern
France. Most of the production is of white wine, based
on the **Savagnin** and **Chardonnay** grape varieties. It can
be still and dry, a **méthode traditionnelle** sparkler, or a
vin jaune. A small amount of light red and rosé is
produced from **Trousseau**, **Poulsard** and **Pinot Noir**.
Wines from the subregion of **Arbois** show more
distinction.

Côtes du Lubéron AC wine of the southern **Rhône**.
Lightweight reds and rosés, best drunk young, are
produced from **Grenache**, **Syrah**, **Cinsault** and
Mourvèdre. Fresh, fruity whites are based on **Ugni
Blanc** and **Clairette**.

Côtes du Marmandais AC wine of southwest
France, mainly soft, fruity red from the classic
Bordeaux grapes plus the local Abouriou and **Fer**, and
a very small quantity of white, from **Sauvignon Blanc**,
Sémillon, **Muscadelle** and **Ugni Blanc**.

Côtes du Rhône AC wine of the **Rhône** region of
France. This AC covers most of the Rhône's basic

production, nearly all of it spicy, fruity red wine, based on the **Grenache**, **Syrah**, **Cinsault** and **Mourvèdre** grape varieties. Côtes du Rhône-Villages comes from one or more of 17 selected villages of the southern Rhône, and generally has more depth and character to it. The villages are **Beaumes-de-Venise**, Cairanne, Chusclan, **Laudun**, **Rasteau**, Roaix, Rochegude, Rousset-les-Vignes, Sablet, Saint-Gervais, Saint-Maurice-sur-Eygues, Saint-Pantaléon-les-Vignes, Séguret, Vacqueyras, Valréas, Vinsobres and Visan.

White Côtes du Rhône (and Côtes du Rhône-Villages) is produced from the **Clairette**, **Marsanne** and **Roussanne** grape varieties; it is rarely impressive.

Côtes du Roussillon AC wine of the **Languedoc-Roussillon** area of southern **France**. Good-value, robust, fruity red and rosé, for early drinking, are made from the **Carignan**, **Cinsault**, **Grenache** and **Mourvèdre** grape varieties. A very small quantity of white is made, mainly from **Macabeo**. Red wines from selected sites, such as Caramany, are entitled to the Côtes du Roussillon-Villages AC, and they are usually superior.

Côtes du Ventoux AC wine of the southern **Rhône**. Most of the production is of full-flavoured, fruity red made from the **Carignan**, **Cinsault**, **Grenache**, **Mourvèdre** and **Syrah** grape varieties. Only a tiny amount of white wine is produced.

Côtes du Vivarais VDQS wine of the southern **Rhône**. Most of the production is of lively, fruity red (and some rosé) made from the **Grenache**, **Mourvèdre**

and **Syrah** grape varieties. Only a tiny amount of white wine is produced.

Counoise Red grape variety of the southern **Rhône**, planted mainly as a minor ingredient in **Châteauneuf-du-Pape**.

Courbu Minor white grape variety of **France**, used as part of the blend to make **Jurançon**.

Cramant Important wine-producing village in the Côtes des Blancs region of **Champagne**.

Cream Sherry Popular style of sweet **Sherry**, made by sweetening an **oloroso**. See also **Pale Cream**.

crémant French term for a **méthode traditionnelle** sparkling wine produced outside **Champagne** (particularly from **Alsace**, **Burgundy**, Die, the **Loire**, **Limoux**, and **Bordeaux**).

Crémant d'Alsace Méthode traditionnelle sparkling AC wine from **Alsace**. It is usually white, based mainly on **Pinot Blanc**, sometimes with **Riesling** and **Auxerrois**.

Crémant de Bordeaux Méthode traditionnelle sparkling AC wine from **Bordeaux**, produced in relatively small quantities from the classic Bordeaux varieties.

Crémant de Bourgogne Méthode traditionnelle sparkling AC wine from **Burgundy**. It is made mainly from the **Chardonnay** grape variety, sometimes with

Aligoté and **Pinot Noir**. Quality has improved a great deal lately, making this a good-value alternative to **Champagne**. Some good rosé is also made from **Pinot Noir**.

Crémant de Die **Méthode traditionnelle** sparkling **AC** wine, made from the **Clairette** grape variety. See also **Clairette** de Die.

Crémant de Limoux **Méthode traditionnelle** sparkling white **AC** wine, produced around the town of **Limoux**, southern **France**. The wine is made from the **Mauzac Blanc**, **Chardonnay** and **Chenin Blanc** grape varieties. It is dry and can be quite complex. Its quality can be good, but without reaching the heights of top **Champagne**. See also **Blanquette de Limoux**.

Crémant de Loire **Méthode traditionnelle** sparkling **AC** wine of the **Loire**. It is similar to sparkling **Saumur**, except that it can come from anywhere in the Anjou and **Touraine** regions, and permitted **yields** are lower: quality should therefore be better. Most of the production is white, based on the **Chenin Blanc**, **Chardonnay** and **Cabernet Franc** grape varieties. Some rosé is produced, from Cabernet Franc and **Gamay**.

Crépy White **AC** wine of the Savoie region of **France**. Very delicate white wine is produced, sometimes slightly **pétillant**, from the **Chasselas** grape. Rarely seen outside the region.

criadera See **solera**; **Sherry**.

crianza Spanish term used to descibe **ageing** and a barrel-aged wine. For many **DO** wines, a minimum ageing period is required before a wine can be labelled crianza. See **Rioja**.

Crimea Peninsula off southern **Ukraine**, part of the **CIS**. Most of the production is of strong, fortified sweet wines.

Criolla Chica Alternative name, used in South America (particularly **Argentina**), for the grape known as **Mission** (**California**) and **Pais** (**Chile**).

Criolla Grande Low-quality grape variety of **Argentina**, producing large quantities of inferior white and rosé wine.

crisp Tasting term, used to describe a pleasantly assertive, fresh wine, usually white, with a good level of balancing **acidity**.

Croatia Part of the former Yugoslavia. The inland vineyards are planted mainly with white varieties: **Laski Rizling** is the most important, and there is also some **Gewürztraminer**, **Riesling**, **Sauvignon Blanc**, and **Sémillon**. The coastal region produces decent reds from **Cabernet Sauvignon** and **Merlot**, plus local grapes such as Plavac Mali, which show good potential.

Croatina Red grape variety of the **Piedmont** and **Lombardy** regions of **Italy**, where it produces fresh, early drinking wines. In **Oltrepò Pavese** it produces **varietal** wine under the name **Bonarda** (a synonym for Croatina, but distinct from **Bonarda Piemontese**).

cross (or crossing) Vine variety bred by crossing two vines of the same species, usually both **Vitis vinifera**. See also **hybrid**.

Crouchen Medium-quality white grape variety originating in **France** but now planted in **South Africa** and **Australia**. In both countries it has been confused with **Riesling**, and was known as Clare Riesling in Australia and **Cape Riesling** in South Africa.

Crozes-Hermitage AC wine of the northern **Rhône**. The red wine is produced from the **Syrah** grape variety. Although not approaching the depth and complexity of **Hermitage**, it can be excellent, with rich, spicy fruit flavours, and the capacity for moderate **ageing**. Delicately scented white Crozes, made from **Marsanne** and **Roussanne**, is at its best when drunk fresh and young.

cru French term, literally meaning 'growth', but usually referring to the quality and status of a particular vineyard site. See **cru bourgeois**; **cru classé**; **grand cru**; **premier cru**.

cru bourgeois Classification of the **châteaux** of the **Médoc**, **Bordeaux**, at a level immediately below **cru classé**. The classification of the crus classés took place in 1855, and has scarcely altered since, so some of the best crus bourgeois now out-perform lesser **classed growths**. They can offer excellent value for money.

cru classé Top classification of the châteaux of **Bordeaux**. There are five subdivisions: *premier grand*

of northern **Portugal**, which may be red
made from a large number of grape
eds must contain at least 20% of the
al grape and be aged for at least 18
and 2 months in bottle. They are firm,
ty and **tannic** in their youth. The
e has traditionally been for more
nes over-mature, red wines. **Garrafeira**
ed at least two years in vat and one in
this period is often exceeded.

contain at least 20% of the **Encruzado**
be aged six months before bottling.
acidity and an attractive lemony aroma
arrafeira whites must be aged for at
in vat and six in bottle, developing a
aracter. Overall quality is improving
potential is very good.

ape variety native to **Greece**, which
t, crisp, sparkling or semi-sparkling

ess of transferring a wine from its
vessel, usually a glass decanter.
e is to separate the wine from its
larly important with mature Vintage
wines, including red **Bordeaux**.
es may also be decanted, in order to

cru classé down t[...]
to in English as 'f[...]
on. Since the clas[...]
1855, there are in[...]
performers. See [...]

Cruet Zone of V[...]

Crusted Port B[...]
vintages. It is bo[...]
without filtratio[...]
deposit, and the[...]
convincing app[...]
style at a more [...]

cuve French fo[...]

cuve close Se[...]

cuvée French t[...]
indicate a part[...]
Thus a produc[...]
prepared from[...]

Cyprus Island[...]
Mediterranea[...]
table wines, C[...]

Czech Repub[...]
Czechoslovak[...]
in Moravia, p[...]
Welschriesli[...]
Reds made fr[...]
Frankovka)[...]
common.

D

Dão DOC wine[...]
or white and is[...]
varieties. The r[...]
Touriga Nacio[...]
months in cask[...]
full-bodied, fru[...]
Portuguese tas[...]
mature, someti[...]
Dão must be ag[...]
bottle, althoug[...]

The whites mus[...]
grape, and mus[...]
They have goo[...]
in their youth. [...]
least six months[...]
rich, honeyed c[...]
steadily, and the[...]

Debina White g[...]
produces the lig[...]
wines of **Zitsa**.

decanting Proc[...]
bottle to anothe[...]
The main purpo[...]
sediment, partic[...]
Port and old re[...]
Younger red win[...]

aerate them and so help to bring out the **aroma** and taste.

deep Tasting term which describes the intensity of a wine's colour, **aroma** and taste.

dégorgement French for **disgorgement**.

degree Alcoholic strength of a wine. 12° means 12% **alcohol** by volume.

dégustation French for wine tasting.

Deidesheim Small town in the **Pfalz** region of **Germany**, which produces high-quality, full-bodied white wines from the **Riesling** grape. There are three **Grosslagen**: Hofstück, Mariengarten and Schnepfenflug an der Weinstrasse. The top **Einzellagen** include Grainhübel, Leinhöhle, Herrgottsacker, Kieselberg and Langenmorgen, and all of these are in Mariengarten.

Delaware Non-vinifera grape variety planted particularly in **New York State** and Japan.

demi-sec French for medium-dry wine.

denominação de origem controlada See **DOC** (**Portugal**).

denominación de origen See **DO**.

denominación de origen calificada See **DOC** (**Spain**).

denominazione di origine controllata (e garantita) See **DOC (Italy)** and **DOCG**.

dessert wine Term loosely used to describe sweet, usually white wines, such as **Sauternes**, late-harvest wines from **Germany**, **Austria**, **California** and **Australia**, and **vins doux naturels**. In fact the term is misleading. **Sauternes**, for instance, is better enjoyed as an apéritif, with foie gras, salty blue cheese, or drunk on its own after a meal, but is rarely at its best with a sweet dessert.

Deutscher Sekt Sekt actually made from German grapes.

Deutscher Tafelwein Table wine from **Germany**, in a quality category below **QbA**. The wine must be made entirely from grapes grown in Germany, with a minimum **alcohol** content of 8.5%. The wine may be labelled with one of four district names: Rhein-Mosel (subdistricts **Rhein**, Mosel and Saar); Bayern (subdistricts Main, Donau, and Lindau), Neckar and Oberrhein (subdistricts Römertor and Burgengau). **Tafelwein** (without the Deutscher) can include wine from other countries (often **Italy**). See also **Landwein**.

developed Tasting term that describes the state of maturity of a wine. A young wine could be described as 'underdeveloped', a mature wine as 'well-developed' and an over-mature wine as 'overdeveloped'.

Dimiat White grape variety of **Bulgaria** producing floral, often sweetish, white wines.

disgorgement Removal of the sediment that develops during secondary **fermentation** in bottle, as in the case of **Champagne** and other **méthode traditionnelle** sparkling wines. After **remuage**, the sediment is concentrated near the mouth of the bottle. The top of the bottle is plunged into chilled brine so that the wine and sediment in the neck freeze. The crown cork is then removed, and the plug of frozen wine and sediment flies out.

Dizy Village in the Vallée de la Marne region of **Champagne**, **France**. Its vineyards, mainly planted with the **Pinot Noir** grape, are rated 95%.

DO (denominación de origen) Guarantee of origin used for Spanish wines, roughly equivalent to the French **AC** system. For each DO region the laws specify the delimited area from which the wines may come, permitted grape varieties, permitted vineyard practices, and **ageing** requirements. The laws are enforced by the DO region's **consejo regulador**, which monitors production and movement of wines within the region. Wines are analysed and tasted before qualifying for the DO. See also **DOC (Spain)**.

DOC 1. **Italy** (denominazione di origine controllata) Guarantee of origin used for Italian wines, roughly equivalent to the French **AC** system. For each DOC region, of which there are more than 200, the laws specify the delimited area from which the wines may come, permitted grape varieties, permitted vineyard practices, and **ageing** requirements. Although the DOC laws encourage quality, they do not guarantee it; many top wines fall outside its specifications, qualifying only as **vini da tavola** or **IGT**. See also **DOCG**.

2. **Spain** (denominación de origen calificada) Quality designation superior to plain **DO**. So far only **Rioja** has qualified as a DOC.

3. **Portugal** (denominação de origem controlada) Guarantee of origin used for Portuguese wines, roughly equivalent to the French **AC** system. It replaces the former **RD** (região demarcada) system.

DOCG (denominazione di origine controllata e garantita) Highest category used for the wines of **Italy**, so far only awarded to a steadily increasing number of former **DOCs**. The wines are analysed and assessed by a tasting panel before qualifying for the DOCG. In the case of **Chianti**, for instance, elevation from DOC to DOCG involved a change in the permitted mix of grape varieties and lower yields.

dolce Term found on Italian labels meaning sweet. Sweeter than **amabile** or **abboccato**.

Dolcetto Red grape variety of the **Piedmont** region of **Italy**. It produces deep-coloured, easy-drinking, dry wines, usually of good quality. There are seven **DOC** zones. The best are Dolcetto d'Alba and Dolcetto di Diano d'Alba, deep, balanced and smooth. Dolcetto di Dogliani and di Ovada are also firm and structured, while Dolcetto d'Asti, delle Langhe Monregalesi and d'Acqui are more lightweight.

Dôle Red wine of good quality made in the Valais region of **Switzerland**, from the **Pinot Noir** and **Gamay** grapes.

domaine French term for a wine estate, used particularly in **Burgundy** but also elsewhere in **France**.

Donnaz Dry red **DOC** wine from the **Valle d'Aosta** region of northwest **Italy**, made from the **Nebbiolo** grape. It is usually lighter than Nebbiolo from **Piedmont**, but is still capable of moderate **ageing**. Above average quality, but rarely exported.

Donnici Dry red **DOC** wine from the hills around Cosenza in the **Calabria** region of southern **Italy**, made from the **Gaglioppo** and **Greco** Nero grapes. It is usually light red, fruity and flavoursome, and is best drunk while young and fresh.

Dornfelder Red grape variety produced from a crossing of Helfensteiner and Heroldrebe (each of which is also a **cross**), grown mainly in the **Pfalz** and **Rheinhessen** regions of **Germany**. It produces deep-coloured (for Germany) red wines, with good fruit and **acidity**, with some **ageing** potential. One of Germany's most promising new red varieties.

Dorsheim Village near **Bingen** in the **Nahe** region of **Germany**, in the **Bereich** of Kreuznach, and the **Grosslage** of Schlosskapelle. It produces excellent, full-bodied white wines of high quality from the **Riesling** grape. The steep Goldloch vineyard is probably the best **Einzellage**.

dosage French term for the sweetness added to **Champagne** and other **méthode traditionnelle** wines after the second, fizz-producing **fermentation**, in the form of the **liqueur d'expedition**. Without *dosage* the wine is bone dry and labelled *ultra brut* or *zero brut*. Depending on how much sweetness is added, the wine is labelled (in ascending order of sweetness) **brut**, extra dry, **sec** or **demi-sec**, rich or doux. Most Champagne is sold as *brut*.

double magnum Large format bottle with a capacity of 3 litres (equivalent to four standard bottles of 75 cl). Known as a jeroboam in **Champagne**.

Douro River in northern **Portugal**, which rises in **Spain** as the Duero and enters the sea at Vila Nova de Gaia. The grapes for **Port** are grown in the steep valleys of the river and its tributaries. The river also gives its name to dry red (and some white) **DOC** wines. The reds tend to be rich and **tannic**, needing relatively long **ageing** and can be of a very good quality. Whites are generally mediocre.

Drumborg Cool-climate wine region of **Victoria**, **Australia**, important as a source for grapes for sparkling wines.

dry Tasting term, also found on labels, to describe a wine in which no sweetness is detectable on the **palate**. See also **residual sugar**.

Dry Creek Valley AVA in **Sonoma** county, **California**.

dulce 1. Term used in **Spain** to describe a wine that is sweeter than **semi-seco**. 2. A wine used to give sweetness in the blended **Pale Cream** and Cream styles of **Sherry**.

Duras Red grape grown mainly in the Tarn region of southwest **France**. It is used together with **Fer** and **Négrette** to make **Gaillac Rouge**, a fruity red wine of moderately good quality. The grape has no connection with the **Côtes de Duras**.

E

échantillon French for sample.

Echézeaux Grand cru vineyard of the commune of **Flagey-Echézeaux** in the **Côte de Nuits** region of **Burgundy**. It produces among the finest and most elegant of the region's red wines from the **Pinot Noir** grape. Although technically attached to Flagey-Echézeaux, the vineyard is nearer to **Vosne-Romanée**, and the wines can be declassified to Vosne-Romanée **premier cru**. Quality is good, but generally not as good as the smaller, neighbouring **Grands-Echézeaux**, or the other *grand cru* vineyards of the Côte de Nuits.

Edelfäule German term for **noble rot** or **botrytis**.

Edelzwicker Blended wine from the **AC** region **Alsace**. The best grape varieties in Alsace are nearly always bottled and labelled as **varietals**. Edelzwicker tends to be a blend of the lesser varieties such as **Chasselas**, **Pinot Blanc** and **Silvaner**. A supermarket wine labelled simply '**AC Alsace**' will generally be a similar sort of blend, but it might not bear the word Edelzwicker on the label.

Eden Valley Region in the north of the **Adelaide Hills** area of **Australia**, where fine **varietal** wines are made from the **Riesling**, **Gewürztraminer**, **Shiraz** and **Cabernet Sauvignon** grapes. Eden Valley **Rhine Rieslings** are probably Australia's finest wines from that variety.

Edna Valley AVA of **San Luis Obispo** county, **California**, with a growing reputation for its cool-climate white wines, particularly **Chardonnay**.

égrappage French term for the process of separating grapes from their stems. Red wines can be fermented with or without their stems. The stems can add **tannin** to the wine, but also toughness and bitterness, and many quality red wines are today vinified without them.

Egri Bikavér Red Hungarian wine, also known as Bull's Blood, originally made from the **Kadarka** grape variety, with the later addition of **Cabernet Sauvignon**, **Kékfrankos**, and **Merlot**.

Egypt Wine producing country of North Africa, producing relatively small quantities of mediocre wine, most of it white. Most of the country's vines produce table grapes.

Ehrenfelser White grape variety, a **cross** between **Riesling** and **Silvaner**, planted mainly in northern **Germany**. It ripens earlier than Riesling, and produces higher **must weights** and **yields**. One of the most promising Riesling-Silvaner crosses.

Einzellage Term used in German wine law to indicate an individual vineyard site. The boundaries and names are officially defined, and the names of *Einzellagen* can be used only on quality wines. *Einzellagen* are often large and divided among numerous growers. See also **QbA**; **QmP**.

Eisacktaler German name for **Valle Isarco**.

Eiswein German and Austrian quality white wine
category meaning 'ice wine'. The minimum **must
weight** is the same as for **Beerenauslese** wines, but the
grapes are not affected by **botrytis**. The grapes are left
on the vine after the normal harvesting date, sometimes
as late as Christmas or even January, in the hope that
the temperature will fall so low that the water in the
grapes freezes, leaving the sugar and acid unfrozen.
The grapes are then quickly pressed, leaving their water
content as ice, and yielding juice that will produce
sweet, luscious, long-lived wines with high **acidity**. See
QmP. See also **ice wine**.

Elba DOC wine from the island of Elba, just off the
coast of **Tuscany**, **Italy**. The red is made from the same
grapes as **Chianti**, and is usually a light wine for early
drinking. The whites, made mainly from the **Trebbiano**
grape, are dry and full-bodied with a crisp finish. A
sparkling, **spumante** white is also made. The sweet, red
dessert wine **Aleatico** is also made on Elba.

Elbling Ancient white grape variety planted in the
Mosel region of **Germany**. It is used to make still
varietal wines and is occasionally used in the
production of **Sekt**. Elbling is also found in
Luxembourg, where it is the second most-planted
variety, producing thin, tart wine, sometimes sparkling.

Emilia-Romagna Wine region just north of **Tuscany**,
in central **Italy**. The most famous **DOC** wine from this
region is the fizzy **Lambrusco**, which is usually red, and

can be dry or sweet, sparkling or semi-sparkling. White wines include **Albana** di Romagna, Italy's first white **DOCG** wine, and the DOC wine **Trebbiano di Romagna**. Reds include the DOC **Sangiovese** di Romagna. See also **Bianco di Scandiano**; **Colli Bolognesi**; **Colli di Parma**.

encépagement French for the mix of grape varieties planted in a vineyard, or for the blend of grape varieties in a bottle of wine.

Encruzado White grape variety of **Portugal**, particularly found in the **Dão** reigon.

Enfer d'Arvier Dry red **DOC** wine of the **Valle d'Aosta** region in northwest **Italy**, made from the Petit Rouge grape. The wine, produced in tiny quantities, is dark red with a rich, grapey smell and taste. It improves with moderate **bottle age**.

England Modern wine-producing country only since the 1950s. Most of the vineyards are planted in the south of the country, in the counties of Kent, Sussex, Hampshire, Surrey, Somerset, Norfolk and Suffolk, and on the Isle of Wight. Viticulture and winemaking has mainly followed the Germanic model.

The majority of wines produced are white, from grape varieties such as **Müller-Thurgau**, **Seyval Blanc**, **Huxelrebe**, **Schönburger**, **Reichensteiner** and **Bacchus**. As in **Germany**, **süssreserve** is often added to the wines to round them out before bottling, but even so they are often hard and acidic. Red and rosé wines are less common, because of the difficulties of ripening in

England's relatively short, cool summer. Some encouraging results have been achieved with **Pinot Noir**, as well as Triomphe d'Alsace and Leon Millot.

A handful of producers make sparkling **méthode traditionnelle** wines, and these can be among the best wines that England produces.

English wine Wine made from grapes grown out-of-doors in **England** (and Wales). Not to be confused with **British wine**, which is made in Britain from imported grape concentrates or powders.

Enkirch Village of the Mittelmosel in the **Mosel-Saar-Ruwer** region of **Germany**. It comes within the **Grosslage** of Schwarzlay and the best **Einzellagen** are Steffensberg and Herrenberg.

Entre-Deux-Mers White **AC** wine of **Bordeaux**, produced in the region between the rivers Dordogne and Garonne. It is made from the **Sauvignon Blanc** grape, either alone or blended with **Sémillon** and **Muscadelle**, and is usually bone dry, crisp and flavoursome. Quality is increasingly good, and the wines are usually good value for money. Generally the wines should be drunk as young as possible, although new, **oak**-aged versions have some **ageing** potential. Nearly all Entre-Deux-Mers properties also make red wine, which is sold as AC Bordeaux or Bordeaux Supérieur.

Epineuil Red **AC** wine made near **Chablis** in the north of **Burgundy**, from the **Pinot Noir** grape. It is a light, fragrant red, produced in very small quantities. There is also a rosé version.

Erbach Village in the **Rheingau** region of **Germany**, in the **Grosslage** of Deutelsberg. It produces powerful, firm, scented white wines of excellent quality from the **Riesling** grape. The most famous **Einzellage** vineyard is Marcobrunn, and others of repute include Schlossberg, Siegelsberg, Honigberg, Michelmark, Steinmorgen and Hohenrain.

Erbaluce di Caluso DOC wine made around Caluso in the **Piedmont** region of **Italy**. The dry white, made from the Erbaluce grape, is light and creamy with good **acidity**, and should be drunk young. Its acidity means that it makes successful sparkling versions by both the charmat and the **classico** method. Caluso Passito is a sweet, golden-coloured wine also made from Erbaluce grapes, which have been dried before pressing (see **passito**); it can also be fortified.

Erden Village of the Mittelmosel, in the **Mosel-Saar-Ruwer** region of **Germany**, in the **Grosslage** of Schwarzlay. It produces spicy, vigorous white wines, mainly from the **Riesling** grape. The best **Einzellage** vineyards include Treppchen, Prälat and Herrenberg.

Erzeugerabfüllung German term that literally means 'bottled by the producer' (**estate bottled**), though it may also be used by **co-operative cellars**.

espumoso Spanish for sparkling wine. See also **Cava**.

Est! Est!! Est!!! White **DOC** wine from around Lake Bolsena in the **Latium** region of **Italy**, made from the **Trebbiano** and **Malvasia** grapes. It is usually dry, but can be medium dry. Quality is variable, but the best examples have an attractive crisp, fruity, almond taste.

Estaing VDQS wine from the Lot valley in southwest **France**, just east of **Cahors**. Red and white wines are made in extremely small quantities, the reds from **Gamay**, **Cabernet Franc** and **Fer** Servadou grapes, the whites from **Chenin Blanc** and **Mauzac Blanc**.

estate bottled Term used to indicate that a wine has been bottled on the estate where the grapes were grown. It is intended as a guarantee of authenticity.

estufa Oven in which **Madeira** wine is 'cooked' at about 45°C. The cooking process is called *estufagem*.

ethanol Chemical term for what is commonly called alcohol. See **alcohol**.

Etna DOC wine from the slopes of Mount Etna in **Sicily**. Most of the production is of deep, fruity, full-bodied reds, made from the **Nerello** Mascalese grape, which is also used to make **rosato** wines. The **bianco**, made from the Carricante and **Catarratto** grapes, is dry, light and delicate; *bianco superiore* is distinctly better.

Étoile, L' AC wine of the **Jura** region of **France**. Most of the production is of light, fruity white wine, which may be made sparkling by the **méthode traditionnelle**, from the **Savagnin** and **Chardonnay** grapes, sometimes with the addition of the dark **Poulsard** grape. **Vin jaune** is also produced within the *appellation* from the **Savagnin** grape alone.

extract Soluble solids (other than sugar) found in wine, which contribute to its body and structure. In tasting, a wine with good **body** and structure might be described as having good or high extract.

extra sec Term found on **Champagne** labels, indicating a wine drier than **sec** but not as dry as **brut**.

Extremadura Region of western **Spain**, along the border with **Portugal**, which produces a large quantity of wine of very low quality. Little is bottled as wine and much of it is distilled into brandy.

F

Faber White grape variety, a **cross** of **Pinot Blanc** and Müller-Thurgau, planted mainly in the **Rheinhessen** and **Nahe** regions of **Germany**. It is an early ripener, earlier even than Müller-Thurgau, and with more fruit and a higher **must weight** and **acidity**. It can grow well on nearly any soil and will ripen on sites where **Riesling** will not. Faber produces good, fruity wines with Riesling-like character, although it is often used for blending.

Falerio dei Colli Asolani Dry white **DOC** wine grown in the hills between Ascoli Piceno and the coast in the **Marches** region of **Italy**. The wine is produced from the **Trebbiano** grape and is light and fairly neutral with good **acidity**. It is best drunk young.

Falerno Dry red and white **DOC** wine from the **Latium** and **Campania** regions of **Italy**. The red is made from the **Aglianico** grape variety, grown around Mondragone in Campania, and Formia, Gaeta and Fondi in Latium (where it may also contain **Barbera**); fruity and full bodied. The white, in both regions, is produced from the Falanghina grape, but is rarely very good. The name Falerno derives from Falernum, the celebrated wine of ancient Rome (formerly drunk diluted with seawater).

Fara Dry red **DOC** wine grown in the Novara hills in the **Piedmont** region of **Italy**, made from the **Nebbiolo**,

Bonarda and Vespolina grape varieties. It is a full-bodied and perfumed wine which can age well for 5 to 10 years.

Fargues One of the villages entitled to the **AC** of **Sauternes**.

Faro Dry red **DOC** wine produced around Messina, **Sicily**, from the **Nerello** Mascalese grape. It is capable of very good quality, with fine aromas, but sadly very little is made.

fattoria Italian for a farm or estate, commonly used in **Tuscany** for a wine estate.

Faugères Dry red **AC** wine grown just north of Béziers in the **Languedoc-Roussillon** region of **France**. It is made from the **Carignan**, **Grenache**, **Cinsault** and **Syrah** grape varieties. The wine is a deep, beefy, plummy red, and should generally be drunk young. Quality is good, and improving. There is a small amount of white made from the **Clairette**, **Bourboulenc**, Grenache Blanc and **Marsanne** grapes.

Favorita Dry white **DOC** wine grown in the **Roero** and Langhe hills in **Piedmont**, **Italy**, made from the grape variety of the same name. Light, crisp and high in **acidity**, the best examples have some complexity.

Fendant See **Chasselas**.

Fer (also called Fer-Servadou) Red grape variety of good quality and colour, which is used in the wines of **Béarn**, Entraygues, **Estaing**, **Gaillac**, **Madiran**, and **Marcillac**.

fermentation Process whereby grape sugar is converted into **alcohol** and **carbon dioxide** by the action of enzymes produced by **yeast**. This is accompanied by many other chemical transformations. Heat is a by-product. For dry wines, the process is allowed to continue until all the sugar has been turned into alcohol. If the initial level of grape sugar is very high, fermentation may stop naturally before all the sugar has been converted, and a sweet wine is the result. The fermentation of **fortified wines**, such as **Port**, is stopped prematurely by the addition of alcohol in the form of grape spirit. See also **malolactic fermentation**.

Fernão Pires (also called Maria Gomez) White grape variety grown throughout **Portugal** producing **aromatic**, peppery white wines. It is grown in Arruda dos Vinhos, Alenquer, Torres Vedras, the **Douro**, **Alentejo** and **Bairrada** (where it is known as Maria Gomez).

Feteasca **Aromatic** white grape variety grown throughout eastern Europe and particularly in **Romania**.

Fiano di Avellino Dry white **DOC** wine grown around the Avellino hills near Naples in the **Campania** region of **Italy**, made from the Fiano grape. At its best the wine is light coloured, with an **aroma** of nuts and pears, a smooth taste and a lingering **finish**, but quality varies enormously. The sub-denomination of Fiano di Lapiano is considered superior.

fiasco Italian term for flask, used to refer to the traditional wicker-covered bottle which was once commonly used for **Chianti**. There is still a demand for *fiaschi*, mainly from restaurants, but most serious Chianti is now sold in conventional bottles.

Fiddletown AVA within **Amador County**, **California**, which produces mainly rich, red **varietal** wines from the **Zinfandel** grape.

Fiefs Vendéens VDQS wine grown in four locations, Mareuil, Brem, Vix and Pissotte, in the Vendée *département* of the **Loire** region of **France**. The name of the location must appear on the label. The fresh, light red and rosé wines are made from at least 50% of **Gamay** and/or **Pinot Noir** grape varieties, and **Cabernet Sauvignon**, **Cabernet Franc** and **Négrette** are also permitted. The less-common white wine must be at least 50% from the **Chenin Blanc** grape, plus **Sauvignon Blanc** and **Chardonnay**. In Vix and Pissotte, up to 20% of **Melon de Bourgogne** is allowed, and Groslot (**Grolleau**) can be included in the white and rosé wines of Brem.

Figari See **Vin de Corse**.

Finger Lakes Main wine-producing region of **New York State**. Originally the area was planted with native varieties, but recently more **Vitis vinifera** grape varieties have been planted, including **Chardonnay**, **Riesling** and **Gewürztraminer**, which produce mainly sparkling wines.

fining Clarification process whereby solids in a wine are removed. A substance, such as isinglass, gelatine, casein, dried blood, egg white or clay (**bentonite**), is added to the wine, in cask or vat, causing suspended solids to fall to the bottom. The clear wine can then be removed, leaving the solids behind. The same term is used for treatments to remove excess **tannin** from wine. See also **racking**.

finish Tasting term used to describe the intensity and nature of the final taste sensation once a wine is swallowed (or spat out). A 'long finish', where the taste persists for some moments, is one of the hallmarks of a good wine. See also **aftertaste**.

fino Pale, bone dry, pungent **Sherry**, made mainly from the **Palomino** grape variety. Its distinctive tangy **aroma** and flavour are the result of **ageing** the wine in the **solera** system under a layer of **yeast** cells called **flor**. The flor protects the wine from complete **oxidation**, and produces **acetaldehyde**, which is partly responsible for *fino's* distinctive taste. A *fino* from **Jerez** or Puerto de Santa Maria must spend at least three years in the *solera* system before bottling. *Fino* from Sanlúcar de Barrameda is called **manzanilla**.

Once opened, a bottle of fino should be consumed as quickly as any other white wine. Fino, served correctly chilled, is one of the best apéritifs of all, and is excellent with seafood or tapas. Quality is usually at least very good, and the wine is underpriced.

firm Tasting term to describe a wine that is structured, with a positive taste in the mouth. See also **flabby**.

first growth See **premier cru**; **cru classé**.

Fitou Dry red AC wine of the **Languedoc-Roussillon** region of **France** (neighbouring **Corbières**), made mainly from the **Carignan** grape, plus, increasingly, **Grenache**, **Mourvèdre** and **Cinsault**. The wine is dark red, sturdy and fruity, and usually good value for money.

Fixin Village and **AC** wine at the northern end of the **Côte de Nuits** in **Burgundy**. It produces almost entirely red wine from the **Pinot Noir** grape. The best wines, sturdy, deep, strong reds, are from the **premiers crus**, especially La Perrière and Clos du Chapitre, but they do not reach the heights of the great wines from further south in the Côte de Nuits.

The wine from the village of Fixin, which can be very light bodied, may also be sold as **Côte de Nuits-Villages**. The best white Fixin, which is lively and vivacious, is made from the **Pinot Blanc** grape.

flabby Tasting term used to describe a poor wine, which lacks structure and definition and has little **acidity**. See also **firm**.

Flagey-Echézeaux Village in the **Côte de Nuits**, **Burgundy**, whose red wines, made from the **Pinot Noir** grape, are sold under the **AC** of **Vosne-Romanée**. Technically, Flagey contains the **grand cru** *appellations* **Echézeaux** and **Grands-Echézeaux**, although in fact they are nearer to Vosne-Romanée.

Fleurie Red **AC** wine, one of the 10 **crus** of the **Beaujolais** region of **Burgundy**, made from the **Gamay**

grape. The wine is perfumed, with juicy, ripe sweetness, and cherry and chocolate flavours. The quality is usually very good and it is among the best of all **Beaujolais**.

Fleurieu Peninsula Relatively new wine region of **South Australia** producing premium red **varietal** wines, mainly from **Cabernet Sauvignon**, **Merlot**, **Shiraz**, **Chardonnay**, and **Sauvignon Blanc**.

flinty Tasting term usually used to describe the **aroma** of a white wine. Whites made from the **Sauvignon Blanc** grape are sometimes described as having a gunflint aroma.

Floc de Gascogne Apéritif, technically a **mistelle** rather than a wine, made from unfermented grape juice and Armagnac. It is sweet, grapey and **aromatic**, and best served chilled. See also **Pineau des Charentes**; **ratafia**.

flor Thick layer of **yeast** cells that develops on the **fino** and **manzanilla** styles of **Sherry** while they are maturing. The flor protects the wine from oxygen, reduces the **alcohol** and **acidity**, and gives the Sherry its distinctive tangy **aroma** and taste.

Folle Blanche (also called **Gros Plant**) White grape variety, once important for the production of brandy in Cognac and Armagnac (where it is known as Picpoule), but today largely replaced by **Ugni Blanc**. Most Folle Blanche in **France** is now found at the western end of the **Loire** valley, near Nantes, where it is called Gros

Plant. It produces a dry, thin, tart, very acidic wine. There is also a small amount planted in **California**, particularly in San Benito county, where it is used mainly as a blending wine, to add **acidity**, and also in sparkling wine production.

Forst Important wine-producing village in the **Pfalz** region of **Germany**, incorporating the **Grosslagen** of Schnepfenflug and Mariengarten. It produces some of the region's finest white wines from the **Riesling** grape. The wines are full-bodied and richly fragrant, but with great elegance, which is said to derive from the black basalt in the soil. The most important **Einzellage** vineyards are Bischofsgarten, Jesuitengarten, Kirchenstück and Ungeheuer.

fortified wine Wine to which brandy, or neutral grape spirit, has been added. In the case of **Port**, spirit is added to stop **fermentation** prematurely, before all the grape sugar has been turned into **alcohol**. In the case of **Sherry**, the wine is fortified after fermentation. See also **Madeira**; **Marsala**; **vin doux naturel**.

foudre French term for a wooden barrel of unspecified size, but invariably larger than a **barrique** of 225 litres.

foulage French term for the process of gently breaking the skins of grapes before they go into the **fermentation** vat (for reds) or press (for whites). This is done with the aid of a machine called a fouloir; the same machine usually incorporates an égrappoir, which removes the stems from the grapes.

Fourchaume **Premier cru** vineyard of **Chablis**.

Fourneaux **Premier cru** vineyard of **Chablis**.

foxy Tasting term that describes the earthy flavour of
wine made from native American grapes (e.g. Vitis
labrusca). It does not imply the smell or taste of the
animal, but refers to wild, or 'fox' grapes.

France Probably the most important wine-producing
country of the world, producing a huge range of styles
and qualities. There are fine reds based on **Cabernet
Sauvignon** from **Bordeaux**, and this region also
produces **Sauternes**, perhaps the world's greatest sweet
white wine. **Burgundy** is capable of great reds and
whites from **Pinot Noir** and **Chardonnay** respectively.
Champagne produces the world's greatest sparkling
wines; the **Rhône** distinctive, spicy reds; **Alsace**,
fragrant, superlative white **varietals**; the **Loire**, dry
whites from **Sauvignon Blanc**, and luscious sweet wines
from **Chenin Blanc**.

The quality pyramid begins with **vin de table**, followed
by **vin de pays**, **VDQS** and **AC** (see individual entries).
See also **Bergerac**; **Cahors**; **Gaillac**; **Jura**; **Jurançon**;
Languedoc-Roussillon; **Provence**; Savoie.

Franciacorta Italy's first dry **DOCG metodo
classico** sparkling wine grown around Cortefranca
in **Lombardy**. Made from Pinot Biano and/or
Chardonnay with the possible addition of Pinot Nero
and Pinot Grigio. One of the finest of Italy's sparkling
wines, the best examples rival **Champagne** in quality.
Also made in a **crémant**-style version called Saten.

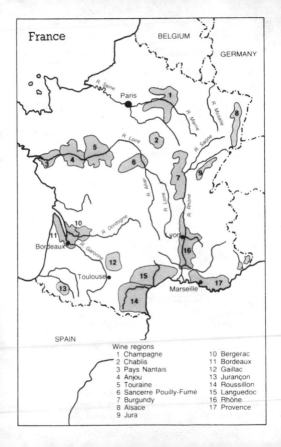

France

BELGIUM
GERMANY

Paris

R. Seine
R. Marne
R. Moselle
R. Loire
R. Allier
R. Saône
R. Rhône
R. Dordogne
R. Garonne

Bordeaux
Toulouse
Lyon
Marseille

SPAIN

Wine regions

1 Champagne
2 Chablis
3 Pays Nantais
4 Anjou
5 Touraine
6 Sancerre Pouilly-Fumé
7 Burgundy
8 Alsace
9 Jura
10 Bergerac
11 Bordeaux
12 Gaillac
13 Jurançon
14 Roussillon
15 Languedoc
16 Rhône
17 Provence

Franconia English for **Franken**.

Franken Important wine-producing region of **Germany**, one of the 13 **Anbaugebiet** areas, centred on Würzburg in northern Bavaria. The wines are almost all dry, full-bodied whites, mainly from the **Silvaner** and **Müller-Thurgau** grapes. Even the **Spätlese** and **Auslese** styles, while broader and more robust, are still essentially dry. There are three **Bereich** subregions, **Mainviereck**, **Maindreieck** and **Steigerwald**.

The wines of Franken have traditionally been sold in the **bocksbeutel**, a squat, flagon-shaped bottle of green glass.

Frankland Up-and-coming cool-climate vineyard area of **Western Australia**.

Frankovka Slovakian synonym for the **Blaufränkisch** grape variety.

Frascati White **DOC** wine grown around the towns of Frascati, Grottaferrata and Monteporzio Catone in the hills above Rome, in the **Latium** region of **Italy**. It is made largely from the **Trebbiano** and **Malvasia** grapes, and should be crisp, fresh, dry to off-dry, with soft, smooth fruit and a nutty flavour. Sweeter **amabile** Frascati (**Cannellino**) is rare and **spumante** Frascati is rarer still. Quality is variable, but from the best producers it can be very good.

Freisa Red grape variety planted mainly in **Piedmont**, **Italy**. It is **DOC** in Freisa d'Asti and Freisa di Chieri, and in the catch-all denomination Freisa del

Piedmonte. Traditionally the wine has been slightly sparkling and off-dry to benefit from the **aromatic** properties of the grape, though there are successful still, dry versions as well.

French Colombard See **Colombard**.

fresh Tasting term used to describe wine with youthful charm, vigour and vibrancy, often marked by **acidity**.

Friuli-Venezia Giulia Region of northeast **Italy**, which has led the Italian white-wine revolution. The combination of an Alpine and Adriatic climate gives rise to a remarkably even growing season. The **DOC** regions are **Aquileia**, **Carso**, **Colli Orientali del Friuli**, **Collio**, **Grave del Friuli**, **Isonzo** and **Latisana**. Each DOC produces a wide range of red and white **varietal** wines.

Native white grape varieties include **Tocai Friulano**, **Verduzzo Friulano**, **Ribolla**, **Malvasia** and **Picolit**, but there are extensive plantings of 'foreign' white varieties including **Müller-Thurgau**, Pinot Bianco, Pinot Grigio, **Riesling Renano**, **Sauvignon Blanc**, and **Traminer**. Generally most are best drunk young.

Although it is most famous for its whites, Friuli actually produces more red wine, again for drinking young, and mainly from **Merlot**, **Cabernet Franc** and **Refosco** grapes.

frizzante Italian term for a wine that is lightly effervescent, but not sufficiently sparkling to be labelled **spumante**. See also **pétillant**.

Fronsac AC wine of **Bordeaux**, grown in an attractive hilly area west of **Saint-Emilion**. It produces chunky, deep red-coloured wines, which are well-flavoured, **tannic** and require some **bottle age**. The main grape varieties are **Cabernet Franc**, **Cabernet Sauvignon**, **Merlot** and **Malbec**. Quality has improved enormously in recent years and the wines have become deservedly well known. See also **Canon-Fronsac**.

Frontignan (formerly **Muscat de Frontignan**) Sweet white **AC** wine from the **Languedoc-Roussillon** area of **France**. This is a **fortified wine**, a **vin doux naturel**, made from the **Muscat** Blanc à Petits Grains grape variety. It is rich and raisiny, but lacks the balancing fruity **acidity** found in **Muscat de Beaumes-de-Venise**.

Fronton See **Côtes du Frontonnais**.

fruity Tasting term used to describe the attractive flavour of a wine made from ripe grapes, which can be reminiscent of a wide range of citrus fruits, red fruits, berries and currants. See also **grapey**.

full Tasting term that describes a wine that is mouth-filling and flavoursome, owing to a high **alcohol** and extract content.

Fumé Blanc Alternative term for wines made from the **Sauvignon Blanc** grape, used in **Australia** and **California**. It originates from California, where it was used to make wines from this variety more fashionable, through association with **Pouilly-Fumé**, and to differentiate them from California's medium-sweet Sauvignon Blanc **varietals**. Today it usually implies an **oak**-aged Sauvignon Blanc.

Fumé de Pouilly See **Pouilly-Fumé**.

Furmint White grape variety of **Hungary** used to make the distinctive sweet wines of **Tokaji**, and tart, dry white wines elsewhere in Hungary. It is susceptible to **botrytis**, which is an important factor in making Tokaji **Aszú**.

fût French term for a small barrel of unspecified size. The claim *'elevé en fûts de chêne'* (matured in **oak** barrels) is increasingly found on labels as a fashionable selling point. See also **barrique**.

G

Gaglioppo Italian red grape variety that produces concentrated, deep wines mainly in **Calabria** (where it is used to make **Cirò**), and also in **Abruzzo**, **Campania**, the **Marches** and **Umbria**.

Gaillac AC wine region in the Tarn *département* near Albi, southwest **France**. It produces red, white (still and sparkling) and rosé wines. The still whites, dry, medium-sweet, or sweet, are somewhat sharp and apple-flavoured, and based on the **Mauzac Blanc** grape, together with Len de l'El, Ondenc, **Sauvignon Blanc**, **Sémillon** and **Muscadelle**. The reds are spicy and peppery and for drinking young. They are based on the **Duras** grape, together with several other varieties including **Fer**, **Négrette**, **Gamay** and **Syrah**. They can be good, especially when the proportion of Gamay is kept low.

The star of the region is the sparkling wine, Gaillac Mousseaux, also based on the Mauzac grape, and produced either by the **méthode traditionnelle**, or by a local method in which the first **fermentation** is finished off in bottle. At its best it is off-dry, scented, apple-flavoured, and of good quality. Gaillac Perlé is a 'barely sparkling' version, which is less good.

Galestro Dry white wine from the **Tuscany** region of **Italy**, based on the **Trebbiano** grape, together with **Malvasia**, Pinot Bianco, **Chardonnay** and Vernaccia.

It is a light, fresh, fruity wine, the result of cold **fermentation**. It was developed by a group of large Tuscan producers, who found themselves with an excess of Trebbiano grapes when the permitted proportion of white grapes in **Chianti Classico** was reduced.

Galicia Region in northwest **Spain**, just north of the border with **Portugal**. There are three **DO** regions. The **Ribeiro** DO produces mainly whites: bland wines from the **Palomino** grape, and more characterful ones from **Albariño**. The Valdeorras **DO** is in decline, producing bland white and red wines from Palomino and **Garnacha** Tintorera respectively. The best wines come from **Rias Baixas**, where fresh whites are made from Albariño, Loureira, Godello and Treixadura grapes.

Gamay (Gamay Noir à Jus Blanc) French red grape variety. It is planted predominantly in the **Beaujolais** region, where it is responsible for every wine from the light, acidic **Beaujolais** Nouveau through to the deliciously vibrant, intensely fruity and sometimes jammy **cru** wines. It is less successful, however, elsewhere in **France**. In the **Loire**, it produces light red wines in **Anjou-Saumur** and **Touraine** and **Fiefs Vendéens**; in **Switzerland** it is used for **Dôle**. Elsewhere in **Burgundy**, **Passe-Tout-Grains** is made from two-thirds Gamay and one-third **Pinot Noir**, vinified together. Bourgogne Grand Ordinaire may be made from 100% Gamay.

Gamay Beaujolais A misleading Californian name for a **clone** of **Pinot Noir**.

Gambellara White **DOC** wine grown in the **Veneto** region of **Italy**, made mainly from the **Garganega** grape. Gambellara **Bianco** is a dry, fresh, fruity white, similar in style to **Soave**.

Recioto di Gambellara is a sweet, intense, golden-coloured white, occasionally sparkling, made from dried grapes (see **recioto**). A small amount of **Vin Santo** is also produced under the Gambellara label.

Garganega White grape used notably in **Soave** in the **Veneto** region of **Italy**, and also in **Gambellara**, **Bianco di Custoza** and **Colli Euganei**. It can produce good wines when **yields** are kept in check.

Garnacha (also called **Grenache**) Red grape variety of Spanish origin, which produces medium- to full-bodied, high **alcohol** wines. It is widely planted in **Rioja** (where it is usually blended with **Tempranillo**) and **Navarra**. As Grenache, it is found in the **Languedoc-Roussillon**, in southern **France**, in the southern **Rhône** in **Tavel**, **Châteauneuf-du-Pape** and **Côtes du Rhône**, and in **Provence**. It is also planted in **Corsica**, **Sardinia** (where it is known as **Cannonau**), **Australia**, **California** and **Algeria**. It can produce dense, structured wines of high quality if yields are kept low, but too often it is over-cropped, resulting in lightish wines of little interest. It is also widely used to produce rosé wines.

garrafeira Portuguese term for a **vintage** red wine which has been matured for two years before bottling plus one year in bottle, or a vintage white wine matured for six months before bottling plus six months in bottle. In practice these minimum periods are often exceeded, as the Portuguese believe 'the older the better'. A *garrafeira* should also be a wine of good quality and with an **alcohol** content at least 0.5% above the minimum specified for the area. See also **Dão**; **Bairrada**.

Gattinara Dry red **DOCG** wine from **Piedmont**, Italy. It is produced mainly from the **Nebbiolo** grape (known locally as **Spanna**), with the option of up to 10% **Bonarda**. In theory it should be capable of the same quality as **Barolo** and **Barbaresco**, but it never seems to reach the same depth, complexity and longevity. At its best it is spicy, with tar on the **nose** and a soft, silky texture.

Gavi See **Cortese**.

Geelong Small wine region in the state of **Victoria**, **Australia**. It has a cool, dry climate and good results have been obtained here with **varietal** wines made from the **Pinot Noir** grape. **Chardonnay**, **Shiraz** and **Cabernet Sauvignon** are also grown.

Geisenheim Village in the **Rheingau** region of **Germany** that produces top-quality, fruity white wines, almost entirely from the **Riesling** grape variety. There are two **Grosslagen**, Burgweg and Erntebringer, and the best **Einzellage** vineyards include Kläuserweg and Rothenberg. The village is also famous for its wine school and research station.

gelatine Animal product sometimes used by winemakers to remove excess **tannin** from wine, or to help remove the taste of rotten grapes.

Germany Wine-producing country important chiefly for its white wines, which range from mediocre to superlative in quality. Some of the best and most distinctive white wines in the world come from the **Riesling** grape, grown on the **Rhine** and Mosel.

The quality pyramid begins with **Deutscher Tafelwein**, **table wine** which can be labelled with one of four broadly based district names. **Landwein**, or 'country' wine, is the next category, with higher natural **alcohol** than *tafelwein*, and 15 designated regions. **QbA**, or 'quality wine from a designated area', comes from one of the 13 **Anbaugebiet** areas, and can be made only from certain permitted grape varieties. **QmP** is the highest category, with five different **prädikat** ratings, which depend on the natural sugar in the grapes at the time of picking, and the degree of selection at harvest. In ascending order they are **Kabinett**, **Spätlese**, **Auslese**, **Beerenauslese**, and **Trockenbeerenauslese**. **Eiswein** should have the same grape sugar level as Beerenauslese.

The 13 *Anbaugebiet* regions are: **Ahr**, **Baden**, **Franken**, **Hessische Bergstrasse**, **Nahe**, **Mittelrhein**, **Mosel-Saar-Ruwer**, **Rheingau**, **Rheinhessen**, **Pfalz**, **Saale-Unstrut**, Sachsen, and **Württemberg**. There is no doubt that the finest wines are made from the Riesling grape variety, but **Müller-Thurgau** and **Silvaner** are also planted widely, along with **Gewürztraminer**, **Ruländer**, **Weissburgunder**, Gutedel, **Morio-Muskat** and

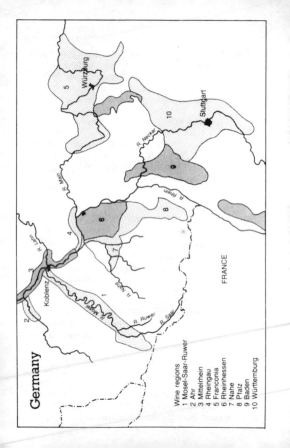

Germany

Wine regions
1 Mosel-Saar-Ruwer
2 Ahr
3 Mittelrhein
4 Rheingau
5 Franconia
6 Rheinhessen
7 Nahe
8 Pfalz
9 Baden
10 Württemburg

FRANCE

Scheurebe, plus more recent crossings such as **Kerner**, **Bacchus**, **Faber**, **Huxelrebe**, **Optima**, **Ortega** and **Ehrenfelser**. Red wines, made from the **Spätburgunder** grape, have improved beyond recognition lately, especially in the hands of good producers.

Gevrey-Chambertin Important village and **AC** in the **Côte de Nuits** area of **Burgundy**. It produces some of the world's finest red wines from the **Pinot Noir** grape. The majority of the wine is produced under the village AC of Gevrey-Chambertin, and this can be of good quality, silky, soft and perfumed.

The **premier cru** wines are better, especially from Clos Saint-Jacques and Clos des Varoilles. They are **tannic** in their youth, but develop mouth-filling, ripe, gamey flavours as they mature.

The best wines of the village come from the **grand cru** vineyards: **Chambertin**, **Chambertin-Clos de Bèze**, **Chapelle-Chambertin**, **Charmes-Chambertin**, **Griotte-Chambertin**, Latricières-Chambertin, **Mazis-Chambertin** and Ruchottes-Chambertin.

Gewürztraminer High-quality white grape variety, which produces distinctive, **aromatic**, floral wines with a deep golden colour. It produces classic **varietal** wines in the **Alsace** region of **France**, usually dry, but sometimes lusciously sweet **vendange tardive** or **Sélection des Grains Nobles**. It is also planted in **Germany** (particularly in the **Pfalz** and **Baden** regions), **Austria**, throughout eastern Europe, the **Alto Adige** in **Italy**, the **United States** (especially **Washington State** and **Oregon**), **New Zealand** and **Australia**.

Ghemme Dry, red **DOC** wine grown near the town of Ghemme in **Piedmont**, **Italy**. It is produced from 60-85% **Nebbiolo** grapes plus Vespolina and **Bonarda**. A robust, sturdy red, it is similar to **Gattinara** in quality.

Gigondas Red (and rosé) **AC** wine produced around the town of Gigondas in the southern **Rhône**, **France**, from the **Grenache** (up to 80%), **Syrah** and **Mourvèdre** (at least 15%), and **Cinsault** grape varieties. The red wine is usually deep coloured, full and supple, with chewy fruit. Quality can be very good, similar to **Châteauneuf-du-Pape** but at a lower price. White wine produced in Gigondas is sold as **Côtes du Rhône**.

girasol Spanish for sunflower, but also used to describe the **gyropalette**.

Girò di Cagliari Red, usually sweet **DOC** wine from **Sardinia**, made from the native Girò grape. It is a bright ruby colour, warm, smooth and similar to **Port** (although unfortified).

Gisborne Important wine region on the north island of **New Zealand**, with a history of producing large quantities of light, but good white wine mainly from the **Müller-Thurgau** grape. Better-quality whites are now made in smaller quantities, particularly from **Gewürztraminer**, **Chenin Blanc**, **Sémillon** and **Chardonnay**. Red wines are generally less successful, although there are some good examples of **Cabernet Sauvignon** and **Merlot**.

Givry AC wine from the **Côte Chalonnaise** area of **Burgundy**, which produces mainly dry red wines from the **Pinot Noir** grape, and a small amount of white from **Chardonnay**. The best reds have a delicate, smoky fragrance, and good Pinot flavour, but quality is very variable.

Glühwein German term for a mulled wine, served hot with the possible addition of sugar and spices.

gobelet Vine training system in which the vine is kept in the form of a low bush. See also **bush vine**.

Goldenmuskateller (also called **Moscato** Giallo) White grape variety of the **Muscat** family, which produces golden yellow, sweet white wines in the **Alto Adige** and **Trentino** regions of **Italy**.

Goulburn Valley Wine region in the state of **Victoria**, **Australia**. Good red **varietals** are produced here, especially **Shiraz**.

goût French for 'taste'. *Goût de terroir* is used to describe a wine that has an earthy taste, or more controversially the taste derived from the special area in which the vines are grown (see **terroir**). *Goût anglais* is used in **Champagne** to describe the English taste for dry, more mature wine. *Goût de grêle* indicates an 'off' flavour caused by grapes damaged by hail.

governo Technique formerly widespread among producers of **Chianti**, in which some grapes are reserved and dried, and added to the bulk of the wine after **vinification**. This causes a second **fermentation**, which increases the **alcohol** content and colour and reduces **acidity**. In the past, this was used to make *normale* Chianti, for early drinking. Today, the extra costs involved mean that the few remaining *governo* practitioners tend to use it for higher-quality, **riserva** Chianti, often with very good results.

Graach Tiny village in the **Bereich** of Bernkastel in the **Mosel-Saar-Ruwer** region of **Germany**. It comes within the **Grosslage** of Münzlay, and the **Einzellage** vineyards are Abtsberg, Domprobst, Himmelreich and Josephshöfer. They produce some of the finest white wines of the Mosel from the **Riesling** grape.

Graciano Red grape variety used as a minor ingredient in the production of **Rioja**, particularly in the Rioja Alta subzone. It produces a wine with a deep colour, highly **aromatic** and with a good **ageing** potential. It is also grown in **Navarra**.

In **France** it is found in small quantities in the Languedoc, under the confusing name **Morrastel**. There are also plantations in **Australia**, **California** (as Xeres), and in **Argentina** (as Graciana).

grafting Process of joining the fruit-bearing part of a vine to another vine's root. Since the coming of **phylloxera**, in the 19th century, most of the world's vineyards have been planted with the traditional **Vitis vinifera** varieties grafted onto American vine rootstocks, which are resistant to phylloxera. The choice of rootstock can be used to manipulate **yield**, vigour, and resistance to other diseases. In some countries and regions, notably Colares in **Portugal** and

Chile, the vineyards are free from phylloxera and ungrafted vines grow unthreatened.

grand cru French quality designation, meaning literally 'great growth', applied differently in different regions. In **Bordeaux**, the châteaux were classified in 1855 (the classification was of all Bordeaux, but only one **château** was from outside the **Médoc** and **Sauternes**): at the top quality level are the *grands crus classés*, subdivided into *premier*, *deuxième*, down to *cinquième* crus, referred to in English as 'first growth', 'second growth', and so on. In **Saint-Emilion** the top quality level is *premier grand cru classé*, followed by *grand cru classé*, followed by *grand cru*. So *grand cru* in Saint-Emilion is a much lower quality level than *grand cru* in the Médoc.

In **Burgundy**, including **Chablis**, the very top vineyard sites are classified as *grand cru*, and in the **Côte d'Or** each has its own *appellation*. Each *grand cru* vineyard may have several different owners. In Burgundy, **premier cru** comes below *grand cru*. In **Alsace**, certain top vineyard sites are designated *grands crus*, for specified grape varieties only, after a fairly recent classification process. In **Champagne**, vineyards rated 100% are referred to as *grands crus*.

gran reserva Spanish term, applied mainly to **Rioja**, which describes a red wine that has been aged for two years in cask and three years in bottle, or a white wine that has been aged for four years, with a minimum of six months in cask. In theory, superior wines are selected for this treatment. In practice, **reserva** is more likely to appeal to the modern international **palate**.

grand vin French term, not officially regulated, that means 'great wine'. In **Bordeaux**, **châteaux** producing a **second wine** sometimes refer to their main wine as the *grand vin*. Nearly all Bordeaux wines are labelled 'Grand vin de Bordeaux'.

grande marque Term used to describe **Champagne** made by the producers that belonged to the former *Syndicat de Grandes Marques de Champagne*, a club founded in 1964 and dissolved in 1997. Most of the great names in Champagne were members, but good quality may also be found outside the *grandes marques*.

Grands-Echézeaux **Grand cru** vineyard of the commune of **Flagey-Echézeaux** in the **Côte de Nuits** region of **Burgundy**. It produces among the finest and most elegant of the region's red wines from the **Pinot Noir** grape. Although technically attached to Flagey-Echézeaux, the vineyard is nearer to **Vosne-Romanée** and the wines can be declassified to Vosne-Romanée **premier cru**. Quality is good and generally better than the larger, neighbouring **Echézeaux**, but not as good as the other *grand cru* vineyards of the Côte de Nuits.

grape Fruit of the vine and the only fruit from which real wine can be made. Of the Vitis genus of plants, there are many species, although only **Vitis vinifera** is of major importance for wine production. Some American varieties, such as *Vitis labrusca* and *Vitis rupestris*, are used to provide rootstock resistant to **phylloxera** (see **grafting**).

There are several thousand varieties of *Vitis vinifera*,

loosely referred to as 'grape varieties'. Of these, some
are best suited to producing grapes for eating, some for
making raisins and others for making wine. The grape
variety used to make a particular wine is one of the
most important factors determining its taste and
character, along with the soil, climate, cultivation and
winemaking technique. Major varieties have their own
entries. See also **cross; hybrid**.

grapey Tasting term used to describe the smell and
taste of fresh grapes. It is often used to describe wines
made from the **Muscat** family of grape varieties.

grassy Tasting term used to describe a herbaceous
smell or the smell of freshly-cut grass.

Grauer Burgunder German name for the **Pinot Gris**
grape variety, usually indicating a drier style of wine
than when the other name, **Ruländer**, is used.

Grave del Friuli Largest **DOC** zone of the **Friuli-
Venezia Giulia** region of **Italy**. It produces red and
white **varietals**, grown on low rolling hills and plains.
Most of the red is **Merlot**, dry, supple and fruity, and of
generally good quality. Other dry reds are made from
Cabernet (mainly Franc, but some Sauvignon), Pinot
Nero and the native **Refosco**. Dry whites are produced
from **Chardonnay**, Pinot Bianco, Pinot Grigio, **Riesling
Renano**, **Sauvignon Blanc**, **Tocai Friulano**, **Traminer**
Aromatico and **Verduzzo Friulano**.

Graves Important **AC** region in the southern part of
Bordeaux. It includes, at its northern end, the city of

Bordeaux itself, and runs along the western (left) bank of the Garonne to just south of **Sauternes**. The name Graves comes from the gravel soil, which is said to give the wines a distinctive **goût** de terroir. Slightly more red than white is produced, mainly from **Cabernet Sauvignon**, plus **Cabernet Franc** and **Merlot** grapes. The whites are dry, made from **Sauvignon Blanc** and **Sémillon** (sometimes 100% Sauvignon). Grapes tend to ripen earlier here than in the rest of Bordeaux, which can be a great advantage when there is rain late in vintage. The best **châteaux** of the northern Graves now have their own AC (see **Pessac-Léognan**) but the southern Graves can produce fine wines at a reasonable price.

Graves de Vayres Minor, little-known **AC** wine of **Bordeaux**, located at the north of the **Entre-Deux-Mers** region, but nothing to do with **Graves** itself. Reds and whites of moderate quality are made with the classic Bordeaux grape varieties.

Great Western Region in the state of **Victoria**, **Australia**, famous mainly for its sparkling wines. The relatively cool climate also allows for production of good still wines, particularly **varietal** wines from **Cabernet Sauvignon** and **Shiraz** grapes.

Grechetto White grape variety grown in the **Umbria** region of **Italy**, particularly used in making **Orvieto** but also increasingly vinified as a **varietal**. Also grown in eastern **Tuscany** (where it is called Pulcinculo) and in northern **Latium** (as Greghetto).

Greco White grape variety of Greek origin, grown in the **Campania** region of southern **Italy**. It is used to make the white **DOC** wines Greco di Tufo, which has a good fruit and crisp flavour, and Greco di Banco, a full-flavoured, sweet dessert wine.

Greece Wine-producing country since ancient times. Today Greece is famed mainly for **Retsina**, which is usually a white wine made from the Savatiano grape, flavoured with pine resin during **fermentation**.

The country's best wines are gradually improving in quality. Fine reds are produced from the **Xynomavro** grape grown in Naoussa, Goumenisa and Amindeo in Macedonia, and from the **Agiorgitiko** grape from Nemea in the Peloponnese. There are also fine **Bordeaux**-style reds from the Côtes de Meliton, and sweet, **Port**-like reds from the **Mavrodaphne** grape from Patras.

A variety of whites is also produced, including the unusual sparkling **Zitsa** made from the **Debina** grape in Epirus, the crisp, dry **Robola** from the island of Kephalonia, dry whites from the **Moscophilero** grape in the Peloponnese, and fine dry whites from the **Assyrtiko** in **Santorini**. There are many sweet whites, especially from the **Muscat** grape, from Patras and the Cyclades, notably Samos. Rhodes produces one of the country's few **méthode traditionnelle** sparkling wines.

Small 'boutique' wineries are starting to spring up around the country, many producing high-quality, high-price wines from northern European grape varieties, especially **Cabernet Sauvignon**.

green Tasting term used to describe a wine that is youthful, acidic, unripe and raw.

Grenache See **Garnacha**.

Grenouilles One of the seven **grand cru** vineyards of **Chablis**.

grey rot Undesirable form of **botrytis**.

Grignolino Red grape variety that produces pale, delicate **DOC** wines in the **Piedmont** region of **Italy**. Grignolino del Monferrato Casalese and Grignolino d'Asti are the best; dry, pale reds, sometimes surprisingly **tannic**, and fragrant and elegant if well made.

Grillo White grape variety grown exclusively in **Sicily**, where it is generally considered the best grape for **Marsala**.

Gringet See **Savagnin**.

Griotte-Chambertin **Grand cru** vineyard of **Gevrey-Chambertin**, in the **Côte de Nuits** area of **Burgundy**. It produces red wine of very high quality, if not quite as big and full-bodied as its neighbour **Chambertin**.

Grolleau (also called Groslot) Red grape variety grown mainly in the **Anjou-Saumur** and **Touraine** regions of the **Loire**. It produces high yields of unexciting, thin, acidic wine, much of it blended with other varieties, such as **Gamay** and **Cabernet Franc**, in the lesser red and rosé wines of the region, particularly **Rosé d'Anjou**. Grolleau is declining in popularity.

Groppello Red grape variety grown mainly in the **Lombardy** region of **Italy**. It is used as part of the blend to make the **DOC** wine **Riviera del Garda Bresciano** and alone to make red **vino da tavola**.

Gros Manseng White grape variety that, together with its better-quality cousin **Petit Manseng**, is used to make **Jurançon** in southwest **France**. It is also used to make **Pacherenc du Vic Bilh** and the rare white wines of **Béarn**.

Gros Plant du Pays Nantais White **VDQS** wine from the western end of the **Loire** valley, the same region as **Muscadet**. Made from the **Folle Blanche** grape (known locally as Gros Plant) it is a dry, thin, tart, very acidic wine, best drunk with local seafood.

Groslot See **Grolleau**.

Grosslage Term used in German wine law to indicate a combination of individual vineyard or **Einzellage** sites, which produce wines of similar style. Quality wines in **Germany** are labelled with the name of their village, followed by either a *Grosslage* or *Einzellage* name. See **QbA**; **QmP**.

Grumello See **Valtellina**.

Grüner Veltliner White grape variety that accounts for about one-third of total plantings in **Austria**. It produces a pale wine, fruity and spicy with markedly high **acidity**, providing a good foil for fatty foods. It is also planted in **Hungary**, the former Yugoslavia, **Czech Republic**, **Slovakia** and **Romania**.

Gutedel See **Chasselas**.

Gutsabfüllung German term meaning **estate bottled**. Stricter and more meaningful than **Erzeugerabfüllung**.

Gutturnio Dry, red **DOC** wine from the Piacenza hills in the **Emilia-Romagna** region of **Italy**, made from the **Barbera** and **Bonarda** grape varieties. It tends to be deep, full and generous, and is usually best drunk young.

gyropalette Mechanical device, often computer-controlled, used in the production of bottle-fermented sparkling wines, such as **Champagne**, to automate the process of **remuage**. The sediment from the secondary **fermentation** is concentrated in the neck of the inverted bottle, prior to **disgorgement**. The gyropalette is much quicker, and less labour intensive, than manual *remuage*. Called a **girasol** in **Spain**, where the technique originated.

H

halbtrocken German term meaning medium dry, used to describe wines with not more than 18 grams per litre of **residual sugar** and with sufficient **acidity** to act as a foil to the sweetness. See also **trocken**.

Hallgarten Village in the **Rheingau** region of **Germany**, which produces fine white wines from the **Riesling** grape. There is one **Grosslage**, Mehrhölzchen, and the individual **Einzellage** sites are Hendelberg, Jungfer, Schönhell and Würzgarten.

hard Tasting term used to describe an **austere** wine, high in **tannin** and **acidity** and lacking in balancing fruit. The severe taste can mellow with time.

Hárslevelü White grape variety grown mainly in **Hungary**, where it gives a smooth and spicy character to **Tokaji**. It also produces powerfully scented, **aromatic varietal** wines, notably Debroi Hárslevelü from the foothills of the Matra mountains. Also grown in **Slovakia**.

Hattenheim Village making some of the finest **Riesling** wines of the **Rheingau** region of **Germany**. There is one **Grosslage**, Deutelsberg, and the individual **Einzellage** sites are Engelmannsberg, Hassel, Heiligenberg, Mannberg, Nussbrunnen, Pfaffenberg, Rheingarten, Schützenhaus, Steinberg and Wisselbrunnen.

Haut-Benauge White **AC** wine produced in small quantities in **Bordeaux**, similar in style to its neighbour, **Entre-Deux-Mers**.

Haut-Médoc Southern half of the Médoc area of **Bordeaux**, where most of the best **châteaux** are found. It includes the communal ACs of **Listrac**, **Margaux**, **Moulis**, **Pauillac**, **Saint-Estèphe** and **Saint-Julien**. It is also an **AC** in its own right, and produces red wines from the classic Bordeaux grape varieties.

Haut Montravel Sweet white **AC** wine from the west of the **Bergerac** region, and produced from the **Sauvignon Blanc**, **Sémillon** and **Muscadelle** grape varieties. It lacks the richness of the great sweet wines of **Bordeaux**, and is declining in popularity.

Haut-Poitou **AC** wine of the **Loire** valley, produced around the city of Poitiers southwest of Tours, which can be red, white, or rosé. The whites, mainly **varietal** wines made from **Sauvignon Blanc** and **Chardonnay** grapes, are crisp, clean and good value. The reds, made from **Gamay**, **Cabernet Franc** and **Pinot Noir**, are simple, with good expression of varietal character.

Hawkes Bay Important wine region on the North Island of **New Zealand**, which produces fine white wines, particularly from **Chenin Blanc**, **Sauvignon Blanc** and **Chardonnay** grapes. This region also shows great potential for red wines, and already there are some fine wines made from **Cabernet Sauvignon** and **Merlot**.

hectare (ha) Unit of area, equal to 100 **ares**, or 10,000 m², or 2.47 acres. In Europe wine **yields** are normally expressed in terms of **hectolitres** of wine per hectare of vineyard.

hectolitre (hl) Unit of volume equal to 100 litres, or about 22 UK gallons. It is used in Europe to measure volume of wine in a tank, or to express the yields per **hectare** of a vineyard.

herbaceous Tasting term for the **aroma** of freshly-cut grass, or a herby taste in wine. Typical of, for example, the **Sauvignon Blanc** grape variety. See also **grassy**.

Hercegovina See **Bosnia Hercegovina**.

Hermitage Important **AC** wine, mainly red with some white, made near Tain l'Hermitage in the northern **Rhône** valley. The red is probably the greatest of the northern Rhône. It is produced largely from the **Syrah** grape, with occasionally a little **Marsanne** and **Roussanne**. At its best, the wine is rich, concentrated, spicy, leathery, curranty and very long-lived.

The whites are made from the Marsanne and Roussanne grapes. They can be dry, fruity and fragrant wines for early drinking, or extraordinarily long-lived, deep and full-flavoured.

Hessische Bergstrasse One of the smallest of **Germany**'s 13 Anbaugebiete. It is situated north of Heidelberg and to the east of the Rhine. About half of the region is planted with **Riesling**, but the **Müller-Thurgau** grape is also important. The wines are similar in style to those of the **Rheingau** and can be of good quality, but they are rarely exported. Most of the production is in the hands of **co-operative** cellars, and the average vineyard size is very small. There are two **Bereich** subregions, Starkenburg and Umstadt.

Heurige 1. Austrian term for young wine, sold soon after vintage. 2. Tavern where such wine is sold, particularly around Vienna.

Hochheim Important area in the **Rheingau** region of **Germany**. It produces powerful white wines of good quality from the **Riesling** grape. Hochheim comes within the **Grosslage** of Daubhaus, and includes the individual **Einzellage** sites of Berg, Domdechaney, Herrnberg, Hofmeister, Hölle, Kirchenstück, Königin Victoriaberg, Riechesthal, Sommerheil, Stein and Stielweg.

hock English term for Rhine wines, derived from the name of the town of **Hochheim** in the **Rheingau**.

hogshead Wooden barrel, of variable capacity depending on country and region, though typically around 300 litres.

hollow Tasting term used to describe a wine which may have a satisfactory initial taste and **finish**, but which lacks flavour in the middle **palate**.

Howell Mountain AVA in Napa county, **California**, planted mainly with the **Cabernet Sauvignon**, **Zinfandel** and **Chardonnay** grape varieties.

Hudson River Valley Small viticultural area of **New York State**, planted mainly with French-American **hybrid** vines, e.g. **Seyval Blanc**, and, more recently, with European grape varieties.

Hungary Central European country, with a long history of wine production. The most famous wine is the legendary **Tokaji**, produced in the northeast of the country, near the Slovak border. The most famous red table wine is **Egri Bikavér**, or Bull's Blood, from Eger; a once full-bodied and concentrated wine, it is now a shadow of its former self. In the northwest, around Sopron, light, fresh reds are made from the **Kékfrankos** grape. Around Lake Balaton, dry and sweet whites are made from various grapes including Ezerjó, Kéknyelü and **Olasz Rizling**. The best whites come from the Badascony region.

The Great Plain is Hungary's major wine region. It produces reds, mainly from **Kadarka**, and whites, from Olasz Rizling. Recently, export-oriented producers have started to make **varietal** wines from west European varieties, including **Cabernet Sauvignon**, **Merlot**, **Sauvignon Blanc**, **Chardonnay** and **Muscat**. Initial results are encouraging and Hungary certainly has the potential to imitate the success of **Bulgaria**.

Hunter Valley Important region in the state of **New South Wales**, **Australia**, divided into the Lower Hunter and the more recently exploited Upper Hunter. It is particularly famous for the high quality and distinct regional character of its **varietal** wines, produced from **Sémillon**, **Chardonnay** and **Shiraz** grapes. Other varieties grown include **Cabernet Sauvignon**, **Merlot**, **Pinot Noir**, **Riesling**, **Sauvignon Blanc** and **Verdelho**. Growing conditions are not always easy, however, with drought a frequent problem during the growing season and heavy rains not uncommon during the harvest.

Huxelrebe Grape variety that is a **cross** of **Chasselas** and Courtillier Musqué. It can give very high yields of ordinary, neutral wine, but at low yields it can achieve good **must weight**, **acidity** and an attractive, **Muscat**-like **aroma** and flavour. In **Germany** it is planted in the **Rheinhessen** and **Pfalz** regions, and good results have also been achieved in **England**.

hybrid Grape variety made by a combination of two different vine species, usually **Vitis vinifera** and one of the American native vines, such as *Vitis labrusca*, or *Vitis rotundifolia*. Examples include **Baco** and **Seyval Blanc**. The purpose of producing a hybrid is usually to combine the attractive fruit flavour of the *vinifera* variety with the disease resistance, or early ripening ability, of the American vine. A hybrid is distinct from a **cross**, which in viticultural terms is a combination of two *vinifera* varieties. The breeding of hybrids should not be confused with the near-universal practice in Europe of **grafting** *vinifera* vines on to American, **phylloxera**-resistant rootstock.

hydrogen sulphide (H_2S) Rotten egg gas. A reduced form of sulphur, which is a fault if it can be detected in bottled wine. Such a wine is said to be reduced. Sometimes vigorous aeration can help eliminate the smell.

I

ice wine English term for Eiswein, particularly used by Canadian wine producers. See **Eiswein**.

Idaho Wine-producing state of the Pacific North-West of the **United States**, much smaller in wine terms than its neighbours **Washington State** and **Oregon**. Most of the vineyards are planted at high altitudes, mainly with the **Riesling** and **Chardonnay** grape varieties, but also with **Cabernet Sauvignon**, **Chenin Blanc**, **Gewürztraminer** and **Pinot Noir**. The climate seems especially suited to the making of sparkling wines, and this may be where Idaho's best prospects lie.

IGT (indicazione geografica tipica) Italian wine class, roughly equivalent to French **vin de pays**. It has been used by some former up-market **vini da tavola**. See **Super Tuscan**.

impériale (also called imperial) Large-format bottle with a capacity of 6 litres, which is equivalent to eight standard bottles of 75 cl. It is used, but only rarely, in the **Bordeaux** region.

India Country whose wine-producing reputation, in the West, is founded on just one estate, which produces good quality **méthode traditionnelle** sparkling wine made from **Ugni Blanc**, **Pinot Noir** and **Chardonnay** grapes, sold under the Omar Khayyam label.

Inferno See **Valtellina**.

Ingelheim am Rhein Town in the **Rheinhessen** region of **Germany**. It is known mainly for the production of good red wine, some of the country's best, made from the **Spätburgunder** grape variety.

invecchiato Italian for aged.

Inzolia (also called Insolia) White grape variety of **Sicily**, where it is used to make good quality white **table wine**, and as a minor part of the blend in **Marsala**.

IPR (indicação de proveniencia regulamentada) Portuguese wine class, roughly equivalent to the French **VDQS**.

Irancy Village southwest of **Chablis** in northern **Burgundy**. It produces the red (and sometimes rosé) **AC** wine Bourgogne Irancy, made from the **Pinot Noir** grape, with the possible addition of César. The wines are delicate, clean reds, with strawberry flavours and are capable of moderate **ageing**.

Irouléguy Red (and rosé) **AC** wine produced in the Pyrenees from the **Tannat**, **Cabernet Franc** and **Cabernet Sauvignon** grape varieties. The rosé is **aromatic** and medium bodied, while the red is fairly rustic, with peppery fruit flavours and high **acidity**, and is best drunk young.

Irsay Oliver Aromatic white grape variety grown in **Slovakia** and **Hungary**. It produces floral, **Muscat**-like wines.

Ischia DOC wine made on the island of Ischia, off the coast of the **Campania** region, **Italy**. The whites are of ordinary quality, produced from the Forastera and Biancolella grape varieties. The small amount of red produced can be better, and is mainly from the Guarnaccia (related to **Garnacha**) grape. Some of the better producers stay outside the DOC system and concentrate on fine whites made from 100% Biancolella.

Isonzo (also called Isonzo del Friuli) **DOC** wine from the Isonzo river area near Gorizia in the **Friuli-Venezia Giulia** region of **Italy**. There are now no fewer than 20 different types of Isonzo. The **bianco** may be dry, **amabile**, or **frizzante**, and is based on the **Tocai Friulano**, **Malvasia**, Pinot Bianco and **Chardonnay** grape varieties. The **rosso** can also be dry, *amabile*, or *frizzante*, and is based on **Merlot**, **Cabernet Franc**, **Cabernet Sauvignon**, **Refosco** and Pinot Nero. The white **varietal** wines are Chardonnay, Malvasia Istriana, Pinot Bianco, Pinot Grigio, **Riesling Italico**, **Riesling Renano**, **Sauvignon**, **Tocai Friulano**, **Traminer** Aromatico and **Verduzzo Friulano**.

The red varietals, particularly the Cabernets, Merlot and Refosco, can be among the best quality wines of the region: Cabernet Franc, Cabernet Sauvignon, Franconia (the local name for Blaufrankisch), Merlot, Pinot Nero and Refosco.

Israel Minor wine-producing country, with relatively new plantings of **Cabernet Sauvignon** and **Sauvignon Blanc**, both varieties producing wines of excellent quality. Other varieties planted include **Chardonnay**, **Chenin Blanc**, **Colombard**, **Merlot**, **Grenache**, **Pinot**

Noir, **Riesling** and **Sémillon**. Previously Israel was known mainly for sweet and **fortified wines**. Much of the wine produced, though by no means all, is **kosher**.

Italy Country which vies with **France** for the honour of producing the largest quantity of wine in the world, with an astonishing variety of qualities and styles. Italy used to be known mainly for inferior examples of wines such as **Valpolicella** and **Chianti**, in wicker-covered flasks. The quality of Italian wines has improved vastly in recent years, however. The country is now increasingly well-known for its truly great wines. There are still many under-achieving zones, particularly in the south of the country, and the potential for further improvement is enormous. The greatest red wines, such as **Barolo**, **Barbaresco**, **Amarone**, **Chianti Classico**, **Vino Nobile di Montepulciano**, and **Brunello di Montalcino**, are produced in the central and northern regions of **Piedmont**, **Veneto**, and **Tuscany**. The northeast has led the Italian white winemaking revolution in **Friuli-Venezia Giulia**.

Quality levels begin with **vino da tavola**, and range up through **IGT** to **DOC** and **DOCG**. Some producers, however, dissatisfied with the DOC/G wine laws, produce high-quality, high-price wines under IGT or *vino da tavola* labels (particularly in Tuscany – see **Super Tuscans**), which do not have to conform to the sometimes restrictive rules. See entries for individual regions: **Abruzzo**; **Apulia**; **Calabria**; **Campania**; **Basilicata**; **Emilia-Romagna**; **Latium**; **Liguria**; **Lombardy**; **Marches**; **Molise**; **Sardinia**; **Sicily**; **Trentino**; **Alto Adige**; **Valle d'Aosta**; **Veneto**; **Umbria**.

Italy

- Milan
- Genoa
- Rome
- Naples
- Cagliari
- Palermo

1 Valle d'Aosta
2 Piedmont
3 Lombardy
4 Trentino-Alto Adige
5 Veneto
6 Friuli-Venezia Giulia
7 Emilia-Romagna
8 Marches
9 Tuscany
10 Umbria
11 Latium
12 Abruzzi
13 Molise
14 Campania
15 Apulia
16 Basilicata
17 Calabria
18 Sicily
19 Sardinia
20 Liguria

Jacquère White grape variety, the most important in the Savoie region of **France**. On its own it produces dry, light, neutral and fairly acidic wines of moderate quality.

Jasnières White **AC** wine of the **Loire** valley. It is produced to the north of Tours on the **Loir** tributary, and made entirely from the **Chenin Blanc** grape variety. The soil is similar to that in **Vouvray**, and the wines are usually dry and elegant, if somewhat **austere**, though sweet versions have been made in good years. At its best, quality can be very good.

Jerez See **Sherry**.

jeroboam Large format bottle of 4.5 litres capacity (six ordinary 75 cl bottles) in **Bordeaux**, or 3 litres (four ordinary bottles) in **Champagne**. See also **double magnum**.

Johannisberg 1. **Bereich** that covers the whole of the **Rheingau** region, or **Anbaugebiet**, of **Germany**. 2. Famous wine-producing village in the Rheingau region of Germany, which produces fine white wines from the **Riesling** grape. The village lies within the **Grosslage** of Erntebringer. The **Einzellage** sites are Goldatzel, Hansenberg, Hölle, Klaus, Mittelhölle, Schwarzenstein, Schloss Johannisberg and Vogelsang.

Johannisberg Riesling Alternative name for the
true **Riesling** grape, grown in Brazil and formerly used
in **California**, where it is now being phased out.

jug wine Term used, particularly in **California**, for the
cheapest sort of wine.

Juliénas Red **AC** wine produced from the **Gamay**
grape, one of the 10 **crus** of the **Beaujolais** region of
Burgundy. The wine is usually high in **tannin** and
acidity (for Beaujolais) with attractive, red-fruit
flavours and a good **ageing** potential in better **vintages**.
Quality is usually very good.

Jumilla DO wine from just south of **Valencia** and to
the west of **Alicante**, **Spain**. Most of the production is
of strong, dark red wines, high in **alcohol** and made
from the **Monastrell** grape, sometimes blended with
the superior **Tempranillo**. **Rosado** wines are made from
the same varieties, and white wine from **Airén**,
Merseguera and **Pedro Ximénez**. Previously many of
the vineyards were planted with ungrafted vines, but
most of these have now been replaced with grafted
vines resistant to **phylloxera**, with consequently more
economic **yields**.

Jura Region of eastern **France** that produces red, white,
and rosé wines, along with **vin gris** and **vin jaune**. The
whites are based on the **Savagnin** and **Chardonnay**
grapes, and the reds on **Trousseau**, **Poulsard**, and
Pinot Noir. There are four ACs: **Arbois**, **Château-
Chalon**, **Côtes du Jura** and **L'Étoile**.

Jurançon 1. White **AC** wine from southwest **France**,
made in the foothills of the Pyrenees from the **Petit
Manseng** and **Gros Manseng** grapes, sometimes with
the addition of **Courbu**. The dry version, Jurançon Sec,
is of good, average quality. The rarer, sweet, late-
harvested Jurançon Moelleux is honeyed and spicy
with cinnamon and clove flavours, delicate and sweet
but with balancing **acidity**, and can be of superb
quality. 2. Family of grape varieties, Jurançon Noir,
Jurançon Rouge and Jurançon Blanc, which have no
connection with AC Jurançon wine. The white variety
is still planted in small quantities in Gascony for
producing Armagnac. Jurançon Noir is used in **Cahors**
and Jurançon Rouge and Noir in **Gaillac**.

K

Kabinett German and Austrian quality white wine category, the first in the prädikat system, coming before **Spätlese**. In **Germany** Kabinett (previously spelled Cabinet) wines can only be made from fully-ripened grapes with a minimum **must weight** depending on variety and region. No **chaptalization** is permitted. The wines are usually light and low in **alcohol**, and may be dry or medium dry. See **QmP**.

Kadarka Most important native red grape variety of **Hungary**, grown all over the country. Previously **Egri Bikavér** (or Bull's Blood) was made almost entirely from this variety, but now, to its detriment, it is usually a blend.

Kaiserstuhl-Tuniberg Bereich of the **Baden** region of **Germany**, facing the vineyards of **Alsace** across the Rhine. Most of the white wine is produced from the **Müller-Thurgau** grape, but fine whites are also made from **Ruländer**. **Spätburgunder** is used to make the rosé **Weissherbst**. There are two Grosslagen, Attilafelsen and Vulkanfelsen.

Kallstadt Village in the Mittelhaardt **Bereich** of the **Pfalz** region of **Germany**. It produces high-quality, fruity white wines from the **Riesling**, **Silvaner** and **Scheurebe** grapes. The village is situated within the **Grosslagen** of Kobnert and Feuerberg.

Kalterer (also called Kalterersee) See **Caldaro**.

Kanzem Village in the **Saar-Ruwer Bereich**, in the **Mosel-Saar-Ruwer** region of **Germany**. In good years it produces superb white wines from the **Riesling** grape. The village is within the **Grosslage** of Scharzberg, and the **Einzellage** sites are Altenberg, Hörecker, Ritterpfad, Schlossberg and Sonnenberg.

Kasel Village in the **Saar-Ruwer Bereich**, in the **Mosel-Saar-Ruwer** region of **Germany**. It produces top-quality white wines from the **Riesling** grape. The vineyards come within the **Grosslage** of Römerlay, and the **Einzellage** sites are Dominikanerberg, Herrenberg, Hitzlay, Kehrnagel, Nies'chen, Paulinsberg and Timpert.

Kazakhstan CIS state with the potential to produce large quantities of decent wine. Wine grape varieties planted include the usual ex-Soviet **Rkatsiteli**, **Saperavi**, **Aleatico**, **Aligoté**, and **Muscat**, along with the more interesting **Cabernet Sauvignon** and **Cabernet Franc**.

Kékfrankos Alternative name, used in **Hungary**, for the **Blaufränkisch** grape.

Kerner White grape variety, a **cross** of Trollinger and Riesling. It produces attractive Riesling-style white wines, with good **ageing** potential, and it has the advantage of ripening in cool climate regions. Kerner is planted throughout **Germany**, (particularly in the **Pfalz** and **Rheinhessen** regions), in **South Africa** and in **England**.

kir White wine (often **Aligoté** from **Burgundy**) mixed with blackcurrant liqueur (**cassis**).

Knights Valley AVA of **Sonoma** county neighbouring **Chalk Hill** and **Alexander Valley** in **California**. It has a growing reputation for rich and elegant **varietal** wines produced from the **Cabernet Sauvignon** grape. **Sauvignon Blanc** and **Johannisberg Riesling** are also planted.

Kocher-Jagst-Tauber Smallest of the three **Bereich** subregions of the **Württemberg** region of **Germany**.

Kosher wine Wine made according to the customs of the Jewish faith, generally under the supervision of a rabbi. Such wines are made in most wine-producing countries.

Kosovo Small, disputed region of the former Yugoslavia. Light, rather acidic, reds were previously made there from **Pinot Noir**, **Cabernet Franc**, **Merlot** and **Gamay** grapes.

Kröv Village in the **Mosel-Saar-Ruwer** region of **Germany**, which produces medium-quality white wine. It is probably most famous for its **Grosslage** name Nacktarsch (meaning 'bare bottom'), which has inevitably led to particularly vulgar labels. The **Einzellage** sites are Burglay, Herrenberg, Kirchlay, Letterlay, Paradies and Steffensberg.

Kumeu Region on the North Island of **New Zealand** which produces fine **varietal** wines from **Cabernet Sauvignon**, **Chardonnay**, **Merlot**, **Müller-Thurgau**, **Pinot Noir**, **Riesling**, **Sauvignon Blanc** and **Sémillon** grapes.

L

La Côte Most westerly of the wine regions of the Vaud area in **Switzerland**. It produces mainly light, floral, elegant white wines from the **Chasselas** grape.

Lacrima Red grape variety of central eastern **Italy**. It is blended with up to 15% **Montepulciano** and **Verdicchio**, and used to make the red, plummy **DOC** wine Lacrima di Morro d'Alba in the **Marches** region. It can be dry or medium sweet, and still or **frizzante**.

Lacryma Christi del Vesuvio DOC wine made around Vesuvius in the **Campania** region of **Italy**. It can be a dry red or rosé, made from the Piedirosso, Sciascinoso and **Aglianico** grapes; or a dry white or fortified **liquoroso** from the Verdeca, Coda di Volpe and Falanghina grapes. The white, red and rosé can be still or sparkling.

Ladoix-Serrigny AC wine of **Burgundy**, made around the villages of Ladoix and Serrigny at the northern end of the **Côte de Beaune**. In practice, most of its production can be classified as **premier cru** or **grand cru Aloxe-Corton**, and much of the rest is declassified into **Côte de Beaune-Villages**, so it is rare to see Ladoix-Serrigny on the label. The quality of the wines, nearly all red and made from the **Pinot Noir** grape, is variable. The best are light to medium-bodied, soft reds, which can be good value.

lagar (pl. *lagares*) Shallow stone trough, traditionally used in the making of **Port**. Lightly crushed grapes are placed in the *lagar* and a team of bare-footed workers (usually men) treads the mixture of grape juice and skins, to maximize the amount of colour, flavour, and **tannin** extracted. When **fermentation** has given an **alcohol** content of about 7% the wine is run out of the *lagares* and mixed with brandy (**aguardente**) to arrest fermentation and to fortify the wine. Some houses still use *lagares*, especially for their best wines; others use more modern **vinification** methods in stainless-steel tanks. See also **autovinificator**.

Lago di Caldaro See **Caldaro**.

Lagrein Red grape variety grown mainly in the **Trentino** and **Alto Adige** regions of **Italy**. It makes a delicate, fragrant rosé wine in Lagrein Rosato (Lagrein Kretzer) and, around Bolzano, the deep, robust, smooth Lagrein Scuro (Lagrein Dunkel).

Lake County Wine region north of the **Napa Valley** in **California**, which was first planted with vines in the 1880s and has recently undergone a revival. It has significant plantings of mainly **Cabernet Sauvignon** and **Sauvignon Blanc** grapes. Lake County is part of the **North Coast AVA** and has two AVAs of its own, Clear Lake and Guenoc Valley.

Lalande-de-Pomerol Red **AC** wine of the **Bordeaux** region, adjacent to **Pomerol**. The wines have a soft, plummy richness, which makes them attractive to drink in their youth (four to five years). There is more **Cabernet Franc** and less **Merlot** in the blend than in

Pomerol, and Lalande never reaches the heights of top Pomerol. Recently there have been signs of an improvement and a search for a more distinctive communal character.

La Mancha DO wine of central **Spain**, and the largest 'quality' wine area of Europe. Most of the wine produced is white and made from the widely planted **Airén** grape variety. Traditionally, it was dark yellow, high in **alcohol**, and of mediocre quality. Recently, cold-temperature **vinification** in stainless-steel tanks has resulted in pale, fresh, and fruity whites, which are very acceptable quaffing wines best drunk young. The **Macabeo**, Pardilla and Verdoncho grapes are also allowed for the white. **Cencibel (Tempranillo)**, **Garnacha** and Moravia are used to make usually pale, easy-drinking reds and **rosado** wines. Given the climate, there is great potential to make excellent wines here, so far largely unexploited.

Lambrusco Family of red grape varieties grown mainly in the **Emilia-Romagna** region of **Italy**. It is used to produce mostly red, but also white and rosé **frizzante** wines sold under the same name. There are four **DOC** wines: Lambrusco di Sorbara, which can be red or rosé, dry or **amabile**; the red Lambrusco Salamino di Santa Croce and Lambrusco Grasparossa di Castelvetro, both of which can be dry or amabile; and Lambrusco Reggiano, which ranges from dry red to sweet pink. The best of these are lightly fizzy, with a sharp **acidity** in the background, good wines to accompany robust food. Sadly, much of what is sold on export markets is non-DOC, sweet red and white

Lambrusco, technically grape **must** rather than wine, and little more than alcoholic lemonade.

Lambrusco Mantovano Red **DOC frizzante** wine of the **Lombardy** region of **Italy**, similar to **Lambrusco** from **Emilia-Romagna**.

Landwein Category of German wine, above **Deutscher Tafelwein**, but below **QbA**, and similar in concept to the French **vin de pays** category. It cannot be sweeter than **halbtrocken**, and there are 15 *Landwein* regions within the four main Deutscher Tafelwein areas: Ahrtaler, Altrheingauer, Bayerischer, Fränkischer, Landwein der Mosel, Landwein der Saar, Nahegauer, Pfälzer, Regensburger, Rheinburger, Rheinischer, Schwäbischer, Starkenburger, Sudbadischer Landwein and Unterbadischer. Because it is so easy to qualify for QbA, the concept of *Landwein* is little used, and the names are rarely seen on labels.

Langhorne Creek Wine region in **South Australia** producing sometimes high-quality red **varietal** wines from **Cabernet Sauvignon**, **Merlot**, and **Shiraz**, plus some whites.

Languedoc-Roussillon Extremely large region on the Mediterranean coast of **France**, which produces a vast quantity of mostly red wine. The wine used to be fairly rough and was high in colour and **alcohol**. It was a major source of France's everyday **vin de table** and was also frequently used for blending to 'beef up' wines of other regions. More recently, there is a great improvement in quality, with major programmes of replantation. Red **AC** wines include **Collioure**,

Corbières, Costières de Nîmes, Coteaux du
Languedoc, Côtes du Roussillon, Fitou and Minervois.
Whites include Clairette de Bellegarde and Clairette du
Languedoc (see **Clairette**), and fortified whites,
Banyuls, Muscat de Frontignan, Muscat de Rivesaltes
and **Maury**. The great marketing success of the region
has been with **vin de pays**, however, particularly with
varietal wines under the vin de pays d'Oc label made
from **Chardonnay, Sauvignon Blanc, Cabernet
Sauvignon, Merlot**, and **Syrah**. Other *vin de pays* areas,
such as Aude and Hérault, provide large quantities of
everyday drinking wine for France and for export
markets.

lanolin Tasting term used to describe a soft, wet-wool
aroma, often found in white wines made from the
Sémillon grape.

La Romanée See Romanée, La.

La Romanée-Conti See Romanée-Conti, La.

La Romanée-Saint-Vivant See Romanée-Saint-
Vivant, La.

Laski Rizling (also called Laskiriesling) Alternative
name, used in **Slovenia**, for the **Welschriesling** grape
variety.

La Tâche Grand cru wine of **Vosne-Romanée**, in the
Côte de Nuits area of **Burgundy**, made from the **Pinot
Noir** grape. This is one of the finest, and most
expensive, red wines in the world. The taste of La

Tâche is difficult to describe – an extraordinary panoply
of smoky, fruity sensations on the **nose**, and intense
concentration on the palate, with truffly, rich and spicy
flavours – but once tasted it is never forgotten.

Late-Bottled Vintage Port See **LBV**.

late harvest Term equivalent to **Spätlese** or **vendange
tardive**, found mainly on New World wine labels. It
indicates that the grapes were harvested later than
usual, and should therefore have a higher concentration of sugar. Such wines are usually rich and sweet,
but they may be fermented to dryness, becoming
powerful and alcoholic.

Latisana (also called Latisana del Friuli) Red, white,
and rosé **DOC** wine of the **Friuli-Venezia Giulia** region
of **Italy**. There are 13 different types, 12 **varietals** and
one **rosato**. The red varietals are Cabernet (made from
Cabernet Franc and/or **Cabernet Sauvignon**), **Merlot**,
Refosco dal Peduncolo Rosso (a **clone** of **Refosco**).
The whites are from **Chardonnay**, Pinot Bianco, Pinot
Grigio, **Sauvignon**, **Tocai Friulano**, **Traminer**
Aromatico and **Verduzzo Friulano**. The *rosato* is made
from Merlot, the Cabernets, Refosco Nostrano and
Refosco dal Peduncolo Rosso.

Latium (also called Lazio) Region on the west coast of
Italy, centred on Rome. The white **DOC** wines **Est!
Est!! Est!!!** and **Capena** come from the north of the
region, along with the alcoholic, sometimes fortified,
sweet red **Aleatico** di Gradoli and the white and red
Cerveteri. **Montecompatri-Colonna**, **Marino**, **Colli**

Albani, **Colli Lanuvini**, Zagarolo and the white **Frascati** are produced in the hills around Rome. **Velletri** can be red or white. **Cesanese** is made in three DOCs in the Ciociaria. From the south comes red and white **Cori** and red, white and rosé **Aprilia**.

Latricières-Chambertin **Grand cru** vineyard of **Gevrey-Chambertin** in the **Côte de Nuits** area of **Burgundy**.

Laudun One of the best villages of the Côtes du Rhône-Villages *appellation* (see **Côtes du Rhône**). It produces fresh, fruity red and rosé from the **Grenache**, **Syrah**, **Cinsault** and **Mourvèdre** grape varieties, and has a good reputation for whites made from **Clairette**, **Roussanne**, and **Marsanne**.

Lavaux One of the three main wine regions of the Vaud area of **Switzerland**, which produces white wines mainly from the **Chasselas** grape. Its wines are richer, deeper and more intense than those of **La Côte**.

Lazio See **Latium**.

LBV (Late-Bottled Vintage Port) Category of **Port**, made from wine from a single year, bottled four to six years after the harvest. Both the vintage year and the year of bottling must appear on the label. Having matured in cask, it is usually made in a 'ready to drink' style, with no need for decanting, although some shippers make a 'traditional' style, which does have a deposit and benefits from **bottle ageing**. The best LBVs offer good-value Port, which is lighter than **Vintage Port** in style, but superior to **Ruby Port**.

Lebanon Wine-producing country of the Middle East, the reputation of which, in the West, is founded almost entirely on one estate, Château Musar in the Bekaa Valley. The vineyards are planted with **Cabernet Sauvignon** and **Cinsault** grapes, plus **Syrah**, **Merlot** and **Pinot Noir**. The **château** wine is dominated by Cabernet and is a concentrated, **tannic**, long-lived, **Bordeaux**-style wine.

lees Deposit of dead **yeast** that falls to the bottom of a vat of wine after **fermentation** and **ageing**. Normally the wine is transferred to another container (racked), leaving this sediment behind. Some wines, notably **Muscadet**, are sometimes aged for a time on the lees (**sur lie**), leading to a distinctive yeasty **aroma** and taste. The lees may be stirred (*bâtonnage* in French) in order to promote uptake of lees character.

Left Bank English term used to describe the **Bordeaux** vineyards of the western bank of the Garonne river and Gironde estuary (viz. **Médoc**, **Graves**, **Pessac-Léognan**, **Sauternes**). By contrast, the vineyards to the east (**Saint-Emilion**, **Pomerol**, and their satellites) are referred to as the **Right Bank**.

legs Tasting term used to describe the pattern formed when drops of wine trickle down the inside of a glass after the wine has been swirled. Persistent legs usually indicate richness in the wine, and a high **alcohol** content.

Leiwen Village in the **Mosel-Saar-Ruwer** region of **Germany**, which produces racy, fruity white wines from the **Riesling** grape. The village comes under the

Grosslage of St Michael, and the **Einzellage** sites are Klostergarten and Laurentiuslay.

Le Montrachet See **Montrachet, Le**.

lemony Tasting term used to describe a citrus fruit flavour and **acidity**, usually in young dry white wines, or as a balancing component in sweet wines.

length Tasting term used to describe the duration of the final taste sensation after a wine has been swallowed (or spat out). 'Good length', where the taste persists for some moments, is an essential characteristic of a well-balanced fine wine.

Léon Small region in northern **Spain**. It produces mainly red wines made mostly from the Prieto Picudo grape, but also from **Tempranillo** and Mencia. Its white wines are made from the **Verdejo** and **Palomino** varieties.

Les Clos Largest of the seven **grand cru** vineyards of **Chablis**.

Les Maranges AC wine of the **Côte de Beaune** area of **Burgundy**, made in the villages of Cheilly-les-Maranges, Dezize-les-Maranges and Sampigny-les-Maranges. It produces light red Burgundy from the **Pinot Noir** grape, of a similar standard to **Côte de Beaune-Villages**.

Lessona **Austere**, dry red **DOC** wine from the Vercelli hills in northern **Piedmont**. It is made mainly from the **Nebbiolo** grape variety, with up to 25% **Bonarda** and Vespolina.

Leverano DOC wine from the Salento peninsula in the
Apulia region of **Italy**. It produces red, white and
rosato wines. The red, which is the best wine, is based
on the **Negroamaro** grape, together with **Malvasia**
Nera, **Sangiovese**, and **Montepulciano**. The dry rosé,
from the same grapes, can also be good. The white,
from **Malvasia**, **Bombino Bianco**, and **Trebbiano**
Toscano, is rarely good.

lie(s) French word for **lees**.

Liebfraumilch Sweet, white **QbA** wine, which is
produced mainly in the **Rheinhessen**, **Pfalz** and **Nahe**
regions of **Germany**, from the **Riesling**, **Silvaner**, or
Müller-Thurgau grapes. As a **QbA** it should have the
name of the **Anbaugebiet** on the label, and theoretically
be typical of its region, but grape names are not
allowed. The wine is immensely popular outside
Germany, the most widely exported German wines,
although it is little known on the home market. At its
best it is pleasantly fruity, sweet, innocuous and
inexpensive.

Lieser Small village near Bernkastel-Kues in the **Mosel-
Saar-Ruwer** region of **Germany**, which produces racy,
elegant white wines. The vineyards are split between
the **Grosslagen** of Beerenlay and Kurfürstlay, and the
Einzellage sites are Niederberg-Helden, Rosenlay,
Süssenberg and Schlossberg.

light Tasting term used to describe a wine low in
alcohol, with little fruit or **body**.

Liguria Small region of **Italy**, situated on the Italian Riviera. There are two main **DOC** zones in west Liguria: the dry red **Rossese di Dolceacqua**; and the red, white and rosé **Riviera Ligure di Ponente**. In the east of the region the white **Cinqueterre** is made, together with red and white **Colli di Luni**.

Limberger See **Blaufränkisch**.

Limousin Forest in **France**, whose **oak** is used for making barrels. Its wood, which has a high phenol content, is less dense, with a wider grain and greater porosity, than oak from **Allier** and Nevers. It has a particular affinity with **Pinot Noir** and **Chardonnay**, particularly in the New World. Limousin oak is the preferred oak for Cognac.

Limoux Wine town in southern **France**, chiefly famed for its sparkling wine (See **Blanquette de Limoux**, **Crémant de Limoux**) but also a good source of **Chardonnay**, either as **Vin de pays** d'Oc or under the **AC** Limoux.

liqueur de tirage Mixture of wine, sugar, and **yeast** added to bottles of **Champagne** (and other **méthode traditionnelle** wines) to induce the bubble-forming, secondary **fermentation** in bottle.

liqueur d'expedition Mixture of wine and, usually, sugar that is used to top-up bottles of **Champagne** (and other **méthode traditionnelle** wines) after **disgorgement**. See also **dosage**.

liquoroso Italian term for a high **alcohol** wine, usually sweet and possibly fortified.

Lirac AC wine of the southern **Rhône** valley, produced in the villages of Lirac, Roquemaure, Saint-Laurent-des-Arbes and Saint-Géniès-de-Comolas. Most of the wine, and the best, is red, with some white and rosé. The red is made mainly from **Grenache** and **Cinsault** grapes, and is light, fruity and plummy. It ages well for three to four years, but is also delicious when drunk young. Light, strawberry-flavoured rosés are made from the same grape varieties. The white is based on the **Clairette** grape. It is fresh and appley, but it is produced in only small quantities and rarely exported.

Lison-Pramaggiore DOC wine of the eastern part of the **Veneto** region of **Italy**. There are 12 different **varietals**, all of which may be still or sparkling. The reds are generally dry and rich, with some class. **Merlot** is the most important, followed by **Cabernet** (Franc and/or Sauvignon) and **Refosco**. The whites are also good, and usually good value. They are **Chardonnay**, Pinot Bianco, Pinot Grigio, **Riesling Italico**, **Sauvignon**, Tocai Italico, and Verduzzo.

Listrac Communal **AC** wine of the **Haut-Médoc** region of **Bordeaux**. It produces good, long-lived, fairly **tannic cru bourgeois** wines, but no **cru classé**.

Livermore Valley AVA of Alameda county, **California**, particularly suited to growing **Sauvignon Blanc** and **Sémillon**. **Chardonnay** and Gray Riesling are the most planted white grape varieties, however, and the main reds are **Cabernet Sauvignon** and Petite Sirah.

Ljutomer Best-known wine-producing area of **Slovenia**, famous for its white wine made from **Laski Rizling**.

Locorotondo Dry white **DOC** wine produced around the town of Locorotondo in **Apulia**, **Italy**. The wine may be still or **spumante**, with gentle fruit and an almond finish. It is made mainly from the Verdeca and **Bianco d'Alessano** grapes.

lodges English name for the cellars, located in Vila Nova de Gaia, used by **Port** producers for **ageing**, blending, and bottling.

Lodi AVA in the San Joaquin Valley of **California**.

Loir Tributary of the **Loire** river.

Loire Longest river in **France**, with important and diverse wine regions located along much of its length. The eastern (Upper) Loire is noted mainly for its fine, dry whites, made from the **Sauvignon Blanc** grape in **Sancerre**, **Pouilly-Fumé**, **Menetou-Salon**, **Quincy**, and **Reuilly**. In **Touraine**, the prominent quality white grape is **Chenin Blanc**, which produces a wide variety of styles in **Vouvray** and **Montlouis**. **Cabernet Franc** makes high-quality red wines in **Chinon**, **Bourgueil** and **Saint-Nicolas-de-Bourgueil**. Similar reds are made in **Saumur-Champigny**, but **Saumur** is chiefly known for its **méthode traditionnelle** sparkling wines. **Anjou-Saumur** produces large quanitites of rosé wine, the best from Cabernet, but its finest wines are whites based on Chenin Blanc, which are either steely dry, as from

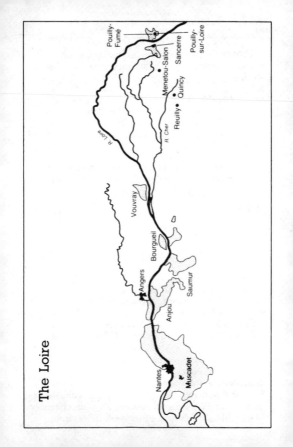

The Loire

Pouilly-Fumé
Pouilly-sur-Loire
Sancerre
Menetou-Salon
Quincy
Reuilly
R. Cher
R. Loire
Vouvray
Bourgueil
Angers
Saumur
Anjou
Nantes
Muscadet

Savennières, or lusciously sweet, as from **Coteaux du Layon**, **Bonnezeaux**, and **Quarts-de-Chaume**. The western end of the Loire is the home of dry, white **Muscadet** and lesser whites made from the Gros Plant (**Gros Plant du Pays Nantais**).

Lombardy (also called Lombardia) Region of northern **Italy**. The wine-growing area is centred on the city of Milan and stretches as far as Lake Garda. South of Milan, **Oltrepò Pavese** produces hearty reds and fragrant whites, together with the base for sparkling wines. Nearer Milan, **San Colombano al Lambro** produces rustic dry reds. In northern Lombardy, **Valtellina** makes sturdy reds based on **Nebbiolo**. To the east, Bergamo produces **Valcalepio**, dry whites based on Pinot Bianco and Pinot Grigio, and dry reds, based on **Merlot** and **Cabernet Sauvignon**. Around Brescia, world-class sparkling whites and rosés are made in **Franciacorta**, as well as still, dry reds and whites (see **Terre di Franciacorta**). See also **Cellatica**, **Botticino**, **Lugana**, **Riviera del Garda Bresciano**, and **Tocai di San Martino della Battaglia**. In Mantova, Colli Morenici Mantovani del Garda produces simple, dry red, white, and rosé, and good, red, dry or **amabile**, sparkling **Lambrusco Mantovano**.

long Tasting term used to describe a wine the flavour of which persists once it is swallowed (or spat out), generally considered to be a sign of quality. See also **finish**; **length**.

Long Island Region of **New York State** which was planted relatively recently with grape varieties including **Chardonnay**, **Sauvignon Blanc**, **Johannisberg Riesling** and **Gewürztraminer**, among the whites, and **Cabernet Sauvignon**, **Pinot Noir** and **Merlot** among the reds.

Lorch Village in the Rhine Gorge, in the **Rheingau** region of **Germany**. It produces moderate to good quality white wines, mainly from the **Riesling** grape. The vineyards come within the **Grosslage** of Burgweg. The **Einzellage** sites are Bodenstal-Steinberg, Kapellenberg, Krone, Pfaffenwies and Schlossberg.

Lorchhausen Village in the **Rheingau** region of **Germany**, which produces light, elegant white wines from the **Riesling** grape. The vineyards come under the **Grosslage** of Burgweg. The **Einzellage** sites are Rosenberg and Seligmacher.

Loupiac Sweet white **AC** wine made on the **Right Bank** of the Garonne river in the **Bordeaux** region. The grapes are the same as those used in **Sauternes** and **Barsac** (**Sémillon**, **Sauvignon Blanc**, and **Muscadelle**), although higher yields are permitted. The wines are in a similar style to those of Sauternes and Barsac, although never as complex, and they have less **ageing** potential.

Loureiro (also called Loureira) White grape variety grown mainly in the **Vinho Verde** region of **Portugal** and **Galicia** in **Spain**. It is one of the best of the permitted varieties for Vinho Verde, with good **acidity**, and an attractive, **grapey** scent.

Lubéron See Côtes du Lubéron.

Lugana Dry white **DOC** wine made near Lake Garda in the **Lombardy** region of **Italy**. The wine may be still or **spumante** and is made mainly from the **Trebbiano** di Lugana grape variety. It is elegant, attractive, medium-bodied and one of the region's finest whites, much better than many other Trebbiano-based wines.

Lussac-Saint-Emilion Red **AC** wine made in a 'satellite' of the main **Saint-Emilion** AC in **Bordeaux**. The wines are produced from the **Merlot**, **Cabernet Franc**, **Cabernet Sauvignon** and **Malbec** grape varieties (the same as Saint-Emilion). Although very pleasant to drink when fairly young, and offering good value, they never reach the heights of the top Saint-Emilions.

Luxembourg Tiny country whose vineyards are located mainly along the banks of the river Mosel, which forms the border with **Germany**. The light, fruity, white wines are mainly Germanic in style, and made from **Müller-Thurgau** (known locally as **Rivaner**), **Riesling**, **Elbling**, **Auxerrois**, **Gewürztraminer** and **Pinot Gris** grapes. Some sparkling wine is made.

M

MA (marque auxillière) Letters found on **Champagne** labels indicating that the name of the wine does not belong to the producer. For example, the letters are found on supermarkets' own-label Champagne. The numbers following the letters identify the producer.

Macabeo (or Maccabeo) White grape variety grown in **Spain**, planted chiefly in the **Rioja** region (where it is known as Viura), **Penedès**, **Conca de Barbera**, and **Jumilla**. It makes wines with good **acidity** and fruity, floral flavour. Also widely planted in **France**, in the **Languedoc-Roussillon**.

Macedonia Former Yugoslav Republic of Macedonia, planted largely with red varieties including **Gamay** and Vranac. Good potential, not yet being realized.

maceration Process whereby red wines derive their colour, **tannin** and some flavour through contact of the fermenting **must** with grape skins. A shorter period of maceration, or skin contact, can also be beneficial for white varieties. See also **carbonic maceration**.

macération carbonique French for **carbonic maceration**.

Mâcon Basic **AC** wine of the **Mâconnais** area of the **Burgundy** region. The white, made from the **Chardonnay** grape, is rarely better than a basic, fairly

ordinary white wine. The red and rosé, made from
Pinot Noir and **Gamay**, are rarely exciting.

Mâcon-Villages AC wine from the **Mâconnais** area of
the **Burgundy** region. Most of the wine is white, made
from the **Chardonnay** grape, and it is usually a good,
medium quality Burgundy. Forty-three villages are
entitled to call their wine Mâcon-Villages, or they can
add their own name, e.g. Mâcon-Clessé, Mâcon-Lugny,
Mâcon-Prissé, and Mâcon-Viré (which are among the
best).

Mâconnais Large area of **Burgundy**, centred on the
town of **Mâcon**, to the north of **Beaujolais** and south of
the **Côte Chalonnaise**. Most of the production is of
white wine from the **Chardonnay** grape. The main ACs
are **Mâcon**, **Mâcon-Villages**, **Pouilly-Fuissé**, **Pouilly-
Vinzelles**, **Pouilly-Loché**, and **Saint-Véran**. The red
grapes planted are **Gamay** plus a smaller amount of
Pinot Noir, which produce less interesting reds under
the **Bourgogne** and **Passe-Tout-Grains** *appellations*.
The wines are seldom great, but they are
straightforward, affordable Burgundies.

Madeira **Fortified wine** made on the island of
Madeira, which belongs to **Portugal**. The unique
method of production involves heating the wine to
around 45°C in an oven, called an **estufa**, for about
three months. The method originates from the time
when sailing ships carried the island's wines through
the tropics, and it was found that they were better after
their hot voyage.

There are four main types, based on grape varieties of the same names: **Sercial**, **Verdelho**, **Bual**, and **Malmsey**. Sercial and Verdelho, the drier styles, are fully fermented then fortified. Bual and Malmsey are sweeter, and **fermentation** is stopped by the addition of brandy. Madeira must be aged for a minimum of three years in cask (five years for Reserve, and 10 years for Special Reserve). Dated Madeiras can be **solera** wines, aged in a similar way to **Sherry**, or the rarer, more expensive, true **vintage** Madeira. It is probably the longest lived of wines, and can survive almost indefinitely, even in an opened, partly-filled bottle.

Madeleine Angevine White grape variety, a **cross** between Precocé de Malingre and Madeleine Royale. It is planted mainly in **England**, where it can produce a soft white wine with **Muscat**-like **aroma**.

Madera County and **AVA** of **California** which produces mainly **jug wine**.

maderized Tasting term used to describe an over-mature, **oxidized** wine.

Madiran Red **AC** wine from the foothills of the Pyrenees, southwest **France**. It produces **tannic**, rather **austere**, long-lived wines, mainly from the **Tannat** grape along with **Cabernet Sauvignon**, **Cabernet Franc** and **Fer**.

maduro Portuguese term for mature. *Vinho maduro* is an 'aged' wine, as opposed to **Vinho Verde** ('green' wine), which is bottled young.

magnum Large-format bottle, with a capacity of 1.5 litres, equivalent to two standard bottles. It is said to be the ideal size for the bottle maturation of great red **Bordeaux**. Some believe that wines age slowly in large bottles, developing greater complexity, and more quickly in small bottles.

Maindreieck Most important of the three **Bereich** subregions of the **Franken** region of **Germany**, which includes the town of Würzburg. It produces good quality white wines, mainly from the **Silvaner** and **Scheurebe** grape varieties.

Mainviereck One of the three **Bereich** subregions of the **Franken** region of **Germany**. It produces some good red wines from the **Spätburgunder** and **Portugieser** grape varieties.

Mainz Important wine town in the **Bereich** of **Nierstein** in the **Rheinhessen** region of **Germany**. Vineyards planted on the outskirts of Mainz come within the **Grosslage** St Alban, and **Einzellage** sites include Edelmann, Hüttberg, Johannisberg, Kirchenstück, Klosterberg, Sand, and Weinkeller.

Maipo Wine region of the **Mendoza** province of **Argentina**.

Maipo Valley One of the foremost wine areas in the **Central Valley** region of **Chile**. The majority of the wines are made from classic European grape varieties, including **Cabernet Sauvignon**, **Merlot**, and **Cabernet Franc**.

Málaga Fortified **DO** wine produced in southern
Spain, mainly from the **Pedro Ximénez**, **Airén**, and
Moscatel grapes. A variety of styles is made from **seco**
(dry) to **dulce** (sweet), from almost white to dark
golden brown. **Arrope** and **vino de color** are sometimes
added to give colour and sweetness. The best wines are
sometimes aged in **solera**, as with **Sherry**.

Malbec Alternative name, used in **Bordeaux**,
Argentina, and **Australia**, for the **Cot** grape variety.

malic acid See **acids**.

Mallorca (Majorca) Island of the Balearics, belonging
to **Spain**. There are two main wine-producing regions,
Binnissalem and Felanitx. The wines, made from
Prensal, Manto Negro, and Negra Moll, have improved
in recent years, since the introduction of modern
winemaking techniques to the island.

Malmsey Grape variety, part of the **Malvasia** family,
grown on the island of **Madeira**, where it gives its name
to a category of wine. Dark, full-bodied and luscious,
Malmsey is the sweetest of Madeiras.

malolactic fermentation Transformation that wines
may undergo, in which the tart malic acid is converted
into smoother, softer lactic acid. Nearly all reds go
through malolactic, while with whites this depends on
the style of wine desired. Despite the name, this is not
technically a **fermentation**.

Malvasia White grape variety grown mainly in central
Italy, where it is used as a minor ingredient in several

wines including **Frascati**, **Chianti** and **Galestro**, as well as in its own right in **Emilia-Romagna**. It is also grown in the **Rioja** area of **Spain**, as well as in **France**, **Australia**, **Portugal**, **Austria**, and **Germany**. It can produce a full-bodied, scented wine, with good **acidity**, but in Italy much of its character is lost in blending with **Trebbiano** and in white Rioja by blending with Viura (**Macabeo**). The **Malmsey** style of **Madeira** takes its name from the grape, and Malvasia is also an ingredient in some white **Port**.

Malvoisie Alternative name, used in the **Loire**, for the **Pinot Gris** grape variety. Also used, confusingly, as a synonym for several other unrelated varieties.

Mammolo Red grape variety which plays a minor role in **Vino Nobile di Montepulciano** and **Chianti** in **Tuscany**.

Mandelaria Red grape variety grown on the Greek islands of Crete, Paros, Rhodes, and **Santorini**.

Mandrolisai DOC wine made in the Barbagia hills of central **Sardinia**. A sturdy red and light rosé are both made, mainly from the Bovale Sardo, **Cannonau**, and **Monica** grapes.

Manduria See **Primitivo di Manduria**.

Manseng See **Gros Manseng**; **Petit Manseng**.

Mantonico di Bianco White wine from around the town of Bianco in the **Calabria** region of **Italy**. It is dry to slightly sweet, made from semi-dried Mantonico grapes, and can develop a nutty, heady **aroma** with age.

manzanilla Style of **Sherry**, very similar to **fino** in taste. Essentially, it is a fino that has been matured in the Spanish coastal town of Sanlúcar de Barrameda, rather than in Jerez de la Frontera or Puerto de Santa Maria. The sea air is said to give the Sherry a more pungent, **aromatic** quality. In fact, the difference in character is due to the different sort of **flor** that develops in Sanlúcar. *Manzanilla* is usually of very high quality, as long as it has not been on the shelf for too long, and is very good value for money. It should be drunk chilled, on its own or with seafood. Once opened, as with any white wine, a bottle of *manzanilla* should be finished quickly.

Maranges, Les See **Les Maranges**.

marc French term for the solid matter (skins, pips, and possibly stalks) left after pressing grapes. It is also used to describe the white spirit made from distilling this residue.

Marches (also called Le Marche) Wine region centred on the town of Ancona on the central eastern coast of **Italy**. The red **Sangiovese** dei Colli Pesaresi and the dry white Bianchello del Metauro are produced in the north of the region. The region's most famous wine, the dry white **Verdicchio** dei Castelli di Jesi, comes from the hills around Ancona, as does the red **Rosso Cònero**. Other wines include the dry white Verdicchio di Matelica, Bianco dei Colli Maceratesi, and Falerio dei Colli Asolani, the bubbly red **Vernaccia di Serrapetrona** and the dry red **Rosso Piceno**.

Marcillac AC wine produced in very small quantities in Aveyron, southwest **France**. The red, based on the **Fer** grape, plus **Gamay** and **Jurançon Noir**, is strong, dry and assertive. A small amount of rosé is also produced.

Margaret River Important wine-producing region of **Western Australia**. The climate is temperate, and **varietal** wines made from the **Cabernet Sauvignon** grape variety do particularly well here. **Sémillon** and **Chardonnay** have also been successful, and experiments with **Pinot Noir** have been encouraging.

Margaux One of the most important communal ACs of the **Médoc**, and also the name of its leading **château**. The *appellation* is based on the village of Margaux, but also takes in the surrounding villages of Soussac, Cantenac, Labarde, and Arsac. There are 21 **cru classé** châteaux and a larger number of **crus bourgeois**, many of the latter also making wine of high quality. At their best, the wines are characterized by delicacy and finesse combined with seductive power.

Maria Gomez See **Fernão Pires**.

Marignan Cru of the **Vin de Savoie** *appellation*.

Marino White **DOC** wine from the hills around Rome in the **Latium** region of **Italy**. The wine can be dry or **amabile**, still or **spumante**, and is made mainly from **Malvasia** and **Trebbiano** grape varieties. It is very similar to **Frascati** in style.

Markgräflerland Bereich subregion of the **Baden** region of **Germany**. It produces mainly white wines, particularly light, spritzy wines from the Gutedel grape.

Marlborough Finest wine region of South Island, **New Zealand**. It produces stunning crisp white wines from the **Sauvignon Blanc** grape, and good results have also been obtained with **Cabernet Sauvignon**, **Chardonnay**, and **Pinot Noir**.

marque auxillière See **MA**.

Marsala Fortified **DOC** wine made in the western part of **Sicily**. The production process is complex, involving the use of concentrated and cooked **musts** and long **ageing** in **oak** barrels. The *oro* (gold) and *ambra* (amber) types are based on white grapes, mainly **Grillo**, **Catarratto**, and **Inzolia**. The *rubino* (ruby) style is based on the Perricone, **Calabrese**, and **Nerello** Mascalese grapes, plus up to 30% of the white varieties. *Fine* and *Superiore* Marsala can be *oro*, *ambra*, or *rubino*, and can range from **secco** through to **dolce** in sweetness. Concentrated musts can be used for all types of *Fine* and *Superiore* (to give sweetness), but cooked must (to give colour and a burnt caramel flavour) is allowed only for ambra. *Vergine* Marsala can be *oro*, *ambra* or *rubino*, but no cooked or concentrated musts can be used.

Some Marsala is aged in a **solera** system, similar to that used for **Sherry**. *Superiore* can have a marvellous, deep, caramel sweetness balanced by piercing **acidity**. *Vergine* makes a deep, dry, complex apéritif, and *Fine* is best used for cooking.

Marsannay AC wine produced just south of Dijon, in the **Côte de Nuits** area of **Burgundy**. The red is made from the **Pinot Noir** grape and is a reasonable quality Burgundy, best drunk fairly young. The rosé, also from Pinot Noir, is dry, with pleasant cherry fruit. Whites are rarely seen.

Marsanne Predominant white grape variety grown in the northern **Rhône** area of **France**, where it is used to make white **Saint-Joseph** and **Crozes-Hermitage**, and still and sparkling **Saint-Péray**. It is permitted in red **Hermitage**, but is rarely used. It is also grown successfully in the **Languedoc-Roussillon**, either as a **varietal vin de pays** or in **AC** blends. It is also planted, to a limited extent, in **Australia**.

Martina Franca (also called Martina) Dry white **DOC** wine produced between Bari and **Brindisi** in the **Apulia** region of **Italy**. It can be still or sparkling, and is made mainly from the Verdeca and Bianco di Alessano grape varieties. The wine is very similar to **Locorotondo** in style.

Martinborough Small region on the North Island of **New Zealand**, which produces particularly fine **varietal** wines from **Sauvignon Blanc**, **Pinot Noir** and **Chardonnay** grapes, along with **Gewürztraminer** and **Rhine Riesling**.

Martinsthal Village in the **Rheingau** region of **Germany**. It produces good quality white wines from the **Riesling** grape variety. The vineyards come within the **Grosslage** of Steinmächer, and the **Einzellage** sites are Langenberg, Rödchen and Wildsau.

Marzemino Red grape variety planted mainly in **Italy**, although probably of Austrian origin. It makes rustic reds for drinking young in the **Trentino** region of **Italy**, and it is one of the **varietals** authorized for the Trentino **DOC**. Elsewhere in Italy, it is used for blending in **Lombardy** and **Emilia-Romagna**.

Mataro Synonym for the **Mourvèdre** grape variety, used particularly in **Australia**.

mature Tasting term used to describe a wine that is fully aged. How long this takes varies enormously with different wines and regions, and it remains very much a matter of opinion. It can take from a few months to several decades for a wine to become mature, depending on the initial content of **acid**, **alcohol**, **tannin**, and fruit. Red wine can be seen to be mature when the colour takes on a ruddy brown at the rim, and on the **nose** and **palate** all the component parts are harmoniously blended. See also **ageing**.

Maury Sweet red or rosé **AC** wine made in the **Languedoc-Roussillon** region from the **Grenache** grape variety. It is a **vin doux naturel** (that is, a **fortified wine**), with a strong, Porty taste. It is sometimes aged to make an **oxidized**, **rancio** style, with a burnt, caramel flavour.

Mauzac Blanc White grape variety of **France**, used to make white wines in **Gaillac** and sparkling wines in **Limoux**, where it goes under the name Blanquette. It is a good, fairly neutral base for sparkling wines, sometimes showing appley character, but still wines based on Mauzac tend to be highly acidic, tart and thin.

Mavrodaphne Red grape variety native to **Greece**, where it produces lightly fortified, deep, sweet, red wines around Patras in the Peloponnese. Quality can be good, especially with a few years' **ageing**.

Mavrud Red grape variety grown particularly in **Bulgaria**, where it can produce deep, **tannic** wines capable of moderate **ageing**.

Mazis-Chambertin Grand **cru** vineyard of **Gevrey-Chambertin** in the **Côte de Nuits** area of **Burgundy**.

McDowell Valley AVA of **Mendocino** county, **California**. It has a short warm season and produces fine **varietal** wines, particularly from **Syrah** and **Zinfandel** grapes; also **Cabernet Sauvignon**, **Chardonnay**, and **Sauvignon Blanc**.

McLaren Vale Important wine-producing area in **South Australia** which produces particularly good white **varietal** wines from the **Chardonnay** grape. Reds from **Cabernet Sauvignon**, **Grenache** and **Shiraz** also do well, as do whites from **Sauvignon Blanc** and **Riesling**.

Médoc 1. General term for the peninsular area of **Bordeaux** to the west of the Gironde estuary, to distinguish it, for example, from **Saint-Emilion** and **Pomerol** to the east and the **Graves** region to the south. The area includes the ACs of Médoc, **Haut-Médoc**, **Margaux**, **Listrac**, **Moulis**, **Saint-Estèphe**, **Saint-Julien** and **Pauillac**.

2. Red **AC** wine of Bordeaux, produced in the northern half of the Médoc peninsula from the classic Bordeaux

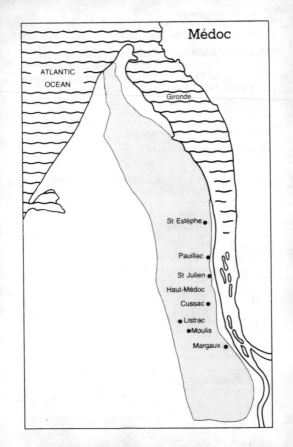

Médoc

ATLANTIC OCEAN

Gironde

St Estèphe

Pauillac

St Julien

Haut-Médoc

Cussac

Listrac

Moulis

Margaux

grape varieties (**Cabernet Sauvignon**, **Cabernet Franc**, **Merlot** and **Petit Verdot**). The wines are usually of good quality, for early drinking, although not approaching the quality of the communal *appellations* of the **Haut-Médoc** to the south. There are no **crus classés**, but several **crus bourgeois**.

Mélinots Premier cru of Chablis.

Melissa DOC wine of the eastern coast of the **Calabria** region of **Italy**, similar to **Cirò**, but generally of lower quality. The white is made mainly from the **Greco** grape and the red from **Gaglioppo**.

Melnik Red grape variety grown particularly in **Bulgaria**, where it can produce deep, **tannic** wines capable of moderate **ageing**.

Melon d'Arbois Alternative name, used in the **Jura**, for the **Chardonnay** grape variety.

Melon de Bourgogne (also called Muscadet) A white grape variety grown almost exclusively in the Pays Nantais region of the **Loire**, where it is used to make the dry, crisp **AC** wine **Muscadet**.

Mendocino Most northerly of the major wine-producing counties of **California**. It produces premium **varietal** wines from **Chardonnay**, **Sauvignon Blanc**, **Zinfandel**, **Pinot Noir** and **Cabernet Sauvignon** grapes. Important **AVAs** include **McDowell Valley**, and the **Anderson Valley** which is well-suited to Chardonnay and Pinot Noir and is becoming popular as a sparkling wine area. Mendocino producers have spearheaded the move towards **organic** winemaking in California.

Mendoza Most important wine producing province of **Argentina**, sub-divided into the main region around Mendoza city, Tupungato, and San Rafael.

Menetou-Salon AC wine made around the village of Menetou-Salon in the eastern **Loire** valley. It is a neighbour of **Sancerre** and the wine is similar to, if not quite as good as, the very best Sancerre and **Pouilly-Fumé**. It is a crisp, refreshing, juicy white made from the **Sauvignon Blanc** grape. Red and rosé Menetou-Salon, made from the **Pinot Noir** grape, can be better than red Sancerre. They are fresh, lean wines with strawberry fruit, which are best drunk slightly chilled.

Méntrida DO wine north east of **La Mancha** in central **Spain** producing dark, strong, high-**alcohol**, high-tannin, red and **rosado** wines from the **Garnacha** and Cencibel grape varieties.

Mercurey AC wine produced around the village of Mercurey in the **Côte Chalonnaise** region of **Burgundy**. Most of the wines are red, made from the **Pinot Noir** grape, and are among the fullest-flavoured and best-structured of the Côte Chalonnaise. A small amount of white wine is produced from the **Chardonnay** grape, and recent improvements in quality among the better producers are encouraging.

Meritage **Californian** term for a **Bordeaux**-style blend; reds and whites must be made from the classic Bordeaux varieties.

Merlot One of the world's major red grape varieties, traditionally grown in **Bordeaux**, where it is the mainstay of the **Saint-Emilion** and **Pomerol** regions. It also plays an important, but secondary role in the great red wines of the **Médoc**. Elsewhere in **France**, it is found in large quantities in the **Languedoc-Roussillon**, and much is bottled as **varietal Vin de pays** d'Oc. Merlot is found the world over, and is particularly successful in **California**, **Argentina** and the rest of south America, **New Zealand**, and **Australia**. It is also widely grown in northeastern **Italy** especially in **Friuli-Venezia Giulia**, **Trentino**, and the **Veneto**.

Merseguera White grape variety of **Spain**, grown in **Valencia**, **Alicante**, and **Jumilla**. It produces dull, bland wine.

méthode champenoise See **méthode traditionnelle**.

méthode traditionnelle Method by which **Champagne** gets its bubbles, by a second **fermentation** which takes place in bottle. The term is currently found on the labels of bottle-fermented sparkling wines from the rest of **France** and all over the world, as the use of the term **méthode champenoise** has gradually been phased out.

methuselah Large format bottle of 6 litres capacity (eight ordinary 75 cl bottles) used for **Champagne**.

metodo classico Italian term for bottle-fermented sparkling wines. See **méthode traditionnelle**.

Meunier See **Pinot Meunier**.

Meursault AC wine of the **Côte de Beaune** area of **Burgundy**. The vineyards surrounding Meursault, one of the largest villages of the **Côte**, produce some of the finest white Burgundies up to **premier cru** level, from the **Chardonnay** grape. There are no **grands crus**. At their best, the whites are pale gold, dry but full, with rich buttery, nutty, creamy aromas and taste. A small amount of red Meursault is produced, from **Pinot Noir**, but much is sold as **Volnay**-Santenots or **Blagny**.

Mexico Wine-producing country of central America. Many of the vineyards are for table-grape production, and most of the country's wine is distilled into brandy. The quality of **table wine** production is gradually improving, and some **Vitis vinifera** grape varieties, including **Riesling**, **Pinot Noir** and **Cabernet Sauvignon**, have been grown successfully, especially in the Baja California area. Production also includes some **méthode traditionnelle** sparkling wines and **fortified wines** similar to **Sherry**.

MIA Abbreviation of **Murrumbidgee Irrigation Area**.

Midi Loose term for the south of **France**, taking in the wine regions of **Languedoc-Roussillon** and **Provence**.

Milawa Wine region in north-east **Victoria**, **Australia**.

millésime French for vintage year.

Minervois AC wine of the **Languedoc-Roussillon** region of **France**. It produces mainly fruity, easy-drinking red wine, which is best drunk young, from the **Carignan** (gradually being reduced), **Grenache** and **Cinsault** grapes, with some **Syrah** and **Mourvèdre**. **Carbonic maceration** is often used to good effect. Minervois wines are generally lighter and less complex than those from neighbouring **Corbières**.

mis(e) en bouteille au château Term found on French labels, indicating that the wine was bottled at the **château**. *Mise en bouteille à la propriété* indicates that the wine comes from a **cave co-opérative**, even if there is a *château* name on the label.

Misket White grape variety of **Bulgaria**, producing floral, scented wines.

Mission Red grape variety, the first **Vitis vinifera** variety to be planted in **California**. It was brought by Jesuit priests in the late 17th century, hence the name Mission. Although now in decline, it is still planted in California, where it produces light, rustic reds. Mission is probably related to the **Pais** grape of **Chile** and the **Criolla Chica** of **Argentina**.

mistelle Alcoholic drink made by the addition of brandy, or grape spirit, to unfermented grape juice. See **Floc de Gascogne**; **Pineau des Charentes**; **Ratafia**.

Mittelhaardt-Deutsche Weinstrasse Bereich subregion of the **Pfalz** region of **Germany**. It produces some of the country's finest white wines from the **Riesling** grape variety. See **Deidesheim**; **Forst**; **Wachenheim**.

Mittelheim Village in the **Rheingau** region of **Germany**, which produces good quality white wines mainly from the **Riesling** grape. Part of Mittelheim, with its neighbour **Winkel**, comes within the **Grosslage** of Honigberg; the remainder within Erntebringer. The **Einzellage** sites are Edelmann, Goldberg and St Nikolaus.

Mittelmosel Area of the **Mosel-Saar-Ruwer** region of **Germany**, approximately corresponding to the **Bereich** subregion of **Bernkastel**.

Mittelrhein Minor **Anbaugebiet** region of **Germany**, which follows the course of the Rhine from just beyond **Lorch**, in the **Rheingau**, almost as far as Bonn. Most of the vineyards are planted with the **Riesling** grape, and they produce attractive, steely wines, which are seldom exported, and base wine for **Sekt**. There are three **Bereich** subregions: **Bacharach**, Rheinburgengau, and Siebengebirge.

moelleux French term used to describe a rich, luscious wine. It is particularly used in the **Loire** region for sweetish whites made from the **Chenin Blanc** grape, such as **Vouvray** and **Montlouis**.

Moldova Important **CIS** wine-producing country, located between **Romania** and **Ukraine**. European varieties are widely planted, and **Chardonnay**, **Cabernet Sauvignon**, and **Merlot** have been produced with great success. Other varieties planted include the white **Aligoté**, **Feteasca**, **Rkatsiteli**, and **Sauvignon Blanc**; and the reds **Gamay**, **Pinot Noir**, and **Saperavi**.

Molette White grape variety grown around **Seyssel** in the Savoie region of **France**. It produces thin, neutral, sometimes bitter wine, which is best used as a base for sparkling wine.

Molinara Red grape variety which produces light, fruity wines. It is chiefly used as a minor part in the blend for **Valpolicella** and **Bardolino** in the **Veneto** region of **Italy**.

Molise Small wine-producing region just south of **Abruzzo**, on the Adriatic coast of **Italy**. The main wine of the region is **Biferno**, but perhaps the best wines of Molise are made outside the **DOC** system, with good **vini da tavola** made from the **Montepulciano** and **Aglianico** grapes.

Monastrell Spanish name for **Mourvèdre**. One of the most widely planted red grape varieties of **Spain**, it produces deep, full-flavoured, high-**alcohol** red and rosé wines. The reds can have good **ageing** potential. It is found mainly in **Alicante** and also in **Almansa**, **Jumilla**, **Penedès**, **Valencia**, and **Yecla**.

Monbazillac Sweet white **AC** wine of the **Bergerac** region, which is made from the same grape varieties as **Sauternes** (**Sémillon**, **Sauvignon** and **Muscadelle**), but never reaching the same heights of quality. The **botrytis** fungus does not appear as often in Monbazillac, and few growers can risk leaving the grapes on the vines in the hopes that it will develop. At its best, Monbazillac is rich and honeyed, but without the depth of Sauternes.

Mondeuse Noire Red grape variety grown in the Savoie region of **France**. In Savoie it produces, at best, dense, deep-coloured, **austere** reds, and at worst, thin, tart wines. In **Bugey** it is successfully blended with other grape varieties, including **Pinot Noir** and **Gamay**. Mondeuse Blanche, a white grape variety, is now rare, even in Savoie.

Monica Red grape variety, thought to be native to **Spain**, but now grown mainly in **Sardinia**, where it makes soft red wines. It is used for **DOC** wines in Monica di Sardegna, producing a soft, light, dry red; and Monica di Cagliari, which is usually a sweet, sometimes fortified, light, ruby coloured wine.

Mont de Milieu Premier cru of **Chablis**.

Montagne de Reims Important vineyard area of the **Champagne** region, especially good for growing the red **Pinot Noir** grape.

Montagne-Saint-Emilion Red **AC** wine made in a 'satellite' area of the main **Saint-Emilion** *appellation* in **Bordeaux**. The grape varieties are the same as for Saint-Emilion (**Merlot**, **Cabernet Franc**, **Cabernet Sauvignon** and **Malbec**), but the wines, although very pleasant to drink when fairly young and offering good value, never reach the heights of the top Saint-Emilions. Producers in the neighbouring commune of Saint-Georges have the option of using the AC of either Montagne-Saint-Emilion or **Saint-Georges-Saint-Emilion**.

Montagny White **AC** wine from the **Côte Chalonnaise** area of **Burgundy**, made from the **Chardonnay** grape variety. Quality can be good, particularly where the wine has been aged in **oak** barrels, although the wines never reach the heights of top white Burgundies from the **Côte d'Or** or **Chablis**. The term **premier cru** is sometimes seen on Montagny wines, but it does not imply increased quality.

Montecarlo DOC wine produced around the town of Montecarlo near Lucca in **Tuscany**. The dry white is very good and is based on the **Trebbiano** Toscano grape. It is also permitted to add more exciting varieties, including **Sémillon**, **Sauvignon** and Pinot Grigio, which add more interesting flavours and aromas. The dry red, made mainly from the **Sangiovese** and **Canaiolo** grapes, can also be good.

Montecompatri-Colonna Dry or medium-dry white **DOC** wine produced in the hills around Rome, near the towns of Montecompatri and Colonna, in the **Latium** region of **Italy**. It is made mainly from the **Malvasia** and **Trebbiano** grape varieties, and is similar in style to **Frascati**.

Montée de Tonnerre Premier cru vineyard of **Chablis**.

Montefalco Red **DOC** wine produced around the town of Montefalco in Perugia, in the **Umbria** region of **Italy**. The dry red is based on the **Sangiovese** grape variety, with **Trebbiano** and Sagrantino.

The best quality red, the full-flavoured, assertive Sagrantino, is made almost entirely from the Sagrantino grape, and is either dry or in the sweet **passito** style (now **DOCG**), made from dried grapes.

Montello e Colli Asolani DOC wine produced in the eastern part of the **Veneto** region of **Italy**. Two **varietal** red wines are produced: **Cabernet** (Franc and/or Sauvignon) and **Merlot**. A dry white, usually sparkling, **Prosecco** is also produced. None is of better than ordinary quality.

Montepulciano Italian red grape variety. It is planted widely throughout **Italy** from **Apulia** to the **Marches**, and is second only in popularity to **Sangiovese**. **Montepulciano** d'Abruzzo and **Rosso Cònero** are two of the more notable wines made from it. See also **Cerveteri**; **Cori**; **Leverano**; **San Severo**. No relation to **Vino Nobile di Montepulciano**.

Monterey County Region of **California** particularly suited to the production of white **varietal** wines, especially from the **Chardonnay**, **Chenin Blanc**, **Riesling**, and **Sauvignon Blanc** grape varieties. Fine reds are also produced from **Cabernet Sauvignon**.

Monthélie AC wine of the **Côte de Beaune** area of **Burgundy**. The village of Monthélie is a neighbour of **Volnay**, and its red wines, made from the **Pinot Noir** grape variety, are in a similar style, but lighter and generally for earlier drinking. Only a tiny amount of white wine is produced.

Montilla-Moriles White **DO** wine of southwest **Spain**, similar in style and in its method of production to **Sherry**. Montilla for export is usually not fortified, however, and is based on the **Pedro Ximénez** grape. It is usually sold under the labels 'dry', 'medium' and 'cream'. Quality can be very good, but most of what is on sale in export markets is mediocre.

Montlouis White AC wine of the **Touraine** area of the **Loire**. The wines, all based on the **Chenin Blanc** grape, are produced in similar styles to **Vouvray**: dry, **demi-sec**, **moelleux**, and sparkling. Quality is usually very good. The dry wines are often very high in **acidity**, and can be quite **austere** in their youth, with a characteristic wet-wool **aroma**.

Montmains Premier cru of **Chablis**.

Montmélian Cru of the **Vin de Savoie** *appellation*. The wines are mainly dry, biting whites, made from the **Jacquère** grape.

Montrachet, Le Grand cru shared by the villages of **Chassagne-Montrachet** and **Puligny-Montrachet** in the **Côte de Beaune** region of **Burgundy**. Le Montrachet is made from the **Chardonnay** grape variety. Its colour begins as a greenish yellow, deepening to gold with age, as the dry but honeyed taste and **aromas** develop. The wine is rich, complex, and mouth-filling, and is best drunk when it is at least 10 years old. It is one of world's finest and most expensive white wines.

Montravel White AC wine from the **Bergerac** region of **France**, made from the **Sémillon**, **Sauvignon Blanc** and **Muscadelle** grape varieties. Most of the wine is dry

to medium-dry, but many producers sell the wine as
Bergerac Sec rather than Montravel.

Morellino di Scansano Dry red **DOC** wine
produced around the town of Scansano in the southern
part of **Tuscany**. It is a dry, cherry-flavoured, rustic red,
of moderate quality, made mainly from the **Sangiovese**
grape.

Morey-St-Denis AC wine from the Côte de Nuits
area of **Burgundy**. The red wine is made from the **Pinot
Noir** grape, and is similar in style to neighbouring
Gevrey-Chambertin. Quality can be very good,
especially from the **grand cru** vineyards.

Morgon Red AC wine, one of the 10 **crus** of the
Beaujolais region of **Burgundy**. Made from the **Gamay**
grape, the wine is perfumed, with juicy, ripe sweetness,
and cherry and chocolate flavours. Its quality is usually
very good. It is relatively long-lived and is among the
best of all Beaujolais.

Morio-Muskat White grape variety made by crossing
Silvaner and **Pinot Blanc (Weissburgunder)**. It is
planted in **Germany**, mainly in the **Rheinhessen** and
Pfalz. It makes blowzy, floral, grapey wine of dubious
quality, and its use is in decline.

Mornington Peninsula Small wine region located
near Melbourne in **Victoria**, **Australia**. Its realtively
cool climate suits it to **Chardonnay** and **Pinot Noir**
production.

Morrastel 1. In **Spain**, a synonym for the **Monastrell** (**Mourvèdre**) grape variety. 2. In **France**, a synonym for the **Graciano** grape variety of **Rioja**.

Moscadello di Montalcino Sweet white **DOC** wine, based on the **Moscato** grape, produced around Montalcino in **Tuscany**. It can be still or **frizzante**, and is of very ordinary quality. A better wine is the fortified **liquoroso** version, made from dried grapes.

Moscatel Name used for grapes of the **Muscat** family in **Spain** and **Portugal**. In Spain, the Moscatel de Málaga variety is used to make sweet white wines in **Málaga** and **Valencia**. **Setúbal** is a fortified white wine of Portugal, based on the Moscatel grape, which is deep, sweet, luscious and capable of long **ageing**, in cask or bottle.

Moscato Italian name for the **Muscat** Blanc à Petits Grains grape variety.

Moscato d'Asti Sweet, **aromatic** white **DOCG** wine made in the same area as **Asti** in **Piedmont**, **Italy**. It can be still or semi-sparkling. Quality is very consistent and it can be a delicious, refreshing wine to drink chilled, on its own, on a summer day.

Moscato Giallo See **Goldenmuskateller**.

Moscophilero Grape variety grown particularly in Mantinia in the Peloponnese area of **Greece**, where it produces scented, fruity white wines.

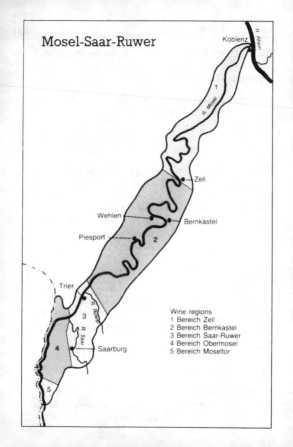

Mosel-Saar-Ruwer

Koblenz

R. Rhein

R. Mosel

1

Zell

Wehlen

Bernkastel

Piesport

2

Trier

R. Ruwer

3

R. Saar

4

Saarburg

5

Wine regions
1 Bereich Zell
2 Bereich Bernkastel
3 Bereich Saar-Ruwer
4 Bereich Obermosel
5 Bereich Moseltor

Mosel-Saar-Ruwer One of the most important of the 13 **Anbaugebiet** regions of **Germany**, named after the Mosel river and two of its tributaries. The region produces mainly white wines, the finest of them made from the **Riesling** grape, on steep, slate vineyard sites. Other varieties planted include **Müller-Thurgau** and **Elbling**. There are five **Bereich** subregions: **Zell**, **Saar-Ruwer**, **Obermosel**, **Moseltor** and **Bernkastel**, which contains the finest vineyards.

Moseltaler Sort of 'Mosel **Liebfraumilch**', a **QbA** wine of the **Mosel-Saar-Ruwer** region which can be made from **Riesling**, **Müller-Thurgau**, **Elbling** or **Kerner** grapes.

Moseltor Smallest **Bereich** subregion of the **Mosel-Saar-Ruwer** region of **Germany**. Its main production is of the base wine for **Sekt** from the **Elbling** grape variety.

mosto Italian for **must**.

Moulin-à-Vent Red **AC** wine, one of the 10 **crus** of the **Beaujolais** region of **Burgundy**. Made from the **Gamay** grape, the wine is full-bodied, even tough in youth, rich and chocolatey, and its quality is usually very good. It is among the longest-lived, and therefore the least characteristic, of all Beaujolais.

Moulis Communal **AC** wine of the **Haut-Médoc** region of **Bordeaux**. It produces good, long-lived, tough, **tannic cru bourgeois** wines but no **cru classé**. In recent years many of the wines have greatly improved in quality, and the best offer great value for money.

Mourvèdre Red grape variety which produces well-structured wines, low in acid and relatively light in colour. It is part of the blend for **Bandol** in **Provence** and for **Châteauneuf-du-Pape** in the **Rhône**, and is widely planted throughout southern **France**. It is widely planted in **Spain** (see **Monastrell**). In **Australia** it is called **Mataro**, and is usually blended with other varieties. It is also found, but in diminishing quantities, in **California**.

mousseux French term for sparkling. It is normally used on sparkling wines that are made by the **Charmat method** (*cuve close*) rather than the more costly **méthode traditionnelle**.

Mudgee Wine-producing region of **New South Wales** in **Australia**. It produces good-quality red wines from the **Cabernet Sauvignon** and **Shiraz** grape varieties, and whites from **Chardonnay** and **Sémillon**. Much of the wine is sold to producers in the **Hunter Valley** region for blending.

muffa nobile Italian term for **noble rot** or **botrytis**.

Mülheim Village in the **Bereich** of Bernkastel in the **Mosel-Saar-Ruwer** region of **Germany**. It produces some very good, elegant white wines mainly from the **Riesling** grape, which rival Bernkastel and Braunenberg. It comes within the **Grosslage** of Kurfürstlay, and the **Einzellage** sites are Amtsgarten, Elisenberg, Helenenkloster and Sonnenlay.

Müller-Thurgau White grape variety, made by crossing **Riesling** and **Silvaner**, or possibly two different varieties of Riesling. It is planted extensively throughout **Germany**, where it produces large quantities of moderately good, light quaffing wines; capable of distinction in **Baden**. It is also grown in the **Alto Adige** in **Italy**, in **Austria**, **Hungary**, Yugoslavia, **New Zealand** and **England**, and anywhere where its early ripening ability is appreciated.

Münster-Sarmsheim Village in the **Nahe** region of **Germany**. It produces top-quality white wines from the **Riesling** grape variety, and it comes within the **Grosslage** Schlosskapelle. The best **Einzellage** site is Dautenpflänzer, followed by Kapellenberg, Königsschloss, Liebehöll, Pittersberg, Röerberg, Steinkopf and Trollberg. The 'Sarmsheim' part of the name does not appear on the label.

Murray River Major river of **Australia**, which provides the irrigation water needed for the important **Riverland** wine-producing area. This is the source of a major part of Australia's wine production, mainly from inferior varieties such as Muscat Gordo Blanco, Sultana, and Doradillo, but also some **Sémillon**, **Chardonnay**, and **Shiraz**.

Murrumbidgee Irrigation Area (MIA) Wine-producing area of **New South Wales** in **Australia**. It produces large quantites of wine, mainly whites from the **Sémillon** and **Trebbiano** grape varieties, and some reds from **Shiraz**. Much of the production ends up in wine boxes, with a handful of quality-conscious producers making fine table wines.

Muscadelle White grape variety that plays a minor role in the sweet wines of **Bordeaux**, e.g. **Sauternes** and **Barsac**, and in dry whites such as **Entre-Deux-Mers**, where it is sometimes added to the blend of **Sémillon** and **Sauvignon Blanc**, to contribute **aroma**. It has some of the **grapey** quality of **Muscat**, but is a distinct variety in its own right.

In **Australia** it is used to make rich, dark, dessert wines, known as Liqueur Tokays. The **South African** Muscadel or Muskadel is **Muscat** Blanc à Petits Grains rather than Muscadelle.

Muscadet White **AC** wine of the western part of the **Loire**, made from the grape of the same name, also known as **Melon de Bourgogne**. Muscadet is a crisp, dry white, usually fairly simple, and is ideal for drinking as a refreshing apéritif or with the oysters and other seafood of the region.

Most Muscadet is sold as Muscadet de Sèvre et Maine. It is produced on the gently hilly banks of the Sèvre and Maine rivers, two tributaries of the Loire. Some Muscadet is sold as **sur lie**, meaning that the wine is matured on the **lees**, and, in theory, bottled straight from the barrel. The wine can develop a delicious yeasty complexity, sometimes with a slightly **pétillant** prickle on the tongue.

A further AC, Muscadet Côtes de Grand-Lieu was introduced in 1994.

Muscadet is normally drunk very young, but from exceptional years it can age surprisingly well, developing great complexity.

Muscat Family of white grape varieties. The best in
quality is the Muscat Blanc à Petits Grains, which is
planted throughout the world. It is mainly found in
France, especially around **Frontignan**, where it makes
luscious **vin doux naturel fortified wines**. In **Italy**
(where it is known as **Moscato**) it is used, particularly
in **Piedmont**, for the light, refreshing **Moscato d'Asti**
and **Asti Spumante**. It is also occasionally found in
California and **Australia**, where it is sometimes called
Frontignan. In **Greece** it makes good sweet white on
the island of Samos. Most of the sweet Australian
Liqueur Muscats are made from another member of
the family, the Muscat of Alexandria. The majority of
the Muscat planted in **Spain** and **Portugal** is also
Muscat of Alexandria, and is mainly found around
Alicante and **Valencia** in Spain and **Setúbal** in Portugal.

A third member of the family is Muscat Ottonel, which
is grown chiefly in **Alsace**, where it is usually used to
make light, dry **varietal** wine, good as an apéritif.

Muscat de Beaumes-de-Venise Sweet white **AC**
wine of the southern **Rhône**, made from the **Muscat**
Blanc à Petits Grains grape variety. It is a **vin doux
naturel**, or **fortified wine**, produced by adding grape
spirit to the partly fermented must. It is probably the
best sweet Muscat of France, with a rich, **grapey aroma**
and taste, with a balancing, fruity **acidity**.

Muscat de Frontignan Sweet white **AC** wine from
the **Languedoc-Roussillon** area of **France**. This is a
fortified wine, a **vin doux naturel**, made from the
Muscat Blanc à Petits Grains grape variety. It is rich

and raisiny, but lacks the balancing fruity **acidity** found in **Muscat de Beaumes-de-Venise**.

Muscat de Lunel Sweet white **AC** wine from the **Languedoc-Roussillon** area of **France**, rarely seen outside its own region. This is a **fortified wine**, a **vin doux naturel**, similar in style to **Muscat de Frontignan**. It is rich and raisiny and sometimes with decent **acidity**, but rarely very inspiring.

Muscat de Mireval Sweet white **AC** wine from the **Languedoc-Roussillon** area of **France**, rarely seen outside its own region. This is a **fortified wine**, a **vin doux naturel**, similar in style to **Muscat de Frontignan**, rich and raisiny, sometimes with decent **acidity**, but rarely very inspiring.

Muscat de Rivesaltes Sweet white **AC** wine from the **Languedoc-Roussillon** area of **France**. This is a **fortified wine**, a **vin doux naturel**, made mainly from the **Muscat** of Alexandria grape, together with some Muscat Blanc à Petits Grains. It is heady and fat, with the **aroma** of boiling marmalade, and sometimes rather coarse.

Muscat de Saint-Jean-de-Minervois Sweet white **AC** wine from the **Minervois** region of **Languedoc-Roussillon**. This is a **fortified wine**, a **vin doux naturel**, similar in style to **Muscat de Frontignan**. It is rich and raisiny, sometimes with decent **acidity**, but rarely very inspiring.

Muscatel Alternative name, used in **Australia**, for the **Muscat** of Alexandria grape variety.

Musigny **Grand cru** of the **Chambolle-Musigny**
appellation in the **Côte de Nuits** area of **Burgundy**. It
produces almost entirely red wines from the **Pinot Noir**
grape. The wines can be of very high quality, but in
recent years many have failed to live up to *grand cru*
standards.

musky Tasting term, not always uncomplimentary, used
to describe a perfumed, **Muscat**-like smell in wine.

must Mixture of unfermented grape juice, skins, and
pips.

must weight Natural sugar content of grape juice
before **fermentation** begins. The sugar level is an
important factor in deciding when to harvest grapes.
It can be measured using a refractometer or a hydro-
meter. Scales used to express must weight include
Baumé, **Brix**, **Oechsle** and specific gravity. The
potential **alcohol** content of a wine is determined by
the must weight.

musty Tasting term used to describe a stale smell and
taste, which may mean that the wine is slightly **corked**,
or which may wear off if the wine is allowed to stand
for a while or decanted.

N

Nackenheim Small town of the **Rheinhessen** region of **Germany**, producing excellent white wine, mainly from the **Riesling** grape variety. The vineyards are split between the **Grosslagen** of Spiegelberg and Gutes Domtal, and **Einzellage** sites include Engelsberg, Rothenberg (named after its red sandstone soil) and Schmittskapellchen.

Nahe One of the 13 major quality wine regions, or **Anbaugebiete**, of **Germany**. It produces some of the finest of the country's white wines from the **Riesling** grape variety, which dominates the best vineyard sites, particularly at **Spätlese** and **Kabinett** level. The region is split into the two **Bereich** subregions of Kreuznach and **Schlossböckelheim**.

Napa Valley Leading wine area of **California**. An **AVA** in its own right, it also takes in all, or part, of the following: **Carneros**, Howell Mountain, Mount Veeder, Oakville, Rutherford, **Stag's Leap** and Wild Horse Valley AVAs. Wine has been produced here from as early as the 1840s, but the number of wineries has risen from fewer than 30 in 1965 to close to 200 today.

The majority of the quality wines of the Napa are **varietals**, although some **Bordeaux**-style blends are appearing (see **Meritage**). The principal wine of the region is the red **Cabernet Sauvignon**, which achieves greater distinction than almost anywhere else in California, the best examples coming from the central part of the valley. Reds from **Pinot Noir** and whites from **Chardonnay** grow best in the Carneros region in the cooler southern part of the Napa. Fine Cabernet and excellent **Zinfandel** are also produced in the north, around Calistoga. Other important varieties include **Sauvignon Blanc**, **Chenin Blanc** and **Merlot**; also **Sémillon** and **Cabernet Franc** are being increasingly planted.

Nasco di Cagliari White **DOC** wine from **Sardinia**, made from the native Nasco grape. The wine can be **dolce** *naturale*, medium-sweet and delicately flavoured, or the drier, slightly bitter **secco**. Both versions can also be fortified.

Navarra DO wine of **Spain**, produced to the north and east of the **Rioja** region. Although similar in style to Riojan wines, they do not reach the quality of the best Rioja. Red Navarra suffers from being made mainly from the **Garnacha** grape (which it is now forbidden to plant in the region), but there is an increasingly important contribution from **Tempranillo** and **Cabernet Sauvignon**. There are signs of steady improvement in quality.

White wines are also produced, also inferior to the best of Rioja. Quality is gradually improving with the introduction of more **Chardonnay** and modern **vinification** techniques.

Good quality rosé is made from Garnacha.

Nebbiolo Red grape variety of **Italy**. It is used particularly in **Piedmont**, where it is the sole ingredient in the great reds **Barolo** and **Barbaresco**, as well as **Nebbiolo d'Alba**. Its name derives from *nebbia* (fog), after the mists that are often present when the grape is harvested in late October. Nebbiolo produces big wines, tough and **tannic** in their youth if made in the old-fashioned style, but capable of **ageing** into wines of rich complexity, with overtones of tar, roses, leather and game.

Nebbiolo d'Alba Red **DOC** wine made around **Roero** and the *commune* of **Alba** in **Piedmont**, **Italy**. It is made entirely from the **Nebbiolo** grape, and the wine is usually dry, although there are sweet and **spumante** versions. The dry wine can be very good, offering an early drinking style of Nebbiolo, unlike **Barolo** and **Barbaresco**, which require long **ageing** in bottle.

nebuchadnezzar Large format **Champagne** bottle, of 15 litres capacity (equivalent to 20 ordinary bottles).

négociant French term for a company or individual who deals in buying and selling (and sometimes making and maturing) wine. This function is particularly important in **Burgundy**, where there are many very small growers without the facilities to make, bottle, mature and market their own wines. In **Bordeaux** many producers sell their **château**-produced and bottled wines to *négociants*, who in turn sell them to wholesalers. Wines sold under a *négociant's* label can vary from more or less good generic blends up to high-class wines from individual estates, sometimes owned by the *négociant*.

négociant-manipulant See **NM**.

Negrara Red grape variety sometimes used in making **Valpolicella** and **Bardolino**.

Négrette Red grape variety planted almost exclusively around Toulouse in southwest **France**, where it figures in the blend for **Côtes du Frontonnais**, **Gaillac**, and Lavilledieu. It produces soft wine of good quality, ideal for drinking young, but the vine is highly susceptible to disease and plantings of Négrette are shrinking. Négrette is called Pinot Saint George in **California**, where it produces ordinary quality wine.

Negroamaro Red grape variety planted mainly in the Salento peninsula in **Apulia**, **Italy**, where it produces **big**, **austere** wines. Negroamaro is usually blended with other grape varieties, in **DOCs** such as **Alezio**, **Brindisi**, **Copertino**, **Leverano**, Lizzano, Matino, Nardò, **Salice Salentino** and **Squinzano**.

Nelson Minor wine-producing area on the South Island of **New Zealand**, planted with the ubiquitous (for New Zealand) **Müller-Thurgau** grape variety, and also producing **varietal** wines from **Cabernet Sauvignon**, **Gewürztraminer**, **Pinot Noir**, **Riesling** and **Sémillon**.

Nerello Pair of red grape varieties native to **Sicily**. Nerello Cappuccio is used mainly for blending, to add alcohol and colour to lighter wines. Nerello Mascalese is of a higher quality, and can produce good-quality **varietal** wines, as well as the **DOC** wine **Etna**.

Nero d'Avola See **Calabrese**.

Neuburger White grape variety of **Austria**, a **cross** of **Weissburgunder** and **Silvaner**. It is an early ripener and produces a high **must weight**, yielding a full-bodied wine, sometimes with a distinctive nutty taste.

Neuchâtel Wine-growing region of **Switzerland** which produces white wine from the **Chasselas** grape variety and reds from **Pinot Noir**.

Neusiedlersee Lake region in **Austria**'s **Burgenland**, source of some of the best sweet whites and reds.

Neustadt Town of the **Pfalz** region of **Germany**, producing mainly white and some red wines of decent average quality. The vineyards come within the **Grosslage** of Meerspinne.

Nevers Forest in **France** where some of the best **oak** is grown for making barrels for **ageing** wine. Its wood is dense with a narrow grain and a high phenol content. It imparts a fine **aroma** and flavour to the wine; commonly used in **Burgundy** and the New World particularly with **Cabernet Sauvignon**. See also **Allier**; **Limousin**.

New South Wales State of **Australia** which has five
main, warm-climate vineyard areas: the Upper and
Lower **Hunter Valley**, **Mudgee**, **Murrumbidgee,
Irrigation Area**, and Canberra District. The Lower
Hunter is the best known, producing excellent **varietal**
wines, mainly whites from **Sémillon** and **Chardonnay**
and reds from **Shiraz** and **Cabernet Sauvignon**. Orange
is a newer, cooler-climate region.

New York State State of the eastern **United States**
which has traditionally produced wines from non-**Vitis
vinifera** grape varieties such as **Catawba**, **Concord**, and
Delaware. The wines have a curiously earthy (**foxy**)
taste, which has limited their appeal outside the region.
More recently, many of the vineyards have been
replanted with European grape varieties, including
Chardonnay, **Riesling**, **Cabernet Sauvignon**,
Gewürztraminer, **Merlot** and **Sauvignon Blanc**.
All appear as **varietals**, although a large amount of
sparkling wine is also made, particularly in the **Finger
Lakes** region, from blends of white varieties.

New Zealand Country which produces increasingly
fine red and white **varietal** wines. New Zealand's
position on the international wine stage is based firmly
on its reputation for producing fine **Sauvignon Blanc**.
The vibrant, juicy fruit aromas and flavours, with steely
fresh **acidity**, have provided new and strong
competition with the traditional home of Sauvignon,
Sancerre and **Pouilly-Fumé** in the **Loire**.

However, Sauvignon is a relative newcomer to New
Zealand vineyards. In the 1970s, large areas of vineyard

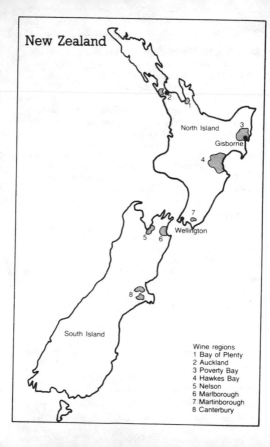

New Zealand

North Island

Gisborne

Wellington

South Island

Wine regions
1 Bay of Plenty
2 Auckland
3 Poverty Bay
4 Hawkes Bay
5 Nelson
6 Marlborough
7 Martinborough
8 Canterbury

were planted with **Müller-Thurgau**, which is still widely planted. By the mid-1980s, the light **table wines** produced from Müller-Thurgau had fallen from favour. Consumers wanted varietal wines from Sauvignon Blanc and, of course, **Chardonnay**. The pioneering plantings of Sauvignon Blanc were made in the early 1970s. Later the variety was planted in the South Island region of **Marlborough**, which has since emerged as the country's best area for Sauvignon. Other regions include Auckland, **Gisborne**, **Hawkes Bay**, and **Martinborough** on North Island, and **Nelson**, Canterbury, and Central Otago on South Island. Among the red wines produced, **Cabernet Sauvignon** is steadily getting better.

Niederhausen Small area of the **Nahe** region of **Germany**. It produces very high-quality white wines, mainly from the **Riesling** grape variety and some from the **Traminer**. The vineyards come within the **Grosslage** of Burgweg, and the **Einzellage** sites include Felsensteyer, Hermannshöhle, Kertz, Klamm, Pfaffenstein, Pfingstweide, Rosenberg, Rosenheck, Steinberg, Steinwingert, Stollenberg and Hermannsberg.

Niederösterreich Largest wine region of **Austria**, planted mainly with the **Grüner Veltliner** grape variety. It produces a pale wine, fruity and spicy with markedly high **acidity**, which provides a good foil for fatty foods.

Nielluccio Most planted native red grape variety of **Corsica** (see **Vin de Corse**), producing moderately good quality wines with high **alcohol**. Some of the best results have been obtained by vinifying it as a rosé wine.

Nierstein 1. A subregion, or **Bereich**, of the **Rheinhessen** region of **Germany**. The *Bereich* contains many fine vineyards, sold under their village and **Einzellage** names, but wine sold as 'Bereich Nierstein' is usually no better than quaffable, fruity white wine. 2. A small town of the **Rheinhessen** which gives its name to the *Bereich* in which it is located. The vineyards of the town come under the **Grosslagen** of Auflangen, Gutes Domtal, Rehbach and Spiegelberg.

NM (**négociant-manipulant**) Letters found on **Champagne** labels, indicating that it comes from a house that both produces (generally from bought-in grapes) and sells the wine. The numbers following the letters identify the producer.

noble rot See **botrytis**.

non-vintage See **NV**.

Norheim Village of the **Nahe** region of **Germany**, producing fine, and sometimes great, white wines mainly from the **Riesling** grape. It comes under the **Grosslage** of Burgweg, and the individual **Einzellage** sites are Dellchen (probably the best), Götzenfels, Kafels, Kirschbeck, Klosterberg, Oberberg, Onkelchen and Sonnenberg.

North Coast Extensive **AVA** of **California**, which includes the counties of Lake, Napa, **Sonoma**, and **Mendocino**.

nose Tasting term which covers all the smell characteristics of a wine, including the **aroma** and **bouquet**.

nouveau French for new, used to indicate a wine produced for drinking immediately after the harvest, e.g. **Beaujolais Nouveau**, often made by **carbonic maceration**. The result is good for the cash flow of the producer, but rarely for the quality of the wine. The Italian equivalent is *novello*.

Nuits-Saint-Georges AC wine and town which gives its name to the northern **Côte de Nuits** region of **Burgundy**'s **Côte d'Or**. Almost all of the production is of plummy, prune-flavoured, chewy, complex red wine, from the **Pinot Noir** grape. The best wines come from the 38 (small) **premier cru** vineyards. There are no **grands crus**.

Nuragus di Cagliari White **DOC** wine of **Sardinia**, made mainly from the Nuragus grape variety. The wine is usually neutral, even bland; there is a rare **frizzante** version.

NV (non-vintage) Term used to describe a wine for which no year of harvest is specified. Basic European **table wine** and branded wines are often NV, so that the blender is able to produce a consistent product by blending wines of different **vintages**. For most

Champagne producers, NV **Brut** is their best-selling wine, and many of the top houses believe that the finest Champagne can be made by blending across vintages – they prefer to think of 'multi-vintage' rather than non-vintage.

oak Family of trees, whose wood is generally agreed to be the best material for the construction of barrels for the storage and **ageing** of fine wines. When a high-quality young wine, with a good concentration of fruit, spends some months or years in oak barrels, this treatment can add an extra dimension of flavour to the wine, rather like the use of seasoning in cooking. The fruit flavours are complemented by the vanilla flavour derived from the oak, and the wood can also give extra **tannin** to the wine, which may increase its ageing potential. Small, new barrels will have a more dramatic effect than large, old ones. Ageing in dirty barrels, whatever the size or wood, can render a wine undrinkable.

There are many varieties of oak, and winemakers will often insist on barrels made from oak of specific forests in **France** (such as **Allier**, Tronçais, **Nevers** and **Limousin**), or from American (white) oak. Oak and barrel-making are both very expensive, and ageing in oak barrels adds significantly to the cost of producing a wine. Some winemakers therefore use the cheaper method of fermenting or ageing wine in the presence of oak chips.

oaky Tasting term that describes a range of sensations, from the smell of freshly sawn wood, the taste and smell of vanilla, to a spicy, cinnamon flavour. The flavours result from **ageing** in **oak** casks or the use of

oak chips, and are attractive in moderation but
undesirable in excess.

Obermosel Bereich, or subregion, of the **Mosel-Saar-
Ruwer** region of **Germany**. It produces mainly basic-
quality wine from the **Elbling** grape variety, much of
which is made into sparkling wine, or **Sekt**.

Ockfen Village on the Saar river in the **Mosel-Saar-
Ruwer** region of **Germany**. It produces high-quality,
floral-scented white wines, mainly from the **Riesling**
grape variety. The vineyards come under the **Grosslage**
of Scharzberg, and the **Einzellage** sites are Bockstein
and Herrenberg (the best two), plus Geisberg,
Heppenstein, Kupp, Neuwies and Zickelgarten.

Oechsle Widely used German scale for measuring the
concentration of sugar in grape must. A reading of 75°
Oechsle represents a density of 1.075 grams per litre,
equivalent to a potential **alcohol** of about 10% vol.
See also **Baumé**; **Brix**.

Oestrich Town of the **Rheingau** region of **Germany**.
It produces full-bodied white wines from the **Riesling**
grape variety, capable of very good quality. The
vineyards are split between the **Grosslagen** of
Gottesthal – where the **Einzellage** sites are Lenchen
(the best), Doosberg, Klosterberg and Schloss
Reichhartshausen – and Mehrhölzchen, which includes
parts of Klosterberg.

Olasz Rizling Alternative name, used in **Hungary**, for
the **Welschriesling** grape variety.

oloroso Rich, nutty, dark style of **Sherry** which takes its flavour from long **ageing** in cask, rather than from **flor**. True *oloroso* is dry, but often it is sweetened to make a commercial blend, sold as 'cream', by adding some **Pedro Ximénez** wine, and sometimes it is darkened with **vino de color**.

Oltrepò Pavese Area of the **Lombardy** region of northern **Italy**, and a **DOC** wine that comes in 15 different varieties. The **rosso** and **rosato** are based on the **Barbera**, **Uva Rara** and **Croatina** grape varieties. The red can be of good quality, full bodied and lightly **tannic**. Buttafuoco is a dry red, usually **frizzante**, and the fizzy Sangue di Giuda can be dry, **amabile**, or **dolce**; both are based on the same varieties as the *rosso*.

The red **varietal** versions are Barbera (which can be a very high quality, robust wine), **Bonarda** (grapey and rustic) and Pinot Nero (which can be good as a still red wine, but is rarely seen). The white varietals are **Cortese** (light and crisp, if somewhat neutral), **Moscato** (produced in a similar style to **Moscato d'Asti**), Pinot Grigio, **Riesling Italico** and **Riesling Renano** (both Rieslings produce delicately perfumed wines of real character).

Oltrepò is also an important source of sparkling wines made by the **metodo classico**, most importantly from the Pinot Nero and **Chardonnay** grapes; the best are sold under the **Classese** or **Talento** labels; the rest are often sold anonymously to bottlers in other regions for the production of commercial blends.

Oppenheim Small town of the **Rheinhessen** region of **Germany**, producing good-quality white wines, mainly from the **Riesling** grape variety. The vineyards come under the **Grosslagen** of Güldenmorgen (**Einzellage** sites are Daubhaus, Gutleuthaus, Herrenberg, Kreuz, Sackträger, Schützenhütte, and Zuckerberg) and Krötenbrunnen (Herrengarten, Paterhof, and Schlossberg).

Optima White grape variety, a **cross** of **Müller-Thurgau** with another cross of **Silvaner** and **Riesling**. It is planted mainly in the **Mosel-Saar-Ruwer**, **Rheinhessen** and **Rheingau** regions of **Germany**, and also in **England**. It yields a wine of low **acidity** and high **must weight**, and can produce wines of up to **Auslese** quality in a good year.

Orange Muscat White grape variety of the **Muscat** family, mainly planted in **California** and **Australia**, where it can produce lusciously sweet dessert wines.

Oregon State of the northwestern **United States**, with a fairly recent reputation for producing **varietal** red wines from the **Pinot Noir** grape variety, especially in the Willamette Valley, and sparkling wines made by the **méthode traditionnelle**. Producers from **Burgundy** and **Champagne** have shown their confidence in the region by investing in Oregon vineyards and wineries in recent years.

organic According to makers of organic wines, they are made without the use of herbicides, chemical fertilizers, or any additives in the winery. In fact there are many exceptions allowed by the various bodies controlling organic viticulture and winemaking. For

instance, almost all organic wine is made with the use
of the chemical **sulphur dioxide**. All good winemakers,
whether or not they describe their wines as 'organic',
try to keep the use of chemicals in the vineyard and
winery to the absolute minimum.

Ortega White grape variety, a **cross** of **Müller-Thurgau**
and **Siegerrebe**, grown mainly in the **Mosel-Saar-
Ruwer**, **Rheinhessen** and **Pfalz** regions of **Germany**,
and to a limited extent in the vineyards of **England**. It
ripens early, and has a relatively high **must weight**, but
its low **acidity** makes it unsuitable for making late-
picked wines of **Spätlese** or of higher quality.

Ortenau Bereich, or subregion, of the **Baden** region of
Germany. It produces good quality white wines from
the **Riesling** grape variety (called Klingelberger locally),
and also some reds from the **Spätburgunder** (including
Affental). The **Bereich** is split into two **Grosslagen**,
Fürsteneck and Schloss Rodeck.

Orvieto White **DOC** wine of the **Umbria** region of
Italy, produced in the hills around the town of Orvieto
from a blend of the **Trebbiano**, Verdello, **Grechetto**,
and **Malvasia** grape varieties. The **classico** area lies at
the centre of the region. The wine is usually a crisp,
smooth, dry wine for early drinking, but it may also be
abboccato, **amabile** or **dolce**.

Ostuni DOC wine of the **Apulia** region of **Italy**. It can
be a light, delicate, dry **bianco** made from the Impigno,
Francavilla, and **Bianco d'Alessano** grape varieties, or a
light, cherry-coloured, early drinking red called

Ottavianello, made mainly from the grape variety of the same name.

oxidation Class of chemical reactions that can result when wine is exposed to an oxidizing agent, most commonly oxygen in the atmosphere. This can occur slowly, if the wine is in a full barrel (a slow, controlled oxidation is part of the maturation process), or rapidly, once a bottle of wine is opened and exposed to the air. Eventually a wine is spoiled by oxidation, and the **alcohol** is oxidized to **acetic acid** and ethyl acetate.

oxidized Tasting term used to describe a stale, 'off' taste, caused by exposure to oxygen in the air. In extreme cases, the wine may smell and taste of vinegar or nail-varnish remover.

P

Pacherenc du Vic Bilh White **AC** wine of southwest **France**, produced in the same area as the red **Madiran**, from the **Gros Manseng**, **Petit Manseng**, and Ruffiac grape varieties. The wine is usually dry and pear-flavoured, although it can be rich and slightly sweet.

Padthaway Relatively cool-climate region of **South Australia**, particularly good for **Chardonnay**, **Sauvignon Blanc**, and **Riesling**.

Pais Pale red grape variety, the most widely planted in **Chile** and probably brought there by Spanish missionaries. It is high yielding and produces thin, poor wines, both red and white, which are only for domestic consumption. Pais is gradually being replaced with European grapes, including **Cabernet Sauvignon**, **Chardonnay**, **Sauvignon Blanc**, and **Merlot**.

palate Tasting term used to describe the flavour and sensation of the wine in the mouth (as opposed to the **nose** and appearance). More generally, a taster can be said to have a 'good palate'.

Palatinate See **Pfalz**.

Pale Cream Style of **Sherry**, which combines the sweetness of **Cream Sherry** with the colour of a **fino**. The style is made by sweetening young *fino* with pale

grape juice concentrate or by removing colour from
dark Sherry using carbon. It never has the complex
flavour of the traditional Sherry styles.

Palette AC wine of **Provence**, made in a tiny region
just east of Aix-en-Provence. Most of the production is
of elegant, herby reds and rosés, made from the
Cinsault, **Grenache**, **Mourvèdre**, and **Syrah** grape
varieties. Small quantities of fresh, spicy white wine are
made from **Clairette**, Grenache Blanc, **Ugni Blanc** and
sometimes **Muscat** and **Sémillon**.

Palmela Wine region on the Atlantic coast of **Portugal**
producing red and rosé wines from the Castelão
Frances grape (also called **Periquita**), and good dry
whites from **Muscat**.

palo cortado Sherry that falls in style somewhere
between an **amontillado** and an **oloroso**. It should
combine the elegance of an *amontillado* with the rich,
nutty character of an *oloroso*.

Palomino White grape variety of **Spain**, used to make
nearly all **Sherry**. Although it excels as a base wine for
fortified wines, such as Sherry, it is rather thin and
neutral when vinified as a **table wine**. It is also planted
in Spain outside the Sherry region, and in **South Africa**,
California and **Australia**.

Parellada White grape variety planted in the **Penedès**
region of **Spain**. It is used to make still and sparkling
white wines. It is particularly important as an
ingredient in the sparkling **Cava**, and is also found in
Tarragona and **Conca de Barbera**. Wine made from

Parellada has high **acidity** (important for sparkling wine) and good fruit when young, but lacks **ageing** potential when it is bottled unblended.

Parrina DOC wine of **Tuscany**, produced above the Argentario peninsula near Grosseto. The dry white **bianco** is made mainly from the **Trebbiano** Toscano grape, and the pleasant red and **rosato** versions are based on **Sangiovese**.

Paso Robles AVA of **San Luis Obispo** county, **California**. It has a growing reputation for rich and well-structured **Zinfandel**, **Cabernet Sauvignon**, and **Chardonnay**, and is pioneering the development of **Nebbiolo** in the US.

Passe-Tout-Grains Red **AC** wine of **Burgundy** made, unusually, from a mixture of **Gamay** and a minimum of one-third **Pinot Noir** grapes. Bourgogne Passe-Tout-Grains, with its light, fresh, fruity flavour, is best drunk relatively young, within three or four years of the vintage. The best examples offer good value for money, though the distinctive flavours of the two grape varieties tend to be masked in a blend.

passito Italian term for the method of making strong, often sweet, wines from the concentrated juice of semi-dried (or *passito*) grapes.

Patrimonio See **Vin de Corse**.

Pauillac Communal **AC** wine of the **Haut-Médoc** area of **Bordeaux**, produced around the small town of the

same name. This is the source of some of the greatest
Claret, including three of Bordeaux's five **premiers crus**
and 15 other **crus classés**. It also boasts a number of
good **cru bourgeois** properties.

The wines of Pauillac are the archetype of Bordeaux
and the blackcurrant taste of the **Cabernet Sauvignon**
grape. The wines are full-bodied, concentrated, and
relatively high in **tannin**. In their youth, they are
austere; at their peak, which may come 10 or (many)
more years after the **vintage**, they are rich, smooth, and
sophisticated. The top wines come from individual
châteaux, but 'generic' Pauillac from a **négociant** can
offer good value for money.

Pécharmant Red **AC** wine from within the **Bergerac**
region of southwest **France**, produced from the **Merlot**,
Cabernet Sauvignon, **Cabernet Franc**, and **Malbec**
grape varieties. The wines are among the finest
produced in Bergerac. They are light but well-
balanced, with a good concentration of blackcurrant
fruit, and capable of moderate **ageing**.

Pedro Ximénez White grape variety planted
throughout **Spain**, but particularly used to make sweet,
dark, thick wines in **Montilla-Moriles** and **Málaga**. PX
is a dark **mistelle** made by adding brandy to the
unfermented juice of concentrated **must** from Pedro
Ximénez grapes. It is added to **Sherry** to make the
sweeter styles. A small amount of Sherry is made from
unblended Pedro Ximénez. It is intensely sweet, with a
dark, almost black colour, and makes a delicious
dessert when poured over ice-cream.

Penedès DO wine of northeast **Spain**, produced in a coastal region just west of Barcelona, and the home of **Cava** production. Most of the wine produced is white, from the native grape varieties of **Parellada**, **Xarel-lo**, and **Macabeo**, usually blended together, and generally not very good as a still wine - there are a few notable exceptions. **Chardonnay** is now permitted under the DO regulations, and is a very welcome addition to the blend.

However, many of the best wines are produced from imported white varieties such as **Chenin Blanc**, **Gewürztraminer**, **Sauvignon Blanc** and **Riesling**. Fine, flavourful reds are also produced from both native grapes, e.g. **Garnacha**, **Tempranillo** and **Cariñena**, and imported varieties (mainly **Cabernet Sauvignon**), or blends of the two.

perfumed Tasting term, used to describe an attractive, delicate **bouquet**.

Periquita (also called Castelão Frances) Red grape variety planted widely in southern **Portugal**, particularly in the **Setúbal** peninsula, and the **Alentejo** and **Ribatejo** regions. It produces a full, robust wine, harsh in its youth, but capable of mellowing with **bottle age**.

perlant See **pétillant**.

perlé See **pétillant**.

Perlwein German term for cheap semi-sparkling wine, made by pumping **carbon dioxide** into the wine, or by

´**fermentation** in pressurised tanks. Quality is almost
always poor.

Pernand-Vergelesses AC wine of the **Côte de
Beaune** area of **Burgundy**. Mainly red wine is
produced, from the **Pinot Noir** grape variety, plus
some white from **Chardonnay** (and **Aligoté**). The reds,
especially the **premiers crus**, are soft, attractive,
raspberry flavoured wines for relatively early drinking.
Part of the **grand cru** of **Corton** also comes within the
appellation, producing much finer, longer-lived reds.

The whites sold as Pernand-Vergelesses are good-
quality, soft wines, best drunk three to four years after
the **vintage**. Part of the white *grand cru* of **Corton-
Charlemagne** also comes within the *appellation*, and
here the wines are among the longest-lived of all
Chardonnays. They need 10 years or more to develop
their nutty, spicy flavour.

Pessac-Léognan AC wine produced in the northern
part of the **Graves** region of **Bordeaux**. All the **classed
growths** of the Graves come under this appellation,
and the soil here is at its most gravelly; an important
factor in determining the Graves style. Reds are made
from the classic Bordeaux grape varieties, **Cabernet
Sauvignon**, **Cabernet Franc**, and **Merlot**, and there is a
wide variety of styles (and prices). The top wines rank
alongside the best that Bordeaux has to offer, and
Pessac-Léognan is also probably the source of
Bordeaux's most exciting dry whites, made from the
Sauvignon Blanc and **Sémillon** grapes. They are fruity

and concentrated in their youth, and can develop glorious nutty complexity as they mature.

pétillant (also called **perlant**; **perlé**) French term used to describe a semi-sparkling wine, and sometimes found on labels. Also a tasting term used to describe a wine with any hint of a bubble.

Petit Manseng White grape variety planted in southwest **France**. Along with the inferior **Gros Manseng** it is used to make **Jurançon**, **Pacherenc du Vic Bihl** and some of the rare white wines from **Béarn**.

Petit Verdot Red grape variety planted mainly in **Bordeaux**, where it forms a minor part of the blend at some **châteaux**. It produces deep, **tannic**, spicy, dark-coloured wine, which can make an important contribution to the longevity of a blend. However, it is a late ripening variety (indeed it will not ripen at all in poor years in Bordeaux) and so many châteaux no longer grow it.

petrolly Tasting term used, generally with approval, to describe the oily, kerosene smell that can develop in fine mature wine made from the **Riesling** grape, especially when affected by **botrytis**.

Pfalz (formerly Rheinpfalz, also called Palatinate) One of the 13 major quality wine regions, or **Anbaugebiete**, of **Germany**. It produces high-quality white wines, particularly in the northern of the two **Bereich** subregions, Mittelhaardt-Deutsche Weinstrasse (top villages include **Bad Dürckheim**, **Wachenheim**, **Forst**

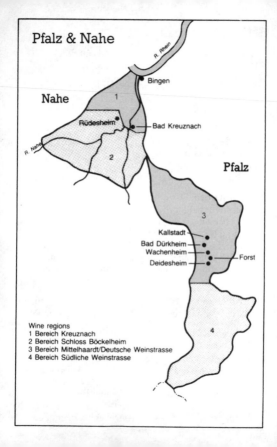

Pfalz & Nahe

Nahe

Pfalz

R. Rhein

Bingen

1

Rüdesheim

Bad Kreuznach

R. Nahe

2

3

Kallstadt
Bad Dürkheim
Wachenheim
Deidesheim

Forst

4

Wine regions
1 Bereich Kreuznach
2 Bereich Schloss Böckelheim
3 Bereich Mittelhaardt/Deutsche Weinstrasse
4 Bereich Südliche Weinstrasse

and **Deidesheim**), and less good wines in the southern Bereich, **Südliche Weinstrasse**.

The **Riesling** grape variety dominates on the best sites, but **Müller-Thurgau** is more widely planted in the region as a whole. **Scheurebe** is used as well to make increasingly successful wines. The Pfalz is also an important source of **Liebfraumilch**.

phylloxera Disease of the vine caused by the aphid *Phylloxera vastatrix*, which attacks the root system. It wiped out most of Europe's vineyards in the late 19th century. The cure was to graft the European **Vitis vinifera** grape varieties on American-vine rootstock (which is resistant to phylloxera), and most of the world's vineyards are now planted in this way. An important exception is **Chile**, where ungrafted vinifera vines grow successfully. Ungrafted vines also survive in **Colares**, **Portugal**, yielding dark, strong, **tannic** wines, and in parts of **South Australia**. Recently phylloxera has ravaged the vineyards of **California**, many of which were planted on rootstocks that were incorrectly thought to be resistant.

Piave DOC wine of the **Veneto** region of **Italy**, produced on the plains on both sides of the Piave river. There are eight types, labelled according to their grape variety. The reds include the native **Raboso** (warm, earthy, and high in **tannin** in its youth) plus the French varieties **Cabernet** (a mixture of Franc and Sauvignon), **Merlot** and Pinot Nero. The whites include **Verduzzo Friulano** and Tocai Italico (fresh and fruity when young, with good **acidity**), plus Pinot Bianco and Pinot Grigio.

Picardan White grape variety, one of 13 permitted in the production of **Châteauneuf-du-Pape**. Neutral, and of little interest.

Picolit White grape variety native to the **Friuli-Venezia Giulia** region of **Italy**, used to make expensive, variable-quality dessert wine.

Picpoul (or Piquepoul) One of the 13 grape varieties allowed in the production of **Châteauneuf-du-Pape**. Picpoul Blanc is part of the blend for the rather dull white Picpoul de Pinet in the **Coteaux du Languedoc** region.

pièce Name used in parts of **France** for a barrel with a capacity of between 205 and 225 litres. See also **barrique**.

Piedmont (also called Piemonte) Important wine-producing region in northwest **Italy**. This is the home, particularly around **Alba**, of the **Nebbiolo** grape, which is used to make the great, long-lived **DOCG** wines **Barolo** and **Barbaresco**. Nebbiolo also thrives in the north of the region, in the Alpine foothills.

The other main red grapes are **Barbera** and **Dolcetto**, which are used to make varietally labelled wines in Alba and neighbouring Asti. See also **Taglio Langhe**. Asti's chief claim to fame for many wine lovers is the sweet, white, sparkling **Asti,** made from the **Moscato** grape. Piedmont is also increasingly important for white wines such as **Arneis**, **Chardonnay**, and **Favorita**.

Piesport Important wine-producing village of the **Mosel-Saar-Ruwer** region of **Germany**. It produces high-quality white wines from the **Riesling** grape variety. The vineyards come within the **Grosslage** of Michelsberg and the **Einzellage** sites are Goldtröpfchen (the best), Domherr, Falkenberg, Gärtchen, Grafenberg, Günterslay, Hofberger, Kreuzwingert, Schubertslay and Treppchen. Wine sold under the *Grosslage* name, as Piesporter Michelsberg, is rarely distinguished and often mediocre, especially when made from grapes other than Riesling.

Pigato DOC wine, and a white grape variety planted in the **Liguria** region of **Italy**. The grape produces full-bodied, dry white wines, often surpassing **Vermentino** in finesse.

Pineau d'Aunis Red grape variety grown in the **Loire** valley, especially in **Touraine**, where it is sometimes part of the blend in Touraine Rouge.

Pineau des Charentes Mistelle made in the Cognac region by the addition of brandy to unfermented (or very slightly fermented) grape juice. It can be white or red, with an appley, **grapey**, sweet flavour, and is generally drunk chilled as an apéritif. Aged versions are better and more expensive.

Pinot Blanc (also called Pinot Bianco; **Weissburgunder**) White grape variety grown in **Alsace** where it is used to make **varietal** Pinot Blanc, as part of the blend for **Edelzwicker**, and as an ingredient in the sparkling **Crémant d'Alsace**. In **Germany** it is called Weissburgunder, and it is probably at its best in trocken and halbtrocken wines.

In **Italy** it is called Pinot Bianco and is widely planted all over the country, particularly in **Friuli-Venezia Giulia**, **Lombardy**, **Trentino**, **Alto Adige** and the **Veneto**. It is **DOC** in many regions, and is also an important part of the blend in Italian **metodo classico** sparkling wines.

It is also planted in **Austria**, **Croatia**, **Slovenia**, **Slovakia**, **Hungary**, and **California**. Almost all 'Pinot Blanc' in **Australia** is, in fact, **Chardonnay**.

Pinot Gris (also called Pinot Grigio; **Ruländer**; Tokay-Pinot Gris) Grape variety that produces wine which is usually a relatively deep-coloured white, but is occasionally slightly tinged with pink. It is most widely planted in **Germany**, where it is called Ruländer (or Grauburgunder when vinified in the modern, drier style), and in **Alsace**, where it is called Tokay-Pinot Gris, producing a spicy, subtly **aromatic** wine.

In **Italy**, it is widely planted as Pinot Grigio, especially in **Friuli-Venezia Giulia**, **Trentino**, **Alto Adige** and **Oltrepò Pavese**. It mainly produces popular, but fairly neutral, low-acid, easy drinking white wine, with only a few examples showing any complexity.

It is also planted in **Austria**, **Luxembourg**, **Romania**, **Switzerland** and **Slovenia**.

Pinot Meunier (or Meunier) Red grape variety which, along with **Chardonnay** and **Pinot Noir**, is used to produce **Champagne**. Although it is the least well-known of the Champagne grapes, it is in fact the most extensively planted variety in the region. It has a reputation for not **ageing** well, but if properly vinified it can make an important contribution to the Champagne blend. Experience has shown that the longest-lived Champagnes tend to be those based on the two Pinots.

Pinot Noir (also called Pinot Nero; Spätburgunder) Important red grape variety, the main red grape of the **Côte d'Or** area of **Burgundy** and also important in **Champagne**. Although capable of greatness in these areas, it is very difficult to cultivate and has had only indifferent success elsewhere in Europe (pale reds from **Alsace**, for example) and parts of the New World, although there have been encouraging successes in **Oregon**, **California**, **Italy**'s **Alto Adige**, and parts of **Australia**.

Pinotage Red grape variety of **South Africa**, a **cross** of **Pinot Noir** and **Cinsault**, producing rich, long-lasting, spicy reds.

pipe Barrel used for storing, maturing, and selling **Port**. 'Shipping pipes' have a capacity of 534 litres; 'Douro pipes', 550 litres; and 'lodge pipes', between 580 and 620 litres. One *pipe* is equivalent to 21 **almudes**, and there are about 12 **canadas** (of 2.1 litres) in one *almude*.

Pollino Pale red **DOC** wine of the **Calabria** region of **Italy**, made in the high-altitude vineyards of the Pollino mountains. The wine is based on the **Gaglioppo** and **Greco** Nero grape varieties, with the possibility of the addition of up to 20% of white varieties, including

Malvasia. This, and the short period of **maceration**, accounts for the wines' pale colour. At their best, the wines are light, fresh, and fruity.

Pomerol Red **AC** wine produced near Libourne in the **Bordeaux** region. It is made from the classic Bordeaux grape varieties, **Cabernet Sauvignon**, **Cabernet Franc** and **Merlot**. Merlot is the most important because it thrives on Pomerol's clay soil. The resulting wines are velvety, smooth and seductive, relatively low in **tannin**, and with great concentration of fruit. The top wines, always in short supply, rank alongside the best of Bordeaux, and the prices reflect this.

Pomino **DOCG** wine produced in high-altitude (700 m) vineyards around the village of Pomino, **Tuscany**, overlapping in part with a corner of the **Chianti** area. The white version is made from Pinot Bianco and **Chardonnay**, plus **Trebbiano**. The rich, soft **rosso** is based on **Sangiovese**, blended with **Cabernet** (Franc and/or Sauvignon), **Merlot** and Pinot Nero. Both are usually very good, especially when aged in **oak**. White and red **Vin Santo** is also made, from the same grapes used for the dry wines.

Pommard Red **AC** wine of the **Côte de Beaune** area of **Burgundy**, made from the **Pinot Noir** grape variety. At its best, Pommard can be a good, sturdy, beefy red Burgundy, with power and richness. Sadly the popularity of the easily pronounceable name in English-speaking countries has resulted in many thin, over-priced, over-alcoholic examples appearing on the market. Taste before you buy.

Port Fortified wine of **Portugal**, produced in the **Douro** valley and matured and bottled in Vila Nova de Gaia. Port is usually red and sweet, although there are white Ports which range from off-dry to sweet. The main grape varieties for red Port are Roriz (the same as **Tempranillo**), **Touriga Nacional**, Touriga Francesa, **Tinta Cão**, **Tinta Barroca**, Mourisco Tinto, Tinta Amarella, and **Tinta Francisca**.

Despite the wide variety of styles of Port available, all red Port starts off life in the same way. At vintage time the grapes are harvested on the steep slopes of the Douro valley and brought to the winery. They are lightly crushed and then fermented, either in the traditional stone **lagar** (with foot treading), or in tank. Once the **alcohol** level has reached about 7%, **aguardente**, or grape spirit, is added in the ratio of 1:4, to stop **fermentation**. The result is a sweet red fortified wine with an alcohol level of about 20%, which is later removed to the Port shippers' **lodges** in Vila Nova de Gaia.

After about two years, the Port shipper will decide on the wine's fate. It might be blended with Ports from different vintages to make an ordinary young **Ruby Port**. Vintage Character denotes a superior Ruby. It may be kept unblended with other years, and bottled after four to six years, as a Late Bottled Vintage. Exceptionally good lots, from a fine year, will be bottled after two years, and these will become Vintage Port - a 'bottle-matured' Port, demanding lengthy maturing and capable of great longevity - the finest and most expensive style.

The alternative route is to make 'wood-matured' or **Tawny Port**. Except for the most basic and commercial Tawnies, which may be blended from red and white Ports, the Port is aged in wooden barrels for at least eight years, and sometimes for many decades. It may be sold as a blend of vintages of indicated age (10-year-old Tawny, 20-year-old Tawny, etc.), or as a dated Tawny from a single year (**Colheita Port**).

Porto Vecchio See **Vin de Corse**.

Portugal Wine-producing country of the Iberian peninsula, most famour for its superb **fortified wine Port**. There is also a wealth of white wines, ranging from the crisp, acidic **Vinho Verde** to the luscious, golden **Setúbal**, together with good reds from **Dão**, **Douro**, and **Bairrada**. See also **Alentejo**; **Algarve**; **Bucelas**; **Colares**; **Palmela**.

Portugieser Alternative name for the **Blauer Portugieser** grape variety.

Potter Valley AVA of **Mendocino** county, **California**. Its vineyards are at high altitude, with a short growing season and a wide day to night temperature variation. Good results have been obtained with **Riesling**, some of it affected by **botrytis**, and both **Chardonnay** and **Pinot Noir** show great promise, but its reputation rests on outstanding **Sauvignon Blanc**.

Pouilly-Fuissé White **AC** wine produced in the Mâconnais area of **Burgundy**, from the **Chardonnay**

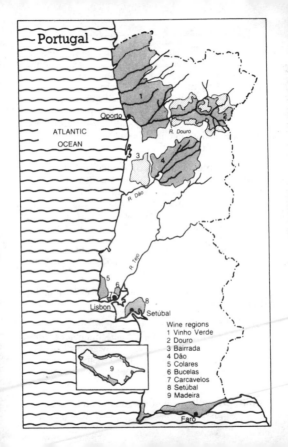

Portugal

ATLANTIC
OCEAN

Oporto

R. Douro

R. Dão

R. Tejo

Lisbon

Setúbal

Faro

Wine regions
1 Vinho Verde
2 Douro
3 Bairrada
4 Dão
5 Colares
6 Bucelas
7 Carcavelos
8 Setúbal
9 Madeira

grape variety. The wine is made from the vineyards of five different villages, Pouilly, Fuissé, Chaintré, Solutré and Vergisson. The best wines, from individual growers, are rich, full, buttery Chardonnays. However, there are also many inferior examples on the market, although quality does seem to be improving.

The nearby appellations of **Pouilly-Loché** and **Pouilly-Vinzelles** make wines in a similar style, but in much smaller quantities.

Pouilly-Fumé White **AC** wine produced in the eastern part of the **Loire** from the **Sauvignon Blanc** grape. The wines can be superb: bursting with juicy fruit, with gooseberry and blackcurrant flavours, sometimes even asparagus, all balanced with racy **acidity**. The wines are in a similar style to the nearby **Sancerre**; although Pouilly-Fumé can have more weight and last longer, it is generally best drunk young. The *fumé* in the name refers to the grey (smoky) appearance of the Sauvignon grapes as they ripen.

Pouilly-Loché AC of **Burgundy**, **France**. See **Pouilly-Fuissé**.

Pouilly-sur-Loire White **AC** wine produced in the same vineyard area as **Pouilly-Fumé**, but made from the **Chasselas** grape rather than **Sauvignon Blanc**. The wines are thin and neutral and may soon disappear because producers are replacing the Chasselas vines with Sauvignon Blanc.

Pouilly-Vinzelles AC of **Burgundy**, **France**. See **Pouilly-Fuissé**.

Poulsard Red grape variety of the **Jura** region of **France**. It produces highly perfumed wine, delicate yet well-structured, with red fruit flavours.

pourriture noble French for **noble rot** or **botrytis**.

Prädikat See QmP.

premier cru French quality designation which literally means 'first growth'. Its application varies in different regions.

In **Bordeaux**, the châteaux were classified in 1855 (the classification was of all Bordeaux, but only one **château** was from outside the **Médoc** and **Sauternes**): at the top quality level are the *grands crus classés*, subdivided into **premier cru**, *deuxième cru*, down to *cinquième cru*, referred to in English as 'first growth', 'second growth', and so on.

In **Burgundy**, including **Chablis**, the very top vineyard sites are classified as **grand cru**, and *premier cru* is the next level down. Each *grand cru* of the **Côte d'Or** has its own **AC**, whereas wines from *premier cru* vineyards are labelled with the village *appellation* plus the name of the *premier cru*. In Chablis, *grand cru* and *premier cru* wines are labelled 'AC Chablis' plus the name of the *cru* : if a wine is a blend from more than one *premier cru* vineyard, it can be labelled 'Chablis Premier cru'.

Premières Côtes de Blaye AC wine of **Bordeaux**, produced on the east side of the Gironde estuary, facing the **Haut-Médoc**. Nearly all the wine produced is red, made from the **Cabernet Sauvignon**, **Cabernet**

Franc, **Merlot**, and **Malbec** grape varieties. These are fresh, fruity, easy-to-drink wines, which are best drunk relatively early, and represent good value for money.

Premières Côtes de Bordeaux AC wine of **Bordeaux**, produced on a long strip of land on the east side of the Garonne river, facing the **Graves** region. Traditionally a sweet white wine area, most of the production is now solid, good-value red and clean, dry white (the white is labelled as AC Bordeaux Blanc), made from the classic Bordeaux grape varieties.

There are still some sweet whites produced, under the *Premières Côtes* AC and as AC **Cadillac**. They can be good-value, light, sweet wines, but they do not have the richness, elegance and concentration of **Sauternes** or **Barsac**.

Pressac Name used for the **Malbec** grape variety in the **Saint-Emilion** and **Pomerol** areas of **Bordeaux**.

Preuses One of the seven **grand cru** vineyards of **Chablis**.

Primitivo Red grape variety grown in **Apulia**, **Italy**, and possibly related to the **Zinfandel** of **California**. Apulian Primitivo was much used as a blending wine, to beef up reds from the north of Italy, but it makes **DOC** wines in **Primitivo di Manduria** and Gioia del Colle.

Primitivo di Manduria Red **DOC** wine produced in the Salento peninsula of the **Apulia** region of **Italy** from the **Primitivo** grape. The wine is strong and full, but lacking in elegance and complexity. It can be dry,

amabile, or fully sweet, and there are also fortified versions.

Priorato Red **DO** wine of north east **Spain**. **Garnacha** and **Cariñena** grape varieties produce strong, high-**alcohol**, sturdy reds with great concentration.

Prosecco White grape variety grown mainly in the **Veneto** region of **Italy**, where it is used to make hillside grown **DOC Prosecco di Conegliano-Valdobbiadene**, as well as ordinary DOC Prosecco from the plains.

Prosecco di Conegliano-Valdobbiadene Usually sparkling **DOC** wine of the eastern **Veneto** region of **Italy**, produced in the hills northwest of Treviso, around the towns of Conegliano and Valdobbiadene. The wine is based on the **Prosecco** grape, with the possible addition of Verdiso, **Chardonnay**, Pinot Bianco, and Pinot Grigio up to 15%. The best wines, usually designated *Superiore di Cartizze*, are almost dry and fully **spumante**, fresh and fruity, with gentle bitter-almond flavours in the background. Ideal for drinking outdoors on a hot day, and good value for money. Sweet Prosecco, which may include **Sauvignon** and **Malvasia**, is a fruity, scented wine with some class.

Provence Region of southeast **France** which produces some fine red and white wines, along with large quantities of often mediocre rosé. The largest **AC** is **Côtes de Provence**, source of much of the rosé, but also of increasingly good reds made from **Mourvèdre**, **Grenache**, **Syrah** and, more recently, **Cabernet Sauvignon**. The small amount of white produced, from

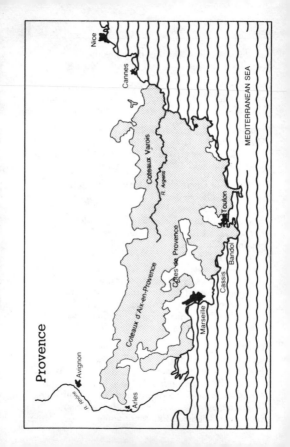

Ugni Blanc and **Clairette** among other grape varieties, is rarely any good.

Cabernet assumes a more important role in the AC **Coteaux d'Aix-en-Provence**, where again red and rosé wine predominate. The separate AC of Coteaux des Baux-en-Provence produces better reds, based mainly on Cabernet Sauvignon, Syrah, and Grenache.

The smaller ACs of Provence are **Bandol** (fine, long-lived reds based on the Mourvèdre grape variety), **Bellet**, **Cassis** (mainly white), and **Palette** (elegant whites and herby reds).

Prugnolo Gentile Red grape variety, a **clone** of **Sangiovese**, used to make **Vino Nobile di Montepulciano**.

Puglia See **Apulia**.

Puisseguin-Saint-Emilion Red **AC** wine made in a 'satellite' of the main **Saint-Emilion** *appellation* in **Bordeaux**, to the northeast of the town of Saint-Emilion. The grape varieties are the same as for Saint-Emilion – **Merlot**, **Cabernet Franc**, **Cabernet Sauvignon** and **Malbec** – and the wines, although very pleasant to drink young (three to five years), and offering good value, never reach the heights of the top Saint-Emilions.

Puligny-Montrachet AC wine of the **Côte de Beaune** area of **Burgundy**. Nearly all the wine produced is white, made from the **Chardonnay** grape. The straight village wines are highly variable in quality. The best are pale gold, dry but full, with rich, buttery, creamy **aromas** and taste.

The **premiers crus** are nearly always better, and the **grand cru**s, **Bâtard-Montrachet**, **Bienvenues Bâtard-Montrachet**, **Chevalier-Montrachet** and Le **Montrachet** (especially the last two) are among the most intensely flavoured and complex white wines in the world. See also **Blagny**; **Chassagne-Montrachet**.

puttonyos See **Tokaji**.

PX See **Pedro Ximénez**.

Q

QbA (Qualitätswein bestimmter Anbaugebiete) German term for quality wines from a specified region. The wine must come from one of the 13 **Anbaugebiet** areas, and can be made only from certain permitted grape varieties. It must not be blended with wine from any other region, and the grapes used to make it will have a high enough **must weight** to raise it above **Landwein** level, but not as high as for **QmP**. Not a great guarantee of quality.

QmP (Qualitätswein mit Prädikat) German term for the highest category of quality wines, classified in ascending order according to the **must weight** of the grapes used to make them: **Kabinett**, **Spätlese**, **Auslese**, **Beerenauslese**, **Trockenbeerenauslese**, and **Eiswein**. The **residual sugar** left in the wine varies considerably within each category, however, and *Auslese*, for instance, can range from bone dry (**trocken**) to lusciously sweet.

Qualitätswein See **QbA**; **QmP**.

Quarts de Chaume Sweet white **AC** wine from the **Coteaux du Layon** area of **Anjou-Saumur** in the **Loire** valley, **France**. The wines are made only from the **Chenin Blanc** grape, which in good years is affected by **botrytis**. They are wines of high quality, rich and luscious, with **acidity** balancing the honeyed fruit.

Queensland Hot-climate wine-producing state of
Australia. It produces good-quality **fortified wine** (in
the style of **Madeira**) and medium-quality **varietal**
wines (in the cooler, high-altitude Granite Belt region)
made from the **Cabernet Sauvignon**, **Chardonnay**,
Sauvignon Blanc, **Sémillon** and **Shiraz** grape varieties.

Quincy AC wine made between Bourges and Vierzon
in the eastern **Loire** valley. The vineyards are to the
west of **Sancerre**, and the wine is similar, although not
as good as the very best Sancerre and **Pouilly-Fumé**:
crisp, pungent, juicy white from the **Sauvignon Blanc**
grape.

quinta Portuguese term for a wine estate producing its
own grapes.

quintal Unit of weight equivalent to 100 kg. The
quintal is used in **Italy** to express yields in terms of
quintals per **hectare**.

QWPSR European term meaning quality wine
produced in a specified region, a general term covering
appellations such as the French **AC**, the Italian **DOC**,
and the Spanish **DO**.

R

Raboso Italian red grape variety, found particularly in the **Veneto** region, where it makes the lively, deep-coloured and high-**tannin DOC** wine **Piave**.

racking Process of transferring a maturing wine from one vessel to another, to aerate it and separate it from any sediment.

Ramandolo See **Colli Orientali del Friuli**.

Ramisco Red grape variety that makes tough, **tannic** wine in the **Colares** region of **Portugal**.

rancio Tasting term used to describe the pungent, intentionally **oxidized** smell of some wood-aged **fortified wine** and **vin doux naturel**.

Rasteau AC wine of the southern **Rhône**. It is a fortified (**vin doux naturel**) wine based on the red **Grenache** grape variety. The traditional style is a sweet, heavy, **tannic** red. However, most Rasteau is fermented without the grape skins, resulting in the '*dorée*' style, a deep, golden colour, honeyed and sweet. The third style receives long **ageing** in **oak** barrels, and the wine develops a **rancio** character. See also **Côtes du Rhône**.

ratafia Mistelle of the **Champagne** region, made by adding brandy to unfermented grape juice. White, rosé, or red, it is similar to **Pineau des Charentes**.

RD Abbreviation of the Portuguese term **Região Demarcada.** See also **DOC.**

recioto Term used in **Italy**, particularly in **Valpolicella**, **Soave**, and **Gambellara** in the **Veneto** region, for sweet dessert wine made from grapes that have been concentrated by drying. The wine is usually still but can be sparkling. The name *recioto* comes from the dialect word *recie*, meaning the 'little ears' of grapes at the top of the bunch. These are the smallest, sweetest berries, which are harvested separately and left to dry on wooden trays until they are ready to be pressed in January.

Recioto della Valpolicella Unusual sweet, heady red **DOC** wine from **Valpolicella**, in the **Veneto** region of **Italy**. About 10 days before the normal vintage, carefully selected grapes (of the usual Valpolicella varieties), are laid out in a dry, airy room. They are allowed to dry until January, when the shrivelled grapes are crushed and fermented slowly. Some barrels stop fermenting at around 13% **alcohol**, and become Recioto della Valpolicella. Others continue to ferment to dryness, reaching about 16% alcohol, and produce the strong, bitter-sweet **Amarone**. The wines are produced in very limited quantities, and quality can be stunningly good with long **ageing** potential.

Recioto di Gambellara Sweet, intense, golden-coloured **DOC** wine, sometimes semi-sparkling, grown in the **Veneto** region of **Italy**. It is made from dried grapes of the **Garganega** and **Trebbiano** di Soave varieties. See also **Gambellara**; **recioto**.

Recioto di Soave Sweet, intense, golden-coloured
DOC wine, occasionally sparkling, made from dried
grapes of the **Garganega** and **Trebbiano** di Soave
varieties. See also **recioto**; **Soave**.

récoltant-manipulant See **RM**.

récolte French term for harvest. See also **vendange**.

Refosco Red grape variety grown in **Friuli** where it
gives deep-coloured full bodied wines with good
plummy fruit.

Região Demarcada (**RD**) Former Portuguese term
for a demarcated wine region, now replaced by **DOC**.
It is roughly equivalent to the French **AC** or Spanish
DO.

Régnié Red **AC** wine, the newest of the 10 **crus** of the
Beaujolais region of **Burgundy**, made from the **Gamay**
grape. The wines are fruity, supple, and full of flavour.
However, their elevation above Beaujolais-Villages AC
has been controversial.

rehoboam Large format **Champagne** bottle, of 4.5
litres capacity (equivalent to six ordinary bottles).

Reichensteiner White grape variety, a **cross** derived
from **Müller-Thurgau** and another crossing (**Madeleine
Angevine** and **Calabrese**), planted in the northern wine
regions of **Germany** and in **England**. It has a relatively
high **must weight** and good **acidity**, but makes rather
neutral wine. In England it has been used to produce

successful **méthode traditionnelle** sparkling wine.

Reims Capital city of the **Champagne** region, where many of the producers have their **cellars**.

remontage French term for the process of pumping **must** from the bottom of a **fermentation** vessel to the top, in order to extract colour and **tannin** from the floating cap of grape skins.

remuage French term for riddling, the process of shaking and turning bottles of **Champagne** and other **méthode traditionnelle** wines. It moves the sediment produced during the second, bubble-forming **fermentation** to the neck of the bottle, ready for **disgorgement**. This can be done by hand or by machine using a **gyropalette**.

rendement French for **yield**.

reserva Term used to describe Spanish wines that have been aged for a certain minimum period, part of it in **oak** barrels. The term refers especially to the red and white wines of **Rioja**.

residual sugar Sugar left in a wine once it has been fermented and is ready for bottling. The quantity of sugar is usually measured in grams per litre. This level determines whether the wine can be described as dry, **sec**, medium dry, **demi-sec**, and so on.

Retsina Wine of **Greece**, made mainly in the **Attica** region, usually from the Savatiano grape. The unique part of the winemaking process is that pine resin is added to the wine, which gives it a distinctive resinous taste. Retsina is nearly always white and it should be drunk as cold and as young as possible. Retsina for export often seems to be less resinated than that found in Greece.

Reuilly AC wine of the eastern part of the **Loire** valley. The white version is made from the **Sauvignon Blanc** grape variety, and is rarely better than a pale imitation of good **Sancerre**. Uninteresting red wines are also made, from **Pinot Noir**, but Reuilly Rosé, made from Pinot Noir or, occasionally, from **Pinot Gris**, can be very good, with a light, pinkish hue, and soft, fresh, **grapey** fruit.

Rhein German name for the Rhine, the river which, together with its tributaries, dominates the fine wine-producing regions of **Germany**. The Rhein rises in the Swiss alps, and flows through the heart of Germany's wine country, fed by the Neckar, Main, **Nahe**, Mosel, and **Ahr**.

Rheingau One of the 13 major quality wine regions, or **Anbaugebiete**, of **Germany**. It produces mainly high-quality white wines from the **Riesling** grape variety, including some of the greatest and most well-known names. The region follows the north bank of the Rhine, from **Lorch** in the west to **Hochheim** in the east, and includes such famous names as Assmannshausen, **Rüdesheim**, **Johannisberg**, **Geisenheim**, and **Hattenheim**.

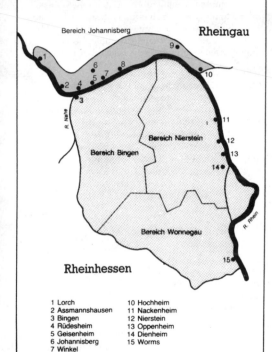

Rheingau & Rheinhessen

Bereich Johannisberg

Rheingau

Rheinhessen

Bereich Nierstein

Bereich Bingen

Bereich Wonnegau

R. Nahe

R. Rhein

1 Lorch	10 Hochheim
2 Assmannshausen	11 Nackenheim
3 Bingen	12 Nierstein
4 Rüdesheim	13 Oppenheim
5 Geisenheim	14 Dienheim
6 Johannisberg	15 Worms
7 Winkel	
8 Hattenheim	
9 Wiesbaden	

The Rheingau is a relatively small Anbaugebiet, and there is only one **Bereich**, Johannisberg. This is divided into 10 **Grosslagen**: Burgweg, Daubhaus, Deutelsberg, Erntebringer, Gottesthal, Heiligenstock, Honigberg, Mehrhölzchen, Steil and Steinmächer.

Rheinhessen Largest of the 13 major quality wine regions, or **Anbaugebiete**, of **Germany**. It is planted with **Riesling**, together with many new **cross**-bred varieties, especially **Scheurebe**. It is not surprising that such a large region produces a wide variety of qualities, from some of Germany's best (especially along the banks of the Rhine, in the east of the region from Dienheim to **Nackenheim**), to bland bulk wine, including much **Liebfraumilch**. The region is divided into three **Bereich** subregions, **Bingen** in the west, **Nierstein** in the east, and **Wonnegau** in the south.

Rheinpfalz (also called Palatinate) See **Pfalz**.

Rhine Riesling The 'true' **Riesling**, as opposed to **Welschriesling** or **Riesling Italico**.

Rhoditis White grape variety of **Greece**, valued for its relatively high **acidity**, and often blended with the lower-acid Savatiano variety.

Rhône Important wine-producing region of southeast **France**. The region divides neatly into distinct halves. The northern Rhône is dominated by red wine made from the **Syrah** grape variety. It includes the great, rich, concentrated wines of **Hermitage** and Côte Rôtie, along with **Saint-Joseph**, **Crozes-Hermitage**, and

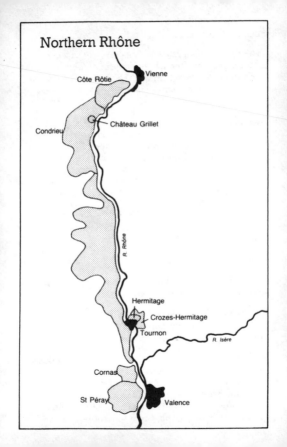

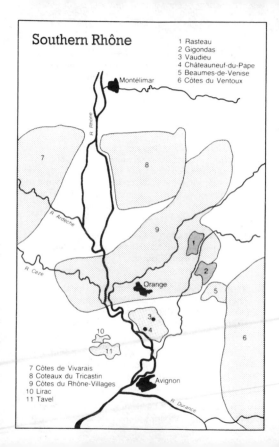

Southern Rhône

1 Rasteau
2 Gigondas
3 Vaudieu
4 Châteauneuf-du-Pape
5 Beaumes-de-Venise
6 Côtes du Ventoux

Montélimar

R Rhône

R Ardèche

R Ceze

Orange

Avignon

R Durance

7 Côtes de Vivarais
8 Coteaux du Tricastin
9 Côtes du Rhône-Villages
10 Lirac
11 Tavel

Cornas. White wine is produced in tiny quantities in **Château Grillet** and **Condrieu** from the **Viognier** grape. Sparkling wine comes from **Saint-Péray** and is made mainly from **Marsanne**.

In the southern Rhône, Syrah is not dominant. This part of the region is centred on **Châteauneuf-du-Pape** and produces red (and some white) wines from no fewer than 13 authorized grape varieties. Also in the south, **Gigondas** produces red wine based mainly on **Grenache**; **Tavel** is rosé, and **Lirac** can be red or rosé, both based on Grenache and **Cinsault**; and **Muscat de Beaumes-de-Venise** and **Rasteau** are fortified **vin doux naturel** wines. See also **Clairette**; **Coteaux du Tricastin**; **Côtes du Rhône** (Côtes du Rhône-Villages); **Côtes du Ventoux**; **Côtes du Vivarais**.

Rias Baixas DO wine of **Galicia**, in northwest **Spain**. Fresh whites, similar to **Portugal**'s **Vinho Verde**, are made from **Albariño**, Loureira, Godello, and Treixadura grapes

Ribatejo Wine-producing region of **Portugal**, along the banks of the River Tejo (Tagus) north of Lisbon. It produces full-bodied, beefy reds based mainly on the **Periquita** grape variety, and **aromatic**, peppery whites largely from the **Fernão Pires** grape.

Ribeiro DO wine of **Galicia**, in northwest **Spain**. Most of the production is of white, bland wines from the **Palomino** grape, and more characterful ones from **Albariño**, Treixadura, and **Torrontés**.

Ribera del Duero DO wine of north-central **Spain**, produced along the banks of the Duero river (which becomes the **Douro** in **Portugal**). Red and **rosado** wines are produced, mainly based on the **Tempranillo** grape variety (known here as **Tinto Fino**), although **Garnacha**, **Cabernet Sauvignon**, **Merlot**, and **Cot** are also planted. The best wines are of superb quality, rich, concentrated, and long lasting, and quality is constantly improving.

Ribolla White grape variety grown mainly in the **Friuli-Venezia Giulia** region of northeast **Italy**. It produces soft, citrus-flavoured, medium-bodied whites in the **DOCs** of **Collio** and **Colli Orientali del Friuli**.

Richebourg **Grand cru** wine of the **Vosne-Romanée**, in the **Côte de Nuits** area of **Burgundy**, made from the **Pinot Noir** grape. This is one of the finest and most expensive red wines in the world, with fat, velvety **body**, and spicy, scented fruit.

riddling See **remuage**.

Rieslaner White grape variety, a **cross** of **Silvaner** and **Riesling**, planted mainly in the **Franken** region of **Germany**. It produces a wine high in **acidity** but rather neutral in flavour.

Riesling Major white grape variety, used to produce the finest wines of **Germany** and some of the best in the **Alsace** region of **France**. It is also widely planted in northern **Italy** (as **Riesling Renano**), as well as the wine-producing countries of the New World.

Riesling has the ability to ripen to a very high **must weight**, without losing too much **acidity**, the key to the balance in Germany's fabulous sweet white wines. Because it ripens late, it can take advantage of **botrytis** in good years, leading to the shrivelled, concentrated grapes that go to make **Beerenauslese** and **Trockenbeerenauslese** wines. However, German wine made from Riesling can cover a wide spectrum of flavours, from steely, dry and **aromatic** wines through to the exotic fruit and honey of the sweetest, which can also develop a **petrolly aroma** and taste with age.

In Alsace, Riesling tends to be made dry, although in exceptional years it can make sweet, rich **vendange tardive** and **Sélection des Grains Nobles** wines. In **California** (where the variety is often called **Johannisberg Riesling**), botrytis can also play a role, but the 'late-harvest' wines seldom have the elegance of their racy German equivalents.

Lighter, spritzy Rieslings are made in the **Alto Adige** region of Italy. **Australia** and **New Zealand** produce mainly dry, fruity wines from Riesling, the best examples capable of elegant **ageing**.

Riesling Italico Italian name for **Welschriesling**.

Riesling Renano Italian name for **Rhine Riesling**.

Right Bank English term used to describe the **Bordeaux** vineyards of the eastern bank of the Gironde estuary (viz. **Saint-Emilion**, **Pomerol**, and their satellites). See also **Left Bank**.

Rioja DOC wine produced along the Ebro valley, from Haro in the west, to just east of the town of Alfaro, in northern **Spain**. The valley is crossed by seven tributaries, from one of which, the Rio Oja, the district is said to take its name.

Red Rioja is made mainly from the **Tempranillo** grape, plus **Garnacha** and sometimes a small proportion of the white Viura (**Macabeo**). The best examples are among the finest red wines of Spain. They are rich, ripe, concentrated and often **oaky**.

The back label is the key to the degree of **oak ageing**: **crianza** is wine in its third year, with one year in cask; **reserva** is aged for at least three years, at least one year in cask; **gran reserva** is wine of a great **vintage**, aged at least two years in oak cask and three years in bottle. Rioja with none of these descriptions will have received little or no oak ageing.

The majority of Rioja is a blend from at least two of the three subregions, Rioja Alta, Rioja Alavesa and Rioja Baja, although examples of single-estate Rioja are available. The two western subregions, Alta and Alavesa, enjoy an Atlantic climate, with snow in the winter, rain in the spring, and short hot summers. To the east, the Rioja Baja has a much more continental climate, with less rain and more sunshine, producing coarser wine for blending.

White Rioja is made from the Viura and **Malvasia** grape varieties. There are two main styles: fresh, fruity, rather neutral whites; and oak-aged whites, with great complexity, depth and **ageing** potential. For oaked white Rioja, **crianza** is wine in its third year, matured for at least 6 months in cask; **reserva** must be aged 24 months, of which at least 6 months is in cask; and **gran**

reserva should be aged 48 months, of which at least 6 months is in cask.

ripasso See **Valpolicella**.

Ripaille **Cru** of the **Vin de Savoie** *appellation*.

riserva Term used in **Italy** to indicate wines of higher than usual quality, which have been aged for a certain minimum period. See **Chianti**.

Rivaner Name used for the **Müller-Thurgau** grape in **Luxembourg**.

Riverland Major wine-producing region of **Australia**, irrigated by the **Murray River**. This is the source of a major part of Australia's wine production, mainly from inferior varieties such as Muscat Gordo Blanco, Sultana, and Doradillo, but also some **Sémillon** and **Shiraz**.

Rivesaltes See **Muscat de Rivesaltes**.

Riviera del Garda Bresciano DOC wine of **Lombardy** in northwest **Italy**, produced southwest of Lake Garda. The red, and refreshing pink **chiaretto**, wine is made from a blend of **Groppello**, **Sangiovese**, **Barbera**, **Marzemino**, and other grape varieties.

Riviera Ligure di Ponente DOC wine produced in a zone covering most of western **Liguria**, northwest **Italy**. **Varietal** red and **rosato** wines are produced from the **Dolcetto** (labelled as Ormeasco), and Rossese (reds only) grapes. The full-bodied white wines, which are better, are made from **Vermentino** or **Pigato**, and are also labelled by grape variety.

Rkatsiteli Russian white grape variety, planted throughout the **CIS** and eastern Europe and also in **China**. It produces fairly neutral tasting wine, but with a good balance of ripeness and **acidity**.

RM (*récoltant-manipulant*) Letters found on **Champagne** labels which indicate that it comes from a grower who both produces and sells the wine. The numbers following the letters identify the grower.

Robola White grape variety of **Greece**, producing a full-bodied, citrus-flavoured white wine of the same name on the island of Cephalonia. Quality can be good, so long as the wine is fresh.

Roche-aux-Moines, La See **Savennières**.

Rochegude See **Côtes du Rhône**.

Roero DOC wine made just north of the **Alba** area of **Piedmont**, northwest **Italy**. Roero is a dry red made from the **Nebbiolo** grape. Roero Arneis (or Arneis di Roero) is a dry white, sometimes sparkling, made from **Arneis**.

Rolle Unusual white grape variety used, along with **Chardonnay**, to make the rare white wine of **Bellet** in **Provence**, and also planted in the **Languedoc-Roussillon**.

Romanée, La Grand cru wine of **Vosne-Romanée**, in the **Côte de Nuits** area of **Burgundy**, made from the

Pinot Noir grape. Although it produces fine wines, they do not approach the splendour of the neighbouring grands crus, **Romanée-Conti**, **Richebourg**, and **La Tâche**.

Romanée-Conti, La **Grand cru** wine of **Vosne-Romanée**, in the **Côte de Nuits** area of **Burgundy**, made from the **Pinot Noir** grape. This is one of the finest, most expensive and longest-lived red wines in the world. It has an extraordinary panoply of smoky, fruity sensations on the nose, and intense concentration on the **palate**, with truffly, rich and spicy flavours.

Romanée-Saint-Vivant, La **Grand cru** wine of **Vosne-Romanée**, in the **Côte de Nuits** area of **Burgundy**, made from the **Pinot Noir** grape. It produces very fine red wines, spicy and scented, although not in the same class as **Romanée-Conti** and **La Tâche**.

Romania Eastern European country with a vast and increasing area under vine. Traditionally, production has been of sweet white wine from native grape varieties, such as **Feteasca** and **Rkatsiteli**, most of it exported to **Russia**. However, large areas have been planted with western grape varieties, including **Cabernet Sauvignon**, **Merlot**, **Pinot Noir**, **Chardonnay**, and **Sauvignon Blanc**. So far little has been exported to the west, but quality is increasing slowly. The handful of wines already available in the West represent good value for money.

Rondinella Red grape variety of the **Veneto** region of **Italy**, playing a secondary role to the major variety,

Corvina, in the production of **Valpolicella** and **Bardolino**. It adds colour, body, and **acidity** to the wine.

rosado Spanish and Portuguese for pink or rosé wine.

rosato Italian for pink or rosé wine.

Rosé d'Anjou Rosé AC wine of the **Loire** valley, produced mainly from the **Grolleau** grape variety. The wine is usually quite a vivid pink, fruity at its best, and can vary between medium-dry and sweet. It is produced in vast quantities, and some of the cheaper wines lack freshness and fruit. The best to be hoped for is a good-value, refreshing, medium-dry wine, to be drunk young and well-chilled, without much thought. See also **Cabernet d'Anjou**; **Rosé de Loire**.

Rosé de Loire Rosé AC wine produced in Anjou and **Touraine** in the **Loire** valley. It is similar to **Rosé d'Anjou**, but is better because the **Grolleau** grape variety is blended with at least 30% **Cabernet Sauvignon**, and it is usually dry.

Rosé des Riceys Rare, still, rosé AC wine of the **Champagne** region, made from the **Pinot Noir** grape variety in exceptionally good years.

Rosette Medium-sweet white AC wine in the **Bergerac** region of southwest **France**, produced from the **Sémillon**, **Sauvignon Blanc**, and **Muscadelle** grape varieties. The wine is light and of rarely more than adequate quality. There are fewer bottles produced each year, and it may die out completely before long.

Rossese di Dolceacqua Red **DOC** wine produced in **Liguria**, northwest **Italy**, from the Rossese grape variety. At best it is a fragant, medium-bodied, fruity red, but too often it is thin and pale-coloured.

rosso Italian for red wine.

Rosso Barletta Dry red **DOC** wine of central **Apulia** in southern **Italy**, made mainly from **Uva di Troia** (plus, occasionally, **Montepulciano**, **Sangiovese** and **Cot**). Quality can be good and it is usually best drunk young.

Rosso Canosa Dry red **DOC** wine of central **Apulia** in southern **Italy** made mainly from **Uva di Troia** (plus, occasionally, **Montepulciano** and **Sangiovese**). A robust red, for relatively early drinking.

Rosso Cònero Red **DOC** wine produced around the town of Ancona in the **Marches** region of **Italy**. Most of the wine is produced from the **Montepulciano** grape variety, although **Sangiovese** is allowed up to 15%. The wine is full, round, high in **tannins**, and capable of long **ageing**. Quality can be exceptionally high and it is very good value for money.

Rosso di Montalcino Red **DOC** wine of **Tuscany**, produced in the same area, and from the same grape variety, as **Brunello di Montalcino**. The idea is that producers select their best grapes for Brunello, and make the rest into Rosso, in an early-drinking style. In poor years, they can make all their wine as Rosso. This benefits the consumer because Rosso is delicious and lovely to drink when relatively young, costs much less than Brunello and the selection process should lead to an improvement in the quality of Brunello.

Rosso di Montepulciano Red **DOC** wine of **Tuscany**, produced in the same area, and from the same grape varieties, as **Vino Nobile di Montepulciano**. As with **Rosso di Montalcino**, the idea is for Vino Nobile producers to declassify lighter years to Rosso, which can be sold after six months' **ageing** rather than two years.

Rosso Piceno Red **DOC** wine of the **Marches** region of **Italy**, made from the **Montepulciano** and **Sangiovese** grape varieties. Quality can be good.

Rotgipfler White grape variety of **Austria**, which along with **Zierfändler** is used to produce the heady, spicy, rich wine Gumpoldskirchner.

Rotling German term for rosé wine, produced by fermenting red and white grapes together (not by blending red and white wine).

Rotwein German for red wine.

rouge French for red.

Roussanne White grape variety that, along with **Marsanne**, is used to make white wines in the northern **Rhône**. Its presence in the blend results in a more vivacious and **aromatic** wine than is available from pure Marsanne. Roussanne is also one of the 13 varieties permitted in red **Châteauneuf-du-Pape** in the southern

Rhône, and it is also planted in **Languedoc-Roussillon**, where it can make good **varietal** or blended **Vin de pays** d'Oc.

Roussette See **Altesse**.

Roussillon See **Languedoc-Roussillon**.

Ruby Port Basic style of young **Port**, full-bodied, sweet, vigorous and fruity. The average age of Ruby is usually around three years. It requires no decanting, and can be drunk immediately after purchase.

Ruchottes-Chambertin **Grand cru** vineyard of **Gevrey-Chambertin** in the **Côte de Nuits** area of **Burgundy**.

Rüdesheim 1. Town of the **Rheingau** region of **Germany**, which produces fine-quality, full-flavoured white wines from the **Riesling** grape variety. The vineyards come within the **Grosslage** of Burgweg, and the best **Einzellage** sites are Berg Roseneck, Berg Rottland, Berg Schlossberg, Klosterberg, Klosterlay, Bischofsberg and Rosengarten.
2. A village of the **Nahe** region of Germany, which produces modest white wines from the **Müller-Thurgau** and **Silvaner** grape varieties. The vineyards come within the *Grosslage* of Rosengarten.

Rueda White **DO** wine of northwest **Spain**, made mainly from the native **Verdejo** grape variety, along with Viura (**Macabeo**) and **Sauvignon Blanc**. Traditionally the region made **fortified wines** from

Palomino, in a similar style to **Sherry**, but today nearly all the production is of young, white table wines. Quality is usually extremely good, and fresh, fruity, nutty Rueda is one of the best white wines of Spain. **Varietal** Sauvignon Blanc can also be extremely good.

Rufina See **Chianti** (Rufina).

Ruländer Alternative name, used in **Germany**, for the **Pinot Gris** grape.

Rully AC wine of the **Côte Chalonnaise** region of **Burgundy**, which produces white wines from **Chardonnay** and reds from **Pinot Noir**. The whites are soft, medium-bodied and nutty, sometimes with a touch of **oak**, and offer good value for money. Reds are lighter bodied, and less successful so far, but there are signs of improvement.

Russia Important wine producing state of the **CIS**. Most of the vineyards are found in the north Caucasus, and are planted with varieties including **Rkatsiteli**, **Aligoté**, **Riesling**, and **Cabernet Sauvignon**, along with lesser quantities of **Traminer**, **Muscat**, **Silvaner**, **Saperavi**, **Merlot**, and **Pinot Gris**. Much of the wine is made sparkling and rather sweet. **Table wine** production has not yet generally reached an acceptable standard for export.

Russian River Valley AVA of **Sonoma** county, **California**, with a relatively cool climate. It produces good **varietal** wines from **Chardonnay**, **Pinot Noir**, **Riesling**, and **Gewürztraminer**. Successful **méthode**

traditionnelle sparkling wines are also made from Chardonnay and Pinot Noir.

Rutherford Important wine area in **California**'s **Napa Valley**.

Rutherglen Small wine-producing town in **Victoria**, **Australia**, with a great reputation for luscious, intensely sweet and complex **fortified wines**, particularly 'Liqueur **Muscat**' and 'Liqueur Tokay' (from **Muscadelle** grapes).

Ruwer See **Mosel-Saar-Ruwer**.

S

Saale-Unstrut Small **Anbaugebiet** region of eastern Germany, planted with **Müller-Thurgau**, **Bacchus**, **Silvaner**, Gutedel, and **Weissburgunder** producing relatively low-**alcohol** wines of, so far, little distinction.

Saar-Ruwer Bereich subregion of the **Mosel-Saar-Ruwer** region or **Anbaugebiet**. The best white wines are made from the **Riesling** grape variety, light but strong-flavoured and steely, with a pronounced slaty character, especially in the Saar valley.

Saarburg Town on the Saar river, in the **Mosel-Saar-Ruwer** region of **Germany**, producing fine, **aromatic**, slaty white wines from the **Riesling** grape variety. The vineyards come under the **Grosslage** of Scharzberg, and the best **Einzellage** sites are Klosterberg, Fuchs, and Schlossberg.

Sablet See **Côtes du Rhône**.

Sacramento Valley **California** wine county, which produces mainly ordinary-quality **jug wine**.

Saint-Amour Red **AC** wine, one of the 10 **crus** of the **Beaujolais** region of **Burgundy**, made from the **Gamay** grape. The wines are among the finest of Beaujolais, juicy, **aromatic** and full of flavour although light and delicate.

Saint-Aubin AC wine of the **Côte de Beaune** region of **Burgundy**. Most of the wine produced is full-bodied red, from the **Pinot Noir** grape variety. The whites, from **Chardonnay**, are more interesting: toasty, with good **acidity** and sometimes a touch of **oak**, offering good value for money, especially those labelled **premier cru**.

Saint-Bris-le-Vineux See **Sauvignon de Saint-Bris**.

Sainte-Croix-du-Mont Sweet white **AC** wine made on the **Right Bank** of the Garonne river in the **Bordeaux** region. The grapes are the same as those used in **Sauternes** and **Barsac**, **Sémillon**, **Sauvignon Blanc**, and **Muscadelle**, although higher **yields** are permitted. The wines are in a similar style to those of Sauternes and Barsac, but never as rich or fine, and they have less **ageing** potential. They represent good value for money.

Saint-Emilion 1. Red **AC** wine of **Bordeaux**, centred on the the town of Saint-Emilion on the north bank of the Dordogne river. It is made from the classic Bordeaux grape varieties, **Cabernet Sauvignon**, **Cabernet Franc** and **Merlot**. Merlot has more importance here than in the **Médoc**, where Cabernet Sauvignon is king.

The wines are classified into *premier grand cru classé*, at the top (13 *châteaux*); **grand cru** *classé* (more than 60); *grand cru* (around 200); and the rest. The wines are soft, **aromatic**, fleshy, and slightly spicy, ready to drink sooner than the great red wines of the Médoc. Quality varies, although the top wines are nearly always reliable, and there is good value to be found lower down the classification. See also **Lussac-**, **Montagne-**, **Puisseguin-** and **Saint-Georges-Saint-Emilion**.

2. An alternative name, used in the Charentes region of **France**, for the **Trebbiano** (**Ugni Blanc**) grape variety.

Saint-Estèphe Red **AC** wine of the **Haut-Médoc** area of **Bordeaux**, and the largest of the four great communal *appellations*. Saint-Estèphe has not enjoyed as high a reputation as the others, **Pauillac**, **Margaux** and **Saint-Julien**. There are only five crus classés, and the wines formerly had a reputation for being **tannic**, tough and unapproachable in their youth, requiring long **ageing**. However, the top **cru classé** are now made in a more approachable style, and today they rank alongside the top wines of the other communes. There are also many good-quality **cru bourgeois** wines available, and these can offer good value for money.

Saint-Georges-Saint-Emilion Red **AC** wine made in a satellite area of the main **Saint-Emilion** appellation, **Bordeaux**. The grape varieties are the same as for Saint-Emilion, **Merlot**, **Cabernet Franc**, **Cabernet Sauvignon** and **Malbec**, and Saint-Georges wines are probably the best of the satellites, if never reaching the heights of the top Saint-Emilions. Producers in Saint-Georges also have the option of using the AC of **Montagne-Saint-Emilion**.

Saint-Joseph **AC** wine of the northern **Rhône**. The red wine is made mainly from the **Syrah** grape variety, sometimes with the addition of the white grapes

Marsanne and **Roussanne**, which are also used to make small quantities of white Saint-Joseph. The reds are more important, and more consistently good, with rich, concentrated blackberry and blackcurrant fruit, although less long-lived than **Hermitage**. Good whites exist, but are difficult to find: the best are full-bodied, with pear and apricot flavours.

Saint-Julien Important communal **AC** of the **Médoc**. It produces very high-quality red **Bordeaux**, with great balance, finesse, rounded fruit flavours and depth, and is capable of lasting as long as the great wines of **Pauillac**. There are 11 **cru classé châteaux**, nearly all making consistently superb wine.

Saint-Nicolas-de-Bourgueil Red **AC** wine of the **Touraine** region in the **Loire** valley, made mainly from the **Cabernet Franc** grape (called Breton locally). It is one of the finest-quality red wines of the Loire, with **grassy**, raspberry fruit flavours, and is capable of short-term **ageing**. **Bourgueil** is similar, but has its own AC.

Saint-Péray White **AC** wine of the northern **Rhône**, made from the **Marsanne** and **Roussanne** grapes. Most of it is turned into a good-quality **méthode traditionnelle** sparkler, although some is bottled as still wine.

Saint-Romain **AC** wine of the **Côte de Beaune** region of **Burgundy**. Production is divided between light, but earthy reds, made from the **Pinot Noir** grape, and dry, flinty whites from **Chardonnay**.

Saint-Véran White **AC** wine of the **Mâconnais** region of **Burgundy**, made from the **Chardonnay** grape variety.

This soft, fresh white should be drunk young, and offers good value for money.

Salice Salentino DOC wine produced in the **Apulia** region of southern **Italy**. Good quality, robust, rich reds are made from the **Negroamaro** grape, along with fresh, floral **rosato** wines.

salmanazar Large format **Champagne** bottle, of 9 litres capacity (equivalent to 12 ordinary bottles).

Sancerre AC wine produced in the eastern part of the **Loire**. Most of the production is of white wine made from the **Sauvignon Blanc** grape variety. These can be superb; bone-dry, but bursting with juicy fruit, with gooseberry and blackcurrant flavours, sometimes even asparagus, all balanced with racy **acidity**. Dry red and rosé Sancerre, made from **Pinot Noir**, are less successful.

San Colombano al Lambro Red DOC wine produced in the **Lombardy** region of northwest **Italy**. This dry, rustic red, which has moderate **ageing** potential, is made from the **Croatina**, **Barbera**, and Uva **Rara** grape varieties.

Sangiovese Red grape variety grown throughout **Italy**, but to best effect in **Tuscany**, where it is responsible for the best part of the blends for **Chianti** and **Vino Nobile di Montepulciano**, and for all of **Brunello di Montalcino**. There are many different clones of Sangiovese, of which one of the best is called Sangioveto (or 'Brunello' in Montalcino). Recent legislation now allows **Chianti Classico** to be 100%

Sangiovese, thus doing away with the anomaly of some of Tuscany's best wines being classed as **vini da tavola**, while leaving other non-**DOCG** blends (e.g. with **Cabernet Sauvignon** or **Merlot**) to be classed as **IGT**. Widely planted in many other parts of Italy, especially in **Emilia-Romagna**, it rarely if ever reaches the same distinction as in Tuscany, largely thanks to the use of productive but inferior clones. It has been grown very successfully in **California**, however, and is also planted in the **Mendoza** province of **Argentina**.

Sangue di Giuda See Oltrepò Pavese.

San Joaquin Valley Hot-climate, wine-producing region of **California**, making mostly large quantities of mass-market **jug wine**. **AVAs** include Lodi, Clarksburg, and **Madera**, and Lodi, in particular, has produced successful **varietal** reds.

Sanlúcar de Barrameda See manzanilla; **Sherry**.

San Luis Obispo County of **California**, with a growing reputation for good-quality **varietal** wines, especially reds from the **Zinfandel** and **Cabernet Sauvignon** grape varieties, and white from **Chardonnay**. **AVAs** include Arroyo Grande, **Edna Valley**, and **Paso Robles**.

San Severo DOC wine produced in the **Apulia** region of southern **Italy**. Large quantities of good-value, simple red, white and **rosato** wine are made. The whites are based on the **Bombino** and **Trebbiano** grapes, the red and rosé on **Montepulciano** and **Sangiovese**.

Santa Barbara County of **California**, which produces mainly white **varietal** wines from the **Chardonnay**, **Chenin Blanc** and **Riesling** grape varieties, together with good-quality red **Pinot Noir**. **AVAs** include Santa Maria Valley and Santa Ynez Valley.

Santa Maddalena (also called St Magdalener) **DOC** wine produced in the **Alto Adige** region of northeast **Italy**. Dry, red, full, fruity wine is produced from the **Schiava** grape variety.

Santenay AC wine of the **Côte de Beaune** area of **Burgundy**. Quite good-value, earthy, fruity, ripe, red Burgundy is made from the **Pinot Noir** grape variety, together with a small quantity of white, made from **Chardonnay**.

Santorini Greek island where fine dry whites are made, mainly from the **Assyrtiko** grape.

Saperavi Russian red grape variety, with good colour and high **acidity**. Planted throughout the **CIS**, and best used for blending with other varieties.

Sardinia Island belonging to **Italy**, making good dry reds from the **Cannonau** grape. It also produces sweet, red **Girò di Cagliari**, sturdy red **Mandrolisai** and soft light reds from the **Monica** grape variety. Dry to sweet white **Nasco di Cagliari**, neutral white **Nuragus di Cagliari** and dry red **Campidano di Terralba** are also made.

Sartène See **Vin de Corse**.

Sassella See **Valtellina**.

Saten Italian term for lightly-sparkling quality wines of **Franciacorta**.

Saumur AC wine of the **Loire** valley, produced around the town of Saumur. Good, white **méthode traditionnelle** sparkling wine (often labelled Saumur d'Origine) is made from the **Chenin Blanc** grape, plus **Cabernet Franc** and, increasingly, **Chardonnay**. Still wines are also made, both white and red, based mainly on Chenin Blanc and Cabernet Franc respectively; both are usually rather thin and **astringent**.

Saumur-Champigny Red **AC** wine produced in vineyards near **Saumur**, in the **Loire** valley. This dry, **grassy**, usually good-quality red is based mainly on the **Cabernet Franc** grape variety, sometimes with **Cabernet Sauvignon**. Best drunk young.

Sauternes Sweet white **AC** wine of **Bordeaux**, produced from the **Sémillon**, **Sauvignon Blanc**, and **Muscadelle** varieties. This is one of the world's finest dessert wines, with marvellous richness and complexity of exotic fruit flavours. Its distinctive rich balance between fruit and **acidity** derives from the action of **botrytis** on the grapes. The particular concentration of Sauternes also has a lot to do with low **yields**, and successive pickings at harvest time, to ensure that every grape is gathered at the optimum degree of ripeness. Consequently, Sauternes can never be 'cheap'. See also **Barsac**.

Sauvignon Blanc Important white grape variety, planted in many wine-producing countries of the world. Its two main homes, in **France**, are **Bordeaux**

and the **Loire**. In the Loire, **Sancerre** and **Pouilly-Fumé** are the archetypal examples of 100% Sauvignon. In Bordeaux, it is sometimes vinified alone to make a crisp dry wine, but more usually blended with **Sémillon** (and **Muscadelle**) to make dry wines (in **Graves** and **Entre-Deux-Mers**), or lusciously sweet dessert wines (in **Sauternes** and **Barsac**).

In **Italy** it is found in **Alto Adige** and **Friuli-Venezia Giulia**. Many New World countries have adopted Sauvignon, but none with more success than **New Zealand**, with zesty, juicy fruit wines that can rival the best of the Loire.

Sauvignon de Saint-Bris Crisp, white **VDQS** wine of northern **Burgundy**, produced in Saint-Bris-le-Vineux, not far from **Chablis**, from the **Sauvignon Blanc** grape variety. At its best, it can rival much generic Sauvignon from the **Loire**, in terms of quality and value for money.

Savagnin (also called Gringet) White grape variety almost unique to the **Jura** region of **France**, where it contributes to the blend for the white **table wines**, and is central to the production of **vins jaunes**.

Savennières White **AC** wine of **Anjou-Saumur**, in the **Loire** valley, probably the finest expression of dry wine produced from the **Chenin Blanc** grape. The wines are highly assertive and acidic in their youth, mellowing, and becoming almost honeyed, as they slowly mature. There are separate ACs for two particularly good sites: Coulée-de-Serrant and La Roche-aux-Moines.

Savigny-lès-Beaune AC wine of the **Côte de Beaune** region of **Burgundy**. Fairly good, if somewhat light, strawberry-flavoured reds are produced from the **Pinot Noir** grape variety, plus a little white from **Chardonnay**.

Savoie See **Vin de Savoie**.

Savuto Red **DOC** wine produced in the **Calabria** region of southern **Italy**. A dry juicy red, it ranges from pale cherry to full ruby in colour, made mainly from the **Gaglioppo**, **Greco** Nero and **Nerello** Cappuccio grape varieties.

Schaumwein German term for basic-quality sparkling wine.

Scheurebe White grape variety, a **cross** of **Silvaner** and **Riesling**, planted throughout the wine regions of **Germany**. It has been underestimated in the past, but has recently been shown to be capable of producing excellent **QmP** quality wines.

Schiava (also called Trollinger; Vernatsch) Red grape variety, planted widely in the **Alto Adige** region of northeast **Italy** (where it is often known as Vernatsch), and in Württemburg in **Germany** (alias Trollinger). It generally produces quite light red wine, lacking in character and **tannin**, and best drunk young and fresh. See also **Caldaro**.

Schloss German for castle. Wines that bear the name of a particular *schloss* must have been produced entirely from vines grown in the estate's vineyards. However, the word *schloss* may also feature in an

Einzellage or district name, so it does not always
indicate an estate wine.

Schloss Böckelheim Bereich subregion of the **Nahe**
region of **Germany**, producing good-quality white
wines, especially from the **Riesling** grape.

Schlossböckelheim Small, but important, village in
the **Nahe** region of **Germany**. It produces very high
quality white wines from the **Riesling** grape. The
vineyards come under the **Grosslage** of Burgweg, and
the best **Einzellage** site is Kupfergrube.

Schönburger White grape variety, a **cross** between
Pinot Noir and Pirovano (itself a cross of **Chasselas**
Rosé and **Muscat** of Hamburg), grown in limited
quantity in the **Rheinhessen** and **Pfalz** regions of
Germany, and also in **England**. The grapes are pink,
producing white wine, with an **aroma** similar to
Gewürztraminer, but slightly **flabby** and lacking in
acidity.

Sciacarello Red grape variety of **Corsica** producing
characterful reds and rosés.

sec French term meaning dry for still wines, but
relatively sweet (sweeter than **brut**) for sparkling wines.

secco Italian term meaning dry for still wines, but off-
dry for sparkling wines.

seco Spanish and Portuguese for dry.

second wine Category of wine produced in **Bordeaux**,
particularly by the **cru classé** châteaux of the **Médoc**.

The production of the very highest quality red Bordeaux involves careful selection of vats of wine, after **fermentation**. Only the very best vats of wine will be blended to form the **grand vin**, which will bear the **château** name. Slightly inferior lots of wine, particularly those made from young vines, may be bottled under a different name and sold at a lower price. This provides consumers with excellent wine from top properties at an affordable price. Second wines are not to be confused with 'second growths', or *deuxièmes crus classés*.

Sekt German term for sparkling wine. Unless the label says Deutscher Sekt, the wine is probably made from low-quality imported base wine, from **Italy**, **France**, or **Spain**. A few producers make an effort to produce quality Deutscher Sekt some using **Riesling** and the **méthode traditionnelle**, but in general quality leaves something to be desired.

Sélection des Grains Nobles Special category of wines from **Alsace**, made from late-picked grapes affected by **botrytis**. Usually made from the **Riesling** or **Gewürztraminer** grapes (sometimes **Muscat** or **Pinot Gris**), they are usually sweet, very concentrated, and of very high quality (and price). See also **vendange tardive**.

semi-secco Italian for medium dry; in practice the taste is medium-sweet.

semi-seco Spanish for medium dry; in practice the taste is medium-sweet.

Sémillon White grape variety, grown in many wine-producing regions throughout the world, but to best effect in **Bordeaux** and **Australia** (especially the **Hunter Valley**). The great white wines of Bordeaux, whether sweet, (e.g **Sauternes** and **Barsac**), or dry, (e.g. **Graves**), are usually a blend of Sémillon with **Sauvignon Blanc**, and possibly also **Muscadelle**.

The variety's particular susceptibility to **botrytis** is of great importance in the sweet wines. The best Australian Sémillon is bottled as a **varietal** wine. It is nearly always dry, and often capable of developing great complexity with **bottle age**. Large plantings of Sémillon also exist in **Chile** and **Brazil**, but **yields** here are so high that the wine rarely has any varietal character. See also **Bergerac**; **Buzet**; **Entre-Deux-Mers**; **Gaillac**; **Haut Montravel**; **Loupiac**; **Monbazillac**; **Montecarlo**; **Montravel**; **Pessac-Léognan**.

Serbia Large republic of the former Yugoslavia, producing mainly red wine from the native Prokupac grape along with **Cabernet Sauvignon**, **Merlot**, **Pinot Noir**, and **Gamay**.

Sercial Grape variety, grown on the island of **Madeira**, where it gives its name to a category of wine. Light, delicate and perfumed, savoury and high in acid, Sercial is the driest, lightest style of Madeira.

Setúbal Fortified white wine of **Portugal**, which is deep, sweet, luscious and capable of long **ageing**, in cask or bottle. Formerly called Moscatel de Setúbal.

Sèvre et Maine See **Muscadet**.

Seyssel White **AC** wine of the Savoie region of **France**. The **méthode traditionnelle** Seyssel **Mousseux** is a

S

light, refreshing sparkler made from the **Molette** and
Altesse grape varieties. The still wine is based on
Altesse, and is dry, full-bodied, spicy, and **aromatic**.

Seyval Blanc White **hybrid** grape variety, a **cross**
between two varieties of Seibel (themselves both
hybrids), widely planted in the vineyards of **England**.
It produces high yields of medium-quality wine, often
with a distinctive grapefruit flavour.

Seyve-Villard 5276 Alternative name for the **Seyval
Blanc** grape variety.

Sfursat See **Valtellina**.

sharp Tasting term, usually used to indicate a wine with
too much **acidity**. A sharp young wine may achieve
better balance with maturity.

Sherry (also called **Jerez**; **Xérès**) **Fortified wine**,
produced in Andalusia in southern **Spain** around the
towns of Jerez de la Frontera, Sanlúcar de Barrameda,
and Puerto de Santa Maria. The most important grape
is the **Palomino**, best grown on the chalky white
albariza soil, and small amounts of **Pedro Ximénez** and
Moscatel are also grown.

Fino is a pale, bone dry, pungent Sherry. Its distinctive,
tangy **aroma** and flavour are the result of **ageing**
the wine in the **solera** system under a layer of **yeast** cells
called **flor**. A *fino* must spend at least three years in the
solera system, in Jerez or Puerto de Santa Maria, before
bottling. Fino from Sanlúcar de Barrameda is called

manzanilla. *Fino* and *manzanilla*, served correctly chilled, are among the best apéritifs of all.

Amontillado is a completely dry, nutty Sherry, with an amber colour, which results when a fino is allowed to mature without being refreshed with younger wines. Less expensive medium-sweet Sherries are often described as *amontillado*, but in fact these are sweetened blends containing only a small amount of true *amontillado*. The same is true of **oloroso**, which is used to describe any dark, sweet Sherry. A true *oloroso* is a rich, nutty, dark style, which takes up its flavour from long **ageing** in cask, rather than from flor. True *oloroso* is dry, but often it is sweetened to make a commercial blend by adding some Pedro Ximénez wine, and sometimes it is darkened with **vino de color**.

Cream Sherry is a sweetened, darkened *oloroso*. **Pale Cream** combines the sweetness of Cream Sherry with the colour of a *fino*. The style is made by sweetening young *fino* with pale grape juice concentrate, or by removing the colour from dark Sherry using carbon. It never has the complex flavour of the traditional Sherry styles. Real Sherry comes only from Spain, though the style is widely imitated in other countries. See also **almacenista**; **Palo cortado**.

Shiraz Alternative name, used in **Australia**, for the **Syrah** grape variety.

short Tasting term, used to describe a wine in which the flavour does not persist on the **palate**, once the wine is swallowed. See **finish**; **length**.

Sicily Island off the coast of southern **Italy**. It was traditionally famed for its **fortified wine Marsala**, but now has a growing reputation for **table wine**, mostly produced outside the **DOC** system. Most of the wines are based on native Italian grape varieties, including the white **Catarratto**, **Inzolia** and **Grillo**, and the red **Calabrese** (or Nero d'Avola) and **Nerello** (both Cappuccio and Mascalese). See also **Alcamo**; **Etna**; **Faro**.

Siegerrebe White grape variety, a **cross** of **Madeleine Angevine** and **Gewürztraminer**, grown to a limited extent in **Germany**, mainly in the **Rheinhessen** and **Pfalz** regions, and also in **England**. It produces wines with a relatively high **alcohol** content, low **acidity**, and powerful **aroma**. Occasionally it is bottled as a **varietal**, but more usually it is used in tiny quantities to add richness and flavour to commercial blends with other grape varieties.

Sierra Foothills Large wine-producing area of **California**, including the **AVAs** of El Dorado, **Fiddletown**, and Shenandoah Valley.

silky Tasting term used to describe a wine with a soft, smooth, yet **firm** texture on the **palate**.

Silvaner (Sylvaner) White grape variety, planted widely in **Germany**, and also in **Alsace** (where it is usually spelled Sylvaner). In Germany it produces a fairly neutral wine, high in **acidity** and lacking in **aroma**, and is usually blended with more characterful varieties, such as **Riesling** and **Scheurebe**. In Alsace, Sylvaner is gradually being replaced by **Pinot Blanc** and **Riesling**; what remains often ends up blended with other Alsatian varieties, and labelled Edelzwicker or just **AC** Alsace. Sylvaner is also important in the **Alto Adige** in northern **Italy**, where it produces crisp, dry, fairly neutral whites.

sin crianza Spanish term, used to describe a wine with little or no **oak ageing**. See **Rioja**.

Single Quinta Port Category of **Port**, which in theory means a Vintage Port made from grapes grown in a single estate, or *quinta*. In fact, there are a number of variations. Some shippers use the Single Quinta category to market Port from an 'off' year, not good enough to declare as their true Vintage Port. Others, confusingly, use a single *quinta* name on Port that is a blend of wines from several *quintas*. The method of production is the same as for Vintage Port, although the required length of maturation in bottle may be shorter, because the wine is usually less concentrated and complex.

Sizzano Dry red **DOC** wine of northern **Piedmont** in **Italy**, produced around the village of the same name. Made from the **Nebbiolo** grape variety (known locally as **Spanna**), plus Vespolina and **Bonarda**, it is light (for Nebbiolo), but full-flavoured and easy to drink in its youth, although capable of up to 10 years' **ageing**.

Slovakia Eastern part of the former Czechoslovakia, and a more important wine country than the **Czech Republic**. Most of the vineyards are concentrated in the south of the country, along the Austrian and Hungarian borders, and planted with white varieties such as **Welschriesling**, **Müller-Thurgau**, and **Grüner Veltliner**. Reds made from **Blaufränkisch** (known locally as **Frankovka**) and Sankt Laurent grape varieties are less common.

Slovenia Republic of the former Yugoslavia, whose winemaking is influenced by its Italian and Austrian neighbours. Among the whites produced, **Laski Rizling** is grown around the town of Lutomer, and **Gewürztraminer**, **Sauvignon Blanc**, and **Pinot Blanc** are also found. The reds are more Italian influenced, with **Refosco**, **Barbera** and lightish **Cabernet** and **Merlot**.

smoky Tasting term used to describe a subtle wood-smoke **aroma**. It is used particularly for some good-quality white wines, made from **Chardonnay**, and many high-quality reds made from **Pinot Noir**, **Syrah** or **Cabernet Sauvignon**, among others.

Soave Dry white **DOC** wine of the **Veneto** region of **Italy**, and one of the best-known of all Italian wines. Soave is made mainly from the **Garganega** grape variety, with some **Trebbiano** and the possible addition of **Chardonnay**. Traditionally, it has been thought of as a rather bland, neutral white, and that reputation remains true for much of what is produced today, although there are exceptions.

The best vineyard sites are on the hills of the Soave **Classico** subregion, and wines from here are nearly always better. Also, some quality-conscious producers have produced characterful Soave by reducing **yields**, making single-vineyard wines from particularly good sites and, in some cases, **ageing** the wines in **barrique**. The best Soave has soft fruit, with a nutty, creamy taste. It is sometimes made **spumante**, by the **Charmat method**. There is also a sweet **recioto** version, made from dried grapes. See **Recioto di Soave**.

soft Tasting term used to describe a wine with a mellow, unaggressive taste and texture. It is also often used to qualify **tannin** (gentle, rather than harsh tannin); and fruitiness (rounded, well-integrated fruit).

solera System by which **Sherry** (and some other fortified wines) are aged. A *solera* can be thought of as a series of rows of **butts** (barrels of 600 litres) piled one on top of the other. When Sherry is required for bottling, it is drawn off from the bottom row of butts (the solera). These are then topped up with slightly younger wine from the row above (a *criadera*), and so on. In fact, the *solera* is often more complicated than this, and the different scales are often not one on top of the other – they may even be in different **bodegas**; but the general principle is the same, i.e. the production of a consistently aged and refreshed final blend. See also **amontillado**; **fino**.

Somontano DO wine of northeast **Spain**, produced in the foothills of the Pyrenees. Most of the production is of red wine, mainly from the local Moristel grape and **Garnacha**, plus some new plantings of **Cabernet Sauvignon** and **Tempranillo**, among other varieties. A little **rosado** is produced, also mainly from Moristel, and a very small quantity of white from **Macabeo**. The reds are light, **aromatic** and easy-drinking, and quality is improving rapidly.

Sonoma Important wine-producing county of **California**, just to the west of **Napa Valley**. The region and microclimates are extremely varied, meaning that almost all the California varieties can be grown successfully somewhere in Sonoma.

The **Alexander Valley AVA** produces fine **Zinfandel**, **Pinot Noir**, **Cabernet Sauvignon** and **Chardonnay**. **Russian River Valley** has a relatively cool climate, producing good Chardonnay, Pinot Noir, **Riesling** and **Gewürztraminer**. Successful **méthode traditionnelle** sparkling wines are also made here, from Chardonnay and Pinot Noir.

The **Dry Creek Valley** AVA produces superb **Sauvignon Blanc**, and excellent reds from Zinfandel and Cabernet Sauvignon. **Knights Valley** has a growing reputation for rich and elegant Cabernets. See also **Carneros**.

Sorni DOC wine of the **Trentino** region of **Italy**. The white version is based on the Nosiola grape variety; the red on **Schiava**. Both are light, fresh and fruity, best drunk young.

South Africa Main wine-producing country of Africa, with vineyards concentrated around the Cape of Good Hope, traditionally making **fortified wines** in the style of **Port** and **Sherry**. Today **varietal table wines** have become more important. **Chenin Blanc** (or **Steen**) is the most important white, though there are also fine whites being made from **Chardonnay** and **Sauvignon Blanc**. The best reds are made from **Cabernet Sauvignon**, **Shiraz**, **Cinsault**, Tinta Barocca, and **Pinotage**, a **cross** of **Pinot Noir** and Cinsault. The major zones are Constantia (legendary sweet whites based on **Muscat**, now seeing a revival); Stellenbosch (best known for **Cabernet**, **Merlot**, Shiraz, and Pinotage, but also producing good Chardonnay and Sauvignon Blanc); Paarl (old-style fortified wines plus a few red and white varietals); and Robertson (mainly whites, including Muscat, **Gewürztraminer**, and Chardonnay).

South Australia Most important wine-producing state of **Australia**, including the regions **Adelaide Hills**, **Barossa Valley**, **Clare Valley**, **Coonawarra**, **Eden Valley**, **McLaren Vale**, **Padthaway**, and **Riverland**. Many of the country's largest wine companies are based here.

Spain Important wine-producing country, best known for **Sherry** and for its reds from **Rioja** and **Ribera del Duero**. Rioja's neighbour, **Navarra**, produces wines in a similar style, although not yet reaching the high quality of top **Rioja**. See also **Léon**. Just west of Ribera, **Rueda** produces some of Spain's best whites. In the northeast of the country, **Penedès** produces good reds and whites, mainly from 'foreign' grape varieties, and is the main centre for **Cava** production; **Priorato** is rich, high-**alcohol** red wine. See also **Alella**; **Ampurdán-Costa Brava**; **Conca de Barberá**; **Somontano**; **Tarragona**; **Terra Alta**.

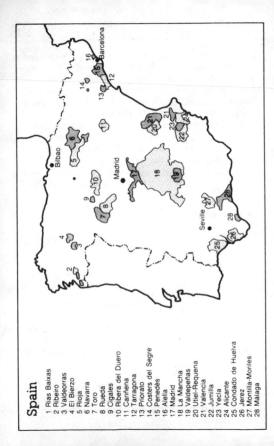

Spain

1 Rias Baixas
2 Ribeiro
3 Valdeorras
4 El Bierzo
5 Rioja
6 Navarra
7 Toro
8 Rueda
9 Cigales
10 Ribera del Duero
11 Cariñena
12 Tarragona
13 Priorato
14 Costers del Segre
15 Penedés
16 Alella
17 Madrid
18 La Mancha
19 Valdepeñas
20 Utiel-Requena
21 Valencia
22 Jumilla
23 Yecla
24 Alicante
25 Condado de Huelva
26 Jerez
27 Montilla-Moriles
28 Málaga

In central Spain, **La Mancha** is a source of vast quantities of easy-drinking reds and whites, while **Valdepeñas** has some rapidly improving reds; see also **Méntrida**. Eastern central Spain is home of large quantities of mediocre red and white; see **Alicante**, **Almansa**, **Jumilla**, **Utiel-Requena** and **Valencia**. In **Galicia** in the northwest, near the Portuguese border, the best wines are fresh, fruity whites from **Rias Baixas**. Other fortified wines apart from Sherry are **Málaga** and **Montilla-Moriles**. See also **Mallorca**.

Spanna Alternative name, used in northern **Piedmont**, for the **Nebbiolo** grape variety, particularly by the makers of **Boca**, **Bramaterra**, **Fara**, **Gattinara**, **Ghemme**, **Lessona**, and **Sizzano**.

Spätburgunder Alternative name, used in **Germany**, for the **Pinot Noir** grape variety.

Spätlese German and Austrian quality white wine category, meaning '**late harvest**'. The ripe grapes are picked at least seven days after the official start of the harvest, resulting in a higher **must weight** than for **Kabinett** wines. The wines can be relatively sweet and honeyed, although many *Spätlese* wines are produced in the **trocken** (dry) or **halbtrocken** styles. See **QmP**.

Spätrot Alternative name for the **Zierfändler** grape variety.

spicy Tasting term, used to describe a herby, **aromatic** flavour. It can derive from the grape variety, for example **Syrah** often has a spicy taste, or from **ageing** the wine in **oak** barrels.

spumante Italian term for fully sparkling wine. See also **frizzante**.

Squinzano DOC wine of the **Apulia** region of southern **Italy**, produced around the town of Squinzano, mainly from the **Negroamaro** grape variety. Red and **rosato** wines are produced, both dry, and both capable of reasonably good quality.

Stag's Leap Important **AVA** in the **Napa Valley** area of **California**. Red **varietal** wines made from **Cabernet Sauvignon** can be of world class, and are as good here as from any part of the Napa.

stalky Tasting term used to describe a fresh, sappy, immature **aroma** and taste, usually used of young, fairly raw red wine.

Steen Alternative name, used in **South Africa**, for **Chenin Blanc**.

Steigerwald Bereich subregion of **Franken**, Germany.

Südliche Weinstrasse Bereich subregion of the **Pfalz**, **Germany**. It produces mainly cheap and cheerful wines, inferior to those of the northern Pfalz Bereich, the Mittelhaardt-Deutsche Weinstrasse.

Südtirol See **Alto Adige**.

sugar Vital ingredient in grapes, sugar is converted into **alcohol** by the action of **yeast** during **fermentation**. In some areas, where grapes do not always have a sufficient level of natural sugar, the addition of sugar (**chaptalization**) is permitted to boost the final alcohol content. The amount of sugar that can be added is controlled by law.

sulphur dioxide Essential additive to nearly all wines, even those described as **organic**, although all good winemakers will keep its use to a minimum. It combines anti-oxidant and disinfectant properties and is used to kill wild **yeast** on grape skins before they are fermented, to sterilize barrels and bottles, and to eliminate any bacterial infection – and prevent **oxidation** – in fermented wine. In some countries, notably the **United States** and **Australia**, the use of sulphur dioxide must be declared on the label.

Super Tuscan Popular term for high-quality wines made in **Tuscany**, **Italy**, which originally fell outside **DOC**/G regulations and were therefore classed, anomalously, as **vini da tavola**. Currently classifications are changing so that the 100% **Sangiovese** wines in **Chianti Classico**, for example, now fall within the Chianti Classico DOCG, and most of the other unorthodox blends or **varietals** can now be classed as **IGT** (see **Tuscany**). The concept of 'super' wines is now spreading to **Piedmont** (see **Taglio Langhe**) and **Veneto**.

supple Tasting term, used to indicate a wine with a **soft**, easy-drinking combination of fruit, **acidity**, and **tannin**.

sur lie Term found on some French wine labels, usually **Muscadet**, to indicate that the wine is matured on the lees, or dead **yeast** cells, and, in theory, bottled straight from the barrel. The wine can develop a delicious yeasty complexity, sometimes with a slightly **pétillant** prickle on the tongue. Many other white wines will have been aged sur lie, without this necessarily being declared on the label.

Süssreserve German term for unfermented grape juice, which is added to fermented wine before bottling to increase the sweetness. The quality and origin of the juice is regulated by law. The same technique is sometimes used for **English wine**.

Swan Valley Wine-producing region of **Western Australia**. It has a hot climate (one of the hottest wine regions in the world), and produces mainly big white wines, from **Chenin Blanc** and **Verdelho**, plus some reds from **Shiraz** and **Cabernet Sauvignon**.

sweaty Tasting term used to indicate a pungent, leathery **aroma**, often associated with wines made from the **Syrah** grape variety.

sweet Tasting term, self-explanatory for white wines, where it indicates a relatively high level of **residual sugar**. It is also used for red wines, which although technically dry may have rich, ripe fruit flavours, which give an impression of sweetness.

Switzerland Wine-producing country known mainly for its white wines from the cantons of Vaud and Valais. Valais, in the upper Rhône valley, produces light, white wines from the **Chasselas** grape, and a red wine, **Dôle**, from **Gamay** and **Pinot Noir**. Vaud includes the vineyards along the shore of Lake Geneva and the wine area of La Côte. Chasselas is again the principal grape variety grown. Among the most notable whites are those from the villages of Aigle and Yvorne in the Chablais region, in the west of Vaud.

Sylvaner See **Silvaner**.

Syrah Red grape variety, grown particularly in the northern **Rhône**, where it makes the great red wines of **Hermitage**, **Cornas** and **Côte Rôtie**, and in **Australia** (where it is known as **Shiraz**) and may be used for blending, often with **Cabernet Sauvignon**, although it makes superb, characterful **varietal** wine. When vinified on its own, Syrah can produce top-quality wines, with a peppery, spicy flavour, sometimes smoky, and often very long lived. The top Rhône wines, especially, need time to show their best. Syrah also provides structure and longevity to many other French wines, particularly elsewhere in the Rhône (where it is often blended with **Grenache**), in **Provence** and in the **Midi** (where it can be found in blended and varietal **Vin de pays** d'Oc and many **AC** wines).

T

table wine 1. General term for any wine that is not **fortified**. 2. General term for a wine not entitled to any quality designation. Defined by the EU as the category of wine below 'quality wine'. See also **tafelwein**; **vin de table**; **vino da tavola**; **vino de mesa**.

Tâche, La See **La Tâche**.

Tafelwein Lowest category of German wine. *Tafelwein* can include wines from outside **Germany** (often from **Italy**), while **Deutscher Tafelwein** must be 100% German.

Taglio Langhe Italian term for the local Piedmontese blend of **Nebbiolo** and **Barbera**, aged in small **oak** barrels.

Talento Italian term grouping **metodo classico** wines from the major producing regions of **Piedmont**, **Oltrepò Pavese**, and **Trentino**.

Tannat Red grape variety of southwest **France**, used as part of the blend to make **Madiran**, **Tursan**, **Irouléguy** and **Béarn**. It produces wines of deep colour, red-fruit flavours, and high **alcohol** and **tannin** (leading to good **ageing** potential).

tannic Tasting term used to describe the level and quality of **tannin** in red wine. Tannin is usually

identified as a dry sensation on the gums and roof of
the mouth, sometimes accompanied by a leathery, or
cold tea, smell and taste. In high-quality young red
wines, the high tannin content can mask the fruit
flavours; as the wine matures, the tannin should
integrate with the fruit and **acidity** to yield a
harmonious, well-knit flavour.

tannin Group of chemical substances which contribute
importantly to the structure and **ageing** potential of red
wines. Tannin is found in grape skins, along with the
pigments that give red wine its colour. A long
maceration during **fermentation** leads to a high level of
tannin. Grape tannin can be supplemented by **oak**-
derived tannins, by ageing the wine in small oak **barrels**.

Tarragona DO wine of northeast **Spain**, produced in a
coastal region southwest of **Penedès**. Traditionally this
was a source of high-**alcohol** dessert wines; today most
of the production is of average-quality white wine.
Production is dominated by **co-operatives** and much of
the wine is sold for blending. There are three
subregions. El Campo de Tarragona produces mainly
white wine from the Penedès grape varieties, **Macabeo**,
Parellada and **Xarel-lo**. The red varieties **Cariñena** and
Garnacha are cultivated in the cooler Conca de Falset
area. Whites from Macabeo and Garnacha Blanca are
produced farther inland, in the more extreme climate
of Ribera de Ebro.

tartaric acid Naturally occuring acid, found in grape
juice and hence in wine. Tartaric acid is the most
important contributor to **acidity** in wine, essential for

balance, a refreshing taste, and good **ageing** potential. White crystals of tartrate salts can be precipitated from wine when chilled; they are harmless and tasteless. Nevertheless, many wine producers chill wines to around -5°C for several days, so that tartrates are precipitated before bottling.

Tasmania Island wine-producing region of **Australia**. Despite its southern location, the climate is highly varied. The usual **varietal** wines are produced, from **Cabernet Sauvignon**, **Pinot Noir** and **Chardonnay**, with mixed results, though there are some fine Cabernets with a distinctive cool-climate definition. The region shows greatest potential for **méthode traditionnelle** sparkling wine production.

tastevin Round, shallow, saucer-shaped cup, usually made of silver or silver plate, used for tasting wine, particularly in **Burgundy**. For serious tasting, especially appreciation of the **nose**, there is no substitute for a proper tasting glass.

Taurasi Red **DOCG** wine of the **Campania** region of southern **Italy**, produced in the hills surrounding the village of the same name, mainly from the **Aglianico** grape variety. This can be one of Italy's better reds, with deep colour and good **ageing** potential, although **austere** tannins can mask the fruit flavours in young Taurasi.

Tavel Rosé **AC** wine of the southern **Rhône**, made chiefly from the **Grenache** and **Cinsault** grape varieties, although others are allowed. It is a deep-coloured pink, always dry and high in **alcohol**, and the best examples have fresh, young strawberry fruit. It is best drunk young.

Tawny Port Style of **Port** that is matured in wooden barrels, rather than in bottle (as with Vintage Port), and hence develops a characteristic tawny colour. Tawny Port of indicated age can be described as 10-year-old, 20-year-old, 30-year-old, or over 40 years old. Most producers will aim for an average age corresponding to these descriptions, but the regulations simply require a 10-year-old, for instance, to have the characteristics expected of a 10-year-old Tawny Port. Dated Tawny, or **Colheita Port**, is Port of a single year, matured in wooden casks. The year of bottling must appear on the label, along with the year of harvest, and the label must state 'matured in wood', to help avoid confusion with Vintage Port. Cheap Tawny is usually made by blending Ruby and White Port.

teinturier General term for those few red grape varieties that have pink (rather than white) juice.

Tempranillo (known as Tempranilla in **Argentina**) Red grape variety grown widely in **Spain**, particularly in the **Rioja** region where it is the most important variety in the blend for red wines, and **Navarra**. It can produce light, fruity wine for drinking young, as well as deep, full-flavoured reds, suitable for long **ageing** in both barrel and bottle. It is known as **Tinto Fino** in **Ribera del Duero**, **Cencibel** in **La Mancha** and **Valdepeñas** and Ull de Llebre in Catalonia. In **Portugal** it is a highly regarded grape for **Port** production, and goes under the name Tinta Roriz. Undoubtedly Spain's best native red variety, with great potential. It is also grown in Argentina, and in the Languedoc, **France**.

tenuta Italian for estate or farm.

Terlano (also called Terlaner) White **DOC** wine of the **Alto Adige** region of northeast **Italy**, produced on both banks of the Adige river, west of Bolzano. Terlano without a **varietal** designation is a fresh, fruity blend with at least 50% Pinot Bianco; it can be still or **spumante**. Apart from this there are seven varietal wines, made from **Chardonnay**, **Müller-Thurgau**, Pinot Bianco, **Riesling Italico**, **Riesling Renano**, **Sauvignon**, or **Silvaner**. Sauvignon is the most promising varietal, although at present it is produced in small quantities.

Teroldego Rotaliano DOC wine of the **Trentino** region of northeast **Italy**, producing deep, well-structured reds capable of moderate **ageing**, and light, flavourful **rosato** (or kretzer), best drunk young. Both are made from the Teroldego grape variety, unique to this region.

Terra Alta DO wine of northeast **Spain**, produced in a region just to the west of **Tarragona**. Like Tarragona, the traditional wines of Terra Alta were high-**alcohol** dessert wines. Now average-quality whites are made from Garnacha Blanca and **Macabeo**, and rather coarse reds from **Cariñena**, **Garnacha** and **Tempranillo**. The region is also an important source of communion wine.

terra rossa Reddish-brown clay-limestone soil found in southern Europe and, notably, in **Coonawarra**,

Australia. Such soil is said to be propitious for the production of fine **Cabernet Sauvignon**.

Terre di Franciacorta DOC still wine made in the same area as **Franciacorta**. The white is made exclusively from Pinot Bianco and is smooth, fruity, and well balanced, best drunk within two to three years. The red is made from the **Cabernet Franc**, **Nebbiolo** and **Merlot** grapes. It is also of good quality, somewhat tough in its youth, with blackcurrant aromas; it becomes smooth, rounded, and fragrant with moderate age.

Terret Red grape variety, one of the 13 permitted for **Châteauneuf-du-Pape**. A white Terret is widely planted in the Languedoc, where it can produce crisp, light white wine.

terroir French term used to embrace all the characteristics of a vineyard site (including soil type, climate, etc). Although New World winemakers have pursued the **varietal** path, the French maintain that it is *terroir* which determines the distinctive identity of a wine.

tête de cuvée Unofficial French term designating the best lots of wine from a grower or *appellation*. In exceptional years an estate may make a separate *tête de cuvée* bottling; or a producer may use the term on the label to distinguish what is considered a superior wine.

Texas Still emerging wine-producing state of the **United States**, where fairly recent plantings of **Vitis**

vinifera grapes are producing **varietal** wines, especially **Chardonnay**, **Cabernet Sauvignon**, and **Sauvignon Blanc**.

Tinta Barroca Red grape variety planted mainly in the **Douro** region of **Portugal**, and used as part of the blend for **Port**. It produces big, full, earthy, **tannic** wines. Also planted in **South Africa**, where it is used to make Port-style wines and **table wines**.

Tinta Cão Red grape variety planted in the **Douro** region of **Portugal**, where it is used as part of the blend for **Port**. It produces fine and complex wine, but at low yields. It is also allowed in **Dão** and red **Vinho Verde**.

Tinta Francisca Red grape variety planted in the **Douro** region of **Portugal**, where it is sometimes used in making **Port**, although it lacks concentration and is not one of the highest quality Port grapes. It is not related to **Pinot Noir**, as was once thought; nor is it related to Touriga Francesa.

Tinta Negra Mole Red grape variety planted on **Madeira**, where it is the most important ingredient in the island's **fortified wines**. Although the wines of Madeira are described by **varietal** names, most are blends consisting mainly of Tinta Negra Mole. It produces wines of high acid and deep colour, but otherwise fairly neutral, allowing the character of the designated grape variety (**Sercial**, **Verdelho**, **Bual**, or **Malmsey**) to show through.

Tinta Roriz See **Tempranillo**.

tinto Spanish and Portuguese for red.

Tinto Fino See **Tempranillo**.

Tocai di San Martino della Battaglia White **DOC** wine of the **Lombardy** region of **Italy**, produced just to the south of Lake Garda from the **Tocai Friulano** grape variety. It is a light, dry white, sometimes with a hint of lemony **acidity**, of moderate quality.

Tocai Friulano White grape variety found in the **Friuli-Venezia Giulia** region of northeast **Italy**, where it makes fresh, crisp white wines, especially in **Collio** and **Colli Orientali del Friuli**. It is also found in the **Veneto** and **Lombardy** regions. It is unrelated to Tokay-Pinot Gris or to the Hungarian Tokay.

Tokaji (also called Tokay) White wine of **Hungary**, produced in the Tokaj-Hegyalja region in the northeast of the country, in 28 villages including Tokaj itself, from the **Furmint** and **Hárslevelü** grape varieties.

When less than half of a particular vineyard is affected by **botrytis**, all the grapes are harvested together and used to make Szamorodni, which can be dry or sweet, depending on the natural sugar content of the grapes. The most famous style is Tokaji Aszú. During the harvest, botrytis-affected (*Aszú*) grapes are kept separate, while the others are fermented to make a base wine, which is stored in casks of 136 litres. The *Aszú* grapes are crushed to make a paste, and the base wine is then poured over it.

The style of wine depends on how many hods, or *puttonyos*, of *Aszú* grapes are used for each cask of base wine: typically, Tokaji Aszú will be labelled as 3, 4, or 5 puttonyos. One to two days after mixing the base wine and *Aszú* grapes, the mixture is pressed and aged in barrel for four to six years. In the cellar, it is affected by a fungus similar to **flor** in **Sherry**. It is pale to deep amber in colour, with appley raisiny **aromas**, and rich, sweet, concentrated apple flavour on the **palate**. Tokaji Aszú Eszencia is an *Aszú* with more than 6 *puttonyos*. Tokaji Eszencia is an exceedingly rare wine made from the free-run juice of *Aszú* grapes; it takes years to ferment, often reaching only a few degrees of **alcohol**. It has traditionally been reserved for the death beds of kings and emperors, where miraculous efficacy is needed. Tokaji is sold in squat 50 cl bottles.

Tokay Anglicized name for **Tokaji**.

Tokay-Pinot Gris See **Pinot Gris**.

tonneau **Bordeaux** measure of volume for bulk wine, originally a wooden cask of 900 litres. The casks have long since disappeared, but wine is still bought and sold using this unit of measure.

Torgiano **DOC** (and **DOCG**) wine of the **Umbria** region of **Italy**. The fresh and fruity **bianco** is made mainly from **Trebbiano** and **Grechetto**, and the **rosso** (known as Rubesco), full-flavoured and high quality, from **Sangiovese** and **Canaiolo**. Torgiano Rosso **riserva**, aged for three years, is entitled to the DOCG designation.

Toro DO wine of northwest **Spain**. Most of the production is good-quality, fruity red wine, made mainly from the **Tempranillo** grape variety plus some **Garnacha**. Quality is improving with each vintage. Some whites are also made, mainly from **Malvasía**.

Torrontés Family of white grape varieties of which the most important is a floral, **aromatic** variety planted in **Argentina**.

tough Tasting term, used to indicate a full-bodied wine (usually red) with an over-high **tannin** content. A tough young wine should mellow as it matures.

Touraine Wine-producing region of the **Loire** valley, centred on the city of Tours. High quality white wines are made from the **Chenin Blanc** grape variety in the ACs of **Vouvray** and **Montlouis**, which can be dry, **demi-sec** or **moelleux**, and still or sparkling. **Jasnières**, produced to the north of Tours, is bone dry Chenin Blanc. The best reds are made from **Cabernet Franc** in **Chinon**, **Bourgueil** and **Saint-Nicolas-de-Bourgueil**. The basic Touraine **AC** includes the white Sauvignon de Touraine (variable in quality, but much cheaper than **Sancerre**). Red AC Touraine, again of variable quality, is made mainly from the **Gamay** grape variety, and occasionally **Pinot Noir**. Touraine Tradition is a blend of Gamay, Cabernet Franc, and **Cot**, which works well.

Three villages can add their names to the Touraine AC. Touraine-Amboise includes good red made from Cot, light fruity red from Gamay, and good dry Chenin Blanc. Touraine-Azay-le-Rideau makes unexciting rosé from **Grolleau** and decent whites, dry or *demi-sec*, from Chenin Blanc. Touraine-Mesland produces excellent red from Gamay and Cabernet Franc, and some decent dry Chenin Blanc.

Touriga Francesa Red grape variety, planted in the **Douro** region of **Portugal**, where it is one of the most important ingredients in the blend for **Port**. It produces good-quality, **aromatic** wine, slightly lighter in colour and weight than **Touriga Nacional**. It is not related to **Tinta Francisca**.

Touriga Nacional Red grape variety, planted in the **Douro** region of **Portugal**, where it is probably the finest ingredient in the blend for **Port**. It produces deep, dark, powerful wines, with intense aromas and black-fruit flavours. It is also found in red **Dão**, where it must make up at least 20% of the blend.

Traben-Trarbach Village of the **Mosel-Saar-Ruwer** region of **Germany**, which produces medium-quality white wines from the **Riesling** grape variety. The vineyards come under the **Grosslage** of Schwarzlay, and the **Einzellage** sites include Burgberg, Gaispfad, Hühnerberg, Königsberg, Kräuterhaus, Kreuzberg, Schlossberg, Taubenhaus, Ungsberg, Würzgarten (the best) and Zollturm.

Traminer **Clone** of the **Gewürztraminer** grape variety, used in **Alsace** (where it is also called Klevener), in **Germany** to produce similarly spicy, but less pungent wine, and in the **Czech Republic**. Also used as a synonym for the true Gewürztraminer throughout the **CIS** and in **Australia**.

Traminer Aromatico An alternative name, used in Italy, for the **Gewürztraminer** grape.

Trebbiano (also called **Ugni Blanc**) White grape variety, producing more wine than any other variety in the world, thanks as much to high **yields** as to the overall area planted. Its home is **Italy**, where it produces more or less characterless white wine throughout the country: it also contributes to the blend for several red wines, including easy-drinking young **Chianti**. In **France** it is the most important variety in the Charentes area, where it is known as **Saint-Emilion**: most of it is distilled to make Cognac, the finest brandy. As Ugni Blanc, it is used to make Armagnac brandy. Ugni Blanc also contributes to the blend for many white wines of the **Midi**, and also for **Bandol** and **Palette** in **Provence**. It is also planted in **Australia** and **California**, mainly for brandy production or for blended whites.

Trebbiano d'Abruzzo Dry white **DOC** wine of the **Abruzzo** region of Italy, made from the **Trebbiano** grape variety. Usually it is dull and best drunk cold. Occasionally it is complex and deep, with good **ageing** potential. Price is a good guide to quality.

Trebbiano di Romagna White **DOC** wine of the **Emilia-Romagna** region of **Italy**. Usually it is clean, but dull and neutral. It can be dry, medium dry, or sweet, and still or sparkling.

Trentino Southern part of the Trentino-**Alto Adige**, Italy's northernmost wine region, the Trentino zone stretches along the Adige and Sarca valleys. The Trentino **DOC** comes in 20 different versions: 17 **varietals**, plus **bianco**, **rosso** and Vino Santo. Of the whites, bianco is a blend of **Chardonnay** and Pinot Bianco and the varietals are **Chardonnay**, **Moscato**, **Müller-Thurgau**, Nosiola, Pinot Bianco, Pinot Grigio, **Riesling Italico**, **Riesling Renano**, and **Traminer** Aromatico. Traditionally, they were blended together more or less indiscriminately to make Trentino Bianco. However, today, with modern winemaking techniques, most producers have chosen to market their wines under varietal designations. Much Chardonnay, Pinot Grigio and Pinot Bianco is also used in sparkling wine production in Trentino. **Rosso** is a blend of Cabernet and **Merlot**, and the red varietals are **Cabernet Franc**, **Cabernet Sauvignon**, **Lagrein**, **Marzemino**, Merlot and Pinot Nero. See **Casteller**; **Sorni**; **Teroldego Rotaliano**; **Valdadige**.

Trier Wine-producing city of the **Mosel-Saar-Ruwer** region of **Germany**. There are vineyards within the city boundaries, which come under the **Grosslage** of Römerlay, but the many **Einzellage** names are rarely used.

trocken German term for dry wines, designed for drinking with food. The **residual sugar** level is controlled; up to 4 grams per litre, or up to 9 grams per litre if specifications of sufficient balancing **acidity** are also met. See also **halbtrocken**.

Trockenbeerenauslese German and Austrian quality white wine category meaning 'selected dried grapes'. Individually selected, shrivelled, overripe grapes, usually affected by **botrytis**, are cut from the bunches, and pressed carefully. A high minimum **must weight** is laid down, but the **fermentation** usually stops when the **alcohol** content has reached only about 6%. This results in exceedingly sweet, rich, and luscious wines, with balancing **acidity**, and long **ageing** potential. They are most successfully made from the **Riesling** grape. See also **QmP**.

Trollinger See **Schiava**.

Tronçais Forest in **France** where some of the best **oak** is grown for making barrels for **ageing** wine. See also **Allier**; **Nevers**.

Trousseau Alternative name, used in **France**, for the **Bastardo** grape variety, which is used with **Poulsard** to make the red wine of **Jura**.

Turkey East Mediterranean country producing large quantities of grapes, only a small proportion of which are turned into wine. Along with a host of native varieties, there are plantings of **Gamay**, **Grenache**, **Carignan**, **Pinot Noir**, **Sémillon**, and **Riesling**. The wines are rarely well made, and frequently oxidised.

Tursan VDQS wine from the foothills of the Pyrenees, in southwest **France**. The tough, **tannic** red and rosé versions are made from the **Tannat**, **Cabernet Sauvignon** and **Cabernet Franc** grape varieties. Charmless, strong-tasting white wines, with little **aroma**, are made from the **Baroque** grape variety.

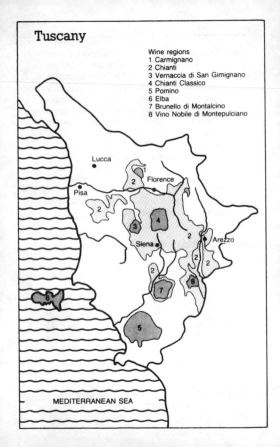

Tuscany

Wine regions
1 Carmignano
2 Chianti
3 Vernaccia di San Gimignano
4 Chianti Classico
5 Pomino
6 Elba
7 Brunello di Montalcino
8 Vino Nobile di Montepulciano

Lucca

Florence

Pisa

Siena

Arezzo

MEDITERRANEAN SEA

Tuscany Major wine-producing region of central **Italy**. Some of the country's best red wines are made here: **Chianti** (particularly Chianti **Classico**), **Brunello di Montalcino**, **Vino Nobile di Montepulciano**, **Morellino di Scansano**, all based on the **Sangiovese** grape variety; **Carmignano**; **Pomino**; and many **IGTs** (increasingly), or **vini da tavola** (less often), based on Sangiovese, **Cabernet Sauvignon**, **Merlot** and **Syrah**, either as **varietals** or as blends. The most prestigious red wines now come from the **Bolgheri** region. White wines can also be fine, although few reach the heights of the best reds. See **Bianco della Val d'Arbia**; **Bianco della Valdinievole**; **Bianco di Pitigliano**; **Bianco Pisano San Torpè**; **Bianco Vergine della Valdichiana**; **Bolgheri**; **Elba**; **Galestro**; **Montecarlo**; **Moscadello di Montalcino**; **Parrina**; **Vin Santo**.

Txakoli See Chacolí de Guetaria.

U

Ugni Blanc See **Trebbiano**.

Ukraine Important wine-producing republic of the **CIS**, with most vineyards centred on the **Crimea** and Odessa regions. There is a wide variety of grapes planted, including **Rkatsiteli**, **Aligoté**, **Cabernet Sauvignon**, **Saperavi**, **Riesling**, **Gewürztraminer**, **Pinot Gris**, and **Feteasca**. Traditional sweet wines and sparkling wines are still produced, along with red and white **varietals** of promising quality.

Ull de Llebre Alternative name, used in Catalonia, for the **Tempranillo** grape variety.

ullage 'Loss' of wine in bottle, owing to a faulty cork, or natural contraction. The level of wine in very old bottles can fall from the neck to the middle of the shoulder, or below. If below mid-shoulder, the wine is said to be 'badly ullaged', and should be regarded with some suspicion, because the risk of **oxidation** is high.

Ullage also refers to the air-space in a barrel or tank, which should be kept to a minimum (preferably zero) to prevent oxidation. Wine aged 'on ullage' in cask will oxidise and may develop **rancio** flavours.

Umbria Wine-producing region of central **Italy**. Umbria's most famous wine is **Orvieto**, usually a crisp, nutty, dry white for early drinking, but sometimes

sweet. There is also high-quality white and red
Torgiano, and good value reds from **Montefalco**
(especially Sagrantino). See also **Colli Martani**; **Colli
Perugini**; **Grechetto**.

unbalanced Tasting term used to describe a wine with
an excess or deficiency of one or more elements, for
instance, **acidity**, **tannin**, or **alcohol**.

Ungstein Wine-producing village in the **Pfalz** region
of **Germany**, producing full, fruity white wines. The
vineyards come within the **Grosslagen** of Hönigsackel,
Hochmess and Kobnert, and the **Einzellage** sites
include Herrenberg, Nussriegel, and Weilberg.

United States Important wine-producing country of
north America. Wine is produced in many states, but
most importantly in **California**, **Oregon** and
Washington State. See also **Finger Lakes**; **Idaho**; **New
York State**; **Texas**.

Ursprungslage German label term, proposed as a
replacement for **Grosslage**. In theory, it should give the
consumer a better idea of the style of wine to expect.

Uruguay Important south American wine-producing
country. Traditionally a producer of inferior rosés and
Tannat-based reds, there has been a recent move to
introduce international grape varieties and more
modern winemaking.

Ürzig Wine-producing village of the **Mosel-Saar-Ruwer**
region of **Germany**, producing good-quality white

United States

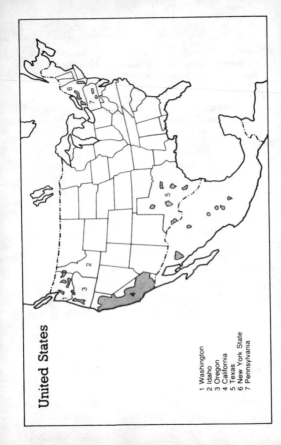

1 Washington
2 Idaho
3 Oregon
4 California
5 Texas
6 New York State
7 Pennsylvania

wine, mainly from the **Riesling** grape variety. The vineyards come within the **Grosslage** of Schwarzlay, and the best **Einzellage** site is Würzgarten.

Utiel Requena DO wine of eastern **Spain**, produced in a mountainous region just to the west of **Valencia**. Fresh, delicate, perfumed **rosado** wine is made from the **Bobal** grape, which is also used to make strong, flavourful, full-bodied reds. **Tempranillo** is gaining in importance, however, and there is the potential to make better-quality **varietal** reds.

Uva di Troia Good-quality red grape variety of southern **Italy**, grown particularly in the **Apulia** region.

Uva Rara Red grape variety, grown in **Oltrepò Pavese** in the **Lombardy** region of **Italy**.

Uzbekistan Wine-producing republic of the **CIS**, located in central Asia, with a long history of wine production. Much of the vineyard area is given over to table grapes, but wine grapes planted include **Aleatico**, **Riesling**, **Muscat**, **Saperavi**, and **Rkatsiteli**. There is good potential to produce commercial wines (as has been achieved in **Moldova**), but it is as yet largely unrealised.

V

VA See **volatile acidity**.

Vaccarese Red grape variety, one of 13 permitted in **Châteauneuf-du-Pape**. It produces wines similar in character to **Cinsault**.

Vacqueyras See **Côtes du Rhône**.

Vaillons Premier cru vineyard of **Chablis**.

Val d'Arbia See **Bianco della Val d'Arbia**.

Valais See **Switzerland**.

Valcalepio DOC wine produced in the Bergamo area of **Lombardy**, northwest **Italy**. The dry **rosso**, made from the **Cabernet Sauvignon** and **Merlot** grapes, can be of good quality. The **bianco**, from Pinot Bianco and Pinot Grigio, is usually quite ordinary.

Valdadige DOC wine of the **Trentino** region of northeast **Italy**. A white **varietal** is made from Pinot Grigio and a red from **Schiava**. **Bianco** is a blend based mainly on **Trebbiano**, Nosiola and Vernaccia, with the possible inclusion of some **Chardonnay**, Pinot Bianco, Pinot Grigio, **Riesling Italico** and **Müller-Thurgau**. **Rosso** and rosato are produced mainly from the **Lambrusco** and **Schiava** grapes, with occasionally **Lagrein**, **Merlot**, **Negrara**, Pinot Nero and Teroldego.

Valdeorras See **Galicia**.

Valdepeñas DO wine zone to the south of **La Mancha**, central **Spain**. The region produces mainly whites, made from the **Airén** grape. However, it is most famous for its reds, sometimes **oak**-aged, from the **Tempranillo** grape (known locally as **Cencibel**, as in La Mancha). Traditionally, the Cencibel was diluted with Airén, but today the best examples are 100% Cencibel: deep, soft, fruity wines, capable of moderate **ageing**, and good value for money.

Valençay VDQS wine produced in small quantities in the southeast corner of **Touraine** in the **Loire**. Fresh reds and rosés are produced mainly from the **Gamay** grape, with the possible addition of **Cabernet Sauvignon**, **Cabernet Franc** and **Merlot**. Crisp whites are made from at least 60% **Arbois**, **Chardonnay** or **Sauvignon Blanc**, with up to 40% Romorantin or **Chenin Blanc**.

Valencia DO wine produced inland from the **Port** of the same name, in eastern **Spain**. Most of the wine produced is dull, bland white, made from the **Merseguera** grape. Easy-drinking reds are made in the south of the region, mainly from **Garnacha** or **Monastrell**. A **mistelle**, called Moscatel de Valencia, is also produced, from a mixture of **Moscatel** juice and brandy.

Valgella See **Valtellina**.

Valle d'Aosta Small, alpine, French-speaking wine region of northwestern **Italy**. There is one **DOC**, Valle d'Aosta (or Valle d'Aoste), and red, white and rosé wines can be made from 22 different grape varieties. The wines are rarely seen outside the region. See **Blanc de Morgex et de La Salle**; **Enfer d'Arvier**.

Valle Isarco (also called Eisacktaler) White **DOC** wine of the **Alto Adige** region of northeast **Italy**. Five pure **varietal** wines are produced: **Müller-Thurgau**, Pinot Grigio, **Sylvaner**, **Traminer** Aromatico, and Veltliner. All are crisp, vibrant, fruity wines, with delicate **aromas** and good **varietal** character.

Valleé de la Marne Vineyard area in the **Champagne** region of **France**. It is planted mainly with the red grape varieties **Pinot Noir** and **Pinot Meunier**.

Valmur One of the seven **grand cru** vineyards of **Chablis**.

Valpolicella Red **DOC** wine from just north of Verona, in the **Veneto** region of **Italy**. It is produced from mainly the **Corvina**, **Rondinella**, and **Molinara** grape varieties. Most of the wine made is fruity, dry, cherry flavoured red for early-drinking, with a distinctive, slightly bitter **finish**. Quality ranges from poor and anonymous, to excellent. Often among the best are those described as Valpolicella **Classico**, indicating that they come from the original, 'classic' zone. Producers in the Pantena valley can add the name Valpantena on their labels. Single-vineyard wines are also usually above average.

Ripasso Valpolicella, which is re-fermented on the **lees** of **Amarone**, is also nearly always better, richer and longer-lasting. See also **Recioto della Valpolicella**.

Valréas See **Côtes du Rhône**.

Valtellina Red **DOC** wine produced in northern **Lombardy**, **Italy**. The sturdy reds are based on the **Nebbiolo** grape. The best wines often carry the Valtellina Superiore DOC, which is further subdivided into four zones: Grumello, Inferno, Sassella, and Valgella.

Even fuller-bodied wines are made by using partly dried grapes, known as *Sfursat* (or *Sforzato*). Nebbiolo grapes are dried before **fermentation**, when the naturally concentrated juice gives a minimum of 14.5% **alcohol**.

vanilla Tasting term used to describe a vanilla-like **aroma**, usually derived from **oak ageing**.

varietal Wine made entirely (or almost entirely) from a single grape variety.

vat General term used to describe a vessel in which wine is stored, or undergoes **fermentation**. They may be made of cement (sometimes resin-lined), wood, fibreglass, mild steel, or stainless steel (generally considered the best).

Vaucoupin (also called Vaucoupain) **Premier cru** vineyard in **Chablis**.

Vaud See **Switzerland**.

Vaudésir One of the seven **grand cru** vineyards of **Chablis**.

Vaudevey Premier cru vineyard of **Chablis**.

VDQS (vin délimité de qualité supérieure) Part of the French system guaranteeing the origin of a wine from a demarcated area. Wines are placed into three main categories, of which VDQS is the middle category just below **AC**. In general, the laws of VDQS will lay down the following: the area entitled to the name; permitted grape varieties; density of vine plants; minimum **alcohol** levels; and yields. Regions are granted VDQS status with the expectation that they will later be promoted to AC if they play their cards right.

vegetal Tasting term, used to describe a vegetable-like **aroma**, sometimes slightly rotting.

Veldenz Small village in the **Mosel-Saar-Ruwer** region of **Germany**. It produces good-quality white wines from the **Riesling** grape. The vineyards come within the **Grosslage** of Kurfürstlay, and the **Einzellage** sites are Elisenberg, Kirchberg, Mühlberg, Grafschafter, Sonnenberg, and Carlsberg.

Velletri DOC wine produced in the **Latium** region of central **Italy**. It makes mainly dry, fresh whites from the **Malvasia** and **Trebbiano** grapes. Warm, fleshy, dry red wines are produced from **Sangiovese**, **Montepulciano** and **Cesanese**.

Veltliner See **Grüner Veltliner**.

velvety Tasting term used to describe a textured, rich sensation of opulence.

vendange French for harvest.

vendange tardive French term used to indicate late-harvest wines, particularly in **Alsace**. Delaying the harvest allows the grapes to become very ripe, with high grape sugar levels. This usually results in sweet, concentrated wines, or completely dry wines high in **alcohol**.

vendemmia Italian for harvest.

vendimia Spanish for harvest.

Veneto Important wine-producing region centred on Venice and Verona in northeast **Italy**. It is most famous for **Soave**, and the similar softly fruity whites **Bianco di Custoza** and **Gambellara**, as well as for **Valpolicella**, **Amarone**, and **Bardolino**, and for the fresh sparkler **Prosecco di Conegliano-Valdobbiadene**. See also **Breganze; Colli Euganei; Lison-Pramaggiore; Montello e Colli Asolani; Piave**.

véraison French term used to describe the change of colour which occurs during the maturation of the grape on the vine, when red-wine grapes change from green to reddish-black.

Verdejo Good quality white grape variety grown in **Rueda**, **Spain**.

Verdelho Grape variety, grown on the island of **Madeira**, where it gives its name to a category of wine. Nutty, and only slightly sweet, Verdelho is the second driest style of Madeira, between **Sercial** and **Bual**. The

variety is also used in making white **Dão** and white
Port. In **Australia** Verdelho is used to make dry,
characterful **table wine**.

Verdicchio White grape variety grown mainly in the
Marches region of **Italy**. It produces **DOC** wines in
Verdicchio dei Castelli di Jesi, fresh, crisp, high-acid,
good-value whites, and the similar, but much rarer,
Verdicchio di Matelica.

Verduzzo Friulano White grape variety native to the
Friuli-Venezia Giulia region of **Italy**. There are two
different types: *verde*, which produces dry, citrus-
flavoured wines (e.g. **Aquileia**, **Latisana**, **Isonzo** and
Grave del Friuli); and *giallo*, or Verduzzo di
Ramandolo, which makes sweet, golden-coloured
dessert wines in **Colli Orientali del Friuli**. Verduzzo
Trevisano, used in the **Veneto** and **Piave**, is not related.

Vermentino White grape variety grown in the south of
France, **Corsica**, and in **Italy**, in **Liguria** and **Sardinia**,
where it makes the **DOC** wines in Vermentino di
Sardegna and Vermentino di Gallura.

Vernaccia di Oristano White **DOC** wine produced
in **Sardinia** from the grape of the same name. The wine
is similar in style to **Sherry** and is usually dry and rather
bitter, although sweeter, fortified versions also exist.

Vernaccia di San Gimignano Dry white **DOCG**
wine produced in **Tuscany**, **Italy**, from the grape of the
same name. The best examples are dry, full-flavoured
and nutty whites.

Vernaccia di Serrapetrona Red, sparkling **DOC** wine produced in the **Marches** region of **Italy**, from the red version of the Vernaccia grape. The wine is usually sweet and softly fruity, but dry versions can also be found.

Vernatsch See **Schiava**.

Vespaiola White grape variety grown in the **Veneto** reigon of **Italy**. See **Torcolato**.

Victoria One of the leading wine states of **Australia**. It produces a wide range of styles: sparkling wines from the **Great Western** region and **Drumborg**; **Sémillon** and **Shiraz** from the **Murray River** Valley; excellent red and white **varietals**, particularly **Pinot Noir** and **Chardonnay**, from the relatively cool-climate **Yarra Valley**, **Mornington Peninsula**, **Geelong**, South Gippsland, and Macedon; excellent **Shiraz** from the Pyrenees and Bendigo in central **Victoria**; and luscious liqueur wines from **Rutherglen** and Milawa.

vieilles vignes French term sometimes found on labels, which indicates that the wine was produced from grapes grown on old, well-established vines.

vigneron French for vine-grower.

vignoble French for vineyard.

Vila Nova de Gaia See **Port**.

vin French for wine.

Vin de Corse AC wine of the French island of
Corsica. Most of the wine produced is red, from a
variety of grapes including **Nielluccio**, **Sciacarello**, and
Grenache. The small amount of white wine produced
is made mainly from **Vermentino**. The names of better
areas – Calvi, Coteaux du Cap Corse, Figari,
Patrimonio, Porto Vecchio, and Sartène – can be
appended to the Vin de Corse AC. See also **Ajaccio**.

vin de garde French term used to indicate a wine
considered capable of improving with **ageing**.

vin de pays Part of the French system guaranteeing
origin from a demarcated area. Wines are placed into
one of three categories, of which *vin de pays* is the
lowest (below **VDQS**). In general the laws of a *vin de
pays* region are more flexible than for **AC** and VDQS.

The main regional categories are: Vin de pays d'Oc
from the Languedoc (blended reds and whites, plus a
wide range of **varietals**); Vin de pays du Jardin de la
France from the **Loire**; Vin de pays du Comté Tolosan
(covering much of south west France); and Vin de pays
des Comtés Rhodaniens (covering the Ardèche,
Beaujolais, **Jura**, Savoie, and the northern **Rhône**).

There are also about 40 departmental categories (such
as Vin de pays de l'Hérault, Vin de pays de l'Aude)
specific to particular French *départements*. Then there
are about 100 local *vin de pays* categories, some of
them rarely used in practice.

The great success of *vin de pays*, particularly d'Oc, has
been in producing and marketing varietal wines (e.g.
Chardonnay, **Sauvignon Blanc**, **Cabernet Sauvignon**,

Merlot, Syrah, Marsanne, Roussanne, Viognier),
providing consumers brought up on New World wines
with an easily recognisable point of reference.

Vin de Savoie General **AC** for wine of the Savoie
region of **France**. Most of the best wine is made from
the **Altesse** grape, producing dry, full-bodied, spicy,
aromatic whites. **Jacquère** is widely planted, producing
dry, biting white wine, which is best used as a base for
sparklers. Dense, deep-coloured, **austere** reds are made
from Mondeuse, plus some **Gamay** and **Pinot Noir**.
Certain **crus** can add their village names to 'Vin de
Savoie', notably **Apremont**, Arbin, Chignin, Cruet,
Jongieux, Marignan, Montmélian, and Ripaille. See also
Crépy; **Seyssel**.

vin de table Lowest category of French wine, with no
indication of regional origin. It comes below the
QWSPR (quality wine) designations **vin de pays**,
VDQS and **AC**.

Vin Délimité de Qualité Supérieure See VDQS.

vin doux naturel French term for a sweet wine,
produced by adding **alcohol** (in the form of grape
spirit) to partially fermented **must**. See **Beaumes-de-
Venise**; **fortified wine**; **Maury**; **Muscat de Beaumes-de-
Venise**; **Muscat de Frontignan**; **Muscat de Lunel**;
Muscat de Mireval; **Muscat de Rivesaltes**; **Muscat de
Saint-Jean-de-Minervois**; **Rasteau**.

vin gris French term for a very pale pink-coloured
wine.

vin jaune Highly distinctive white wine produced in
the **Jura** region from the **Savagnin** grape. Its distinctive
dry, assertive, nutty flavour derives from long barrel
ageing under a layer of **yeast** cells, similar to **flor** in **fino
Sherry**. It is produced in the ACs of **Arbois**, **L'Etoile**,
Château-Chalon and **Côtes du Jura**.

vin mousseux French term for sparkling wine.

Vin Santo Style of wine produced in **Italy**, particularly
in the **Tuscany** region where it is made from the
Malvasia and **Trebbiano** grapes. The grapes are semi-
dried before pressing, and the must is then placed in
small, sealed barrels for **fermentation** and maturation.
The wine remains in barrel, often stored in a roof
space, for at least three years. The result is a golden,
concentrated, **aromatic** wine, ranging from very sweet
to quite dry. Quality is highly variable. *Vin Santo* is also
made in **Gambellara** (**Veneto**) and the **Marches**. In
Trentino it is called Vino Santo.

viña Spanish for vineyard.

vinho Portuguese for wine.

Vinho Verde DOC wine of northern **Portugal**. Most
of the wine produced is a harsh, **austere** red, but in
export markets the white is much better known, made
from several grapes including **Alvarinho** and **Loureiro**.
At its best this is a crisp, high-acid, bone-dry, refreshing
wine; although too often it is off-dry and flat. It is best
drunk as young as possible. (Vinho Verde, 'green wine',
is so called because it is generally sold young.)

vinification Making of wine. Usually the term is used loosely, to cover every stage of winemaking from receiving fruit at the winery through to **fermentation** and beyond.

vino Spanish and Italian for wine.

vino da tavola Italian term for **table wine**. In theory it is the lowest quality designation, below the **QWPSR** (quality wine) designations **DOC** and **DOCG**. The high-quality (often highly priced) **table wines** of **Tuscany** (see **Super Tuscan**), once classified as *vino da tavola* to avoid restrictive DOC/G regulations, particularly in relation to permitted grape varieties, are slowly being reclassified as **IGT** or DOC / DOCG.

vino de color Spanish term for the colouring agent used to make brown **Sherry** and **Málaga**. It is made by re-fermenting a mixture of **arrope** and grape juice.

vino de la tierra Spanish quality term, roughly equivalent to French **vin de pays**.

vino de mesa Spanish for **table wine**.

Vino Nobile di Montepulciano Red **DOCG** wine produced in the **Tuscany** region of **Italy**. It is made mainly from the **Prugnolo Gentile** grape (a **clone** of **Sangiovese**), plus some **Canaiolo**. The wine has similar characteristics to **Chianti**, although until recently quality has lagged behind the best examples of Chianti **Classico**. This is beginning to change now, as Vino Nobile producers are improving all the time, and a

V

distinctive style is emerging, more spicy and full-flavoured. See also **Rosso di Montepulciano**.

Vinsobres See **Côtes du Rhône**.

vintage In general, the year in which the grapes used to make a wine were harvested. In most wine-producing regions, climatic conditions can vary considerably from one year to the next, leading to good and bad vintages. However, with modern winemaking techniques, good producers should be able to make acceptable wines every year in most regions. Vintage has a special significance in **Champagne** and **Port**.

Vintage Character See **Port**.

Vintage Port See **Port**.

Viognier White grape variety grown in the northern **Rhône**, where it is used to make the white wines **Condrieu** and **Château-Grillet**, and sometimes (as a minor ingredient) the red wine **Côte Rôtie**. Also grown successfully in the Languedoc and to a limited extent in **Australia**.

Visan See **Côtes du Rhône**.

viscous Tasting term, used to indicate a heavy, dense wine, often with persistent **legs**.

viticulture Cultivation of vines.

Vitis vinifera Species of vine from which most wine is made. In most regions, however, the *vinifera* vine is grafted on to rootstock of vitis species native to America, such as *Vitis labrusca*, because of their resistance to **phylloxera**.

Viura See **Macabeo**.

volatile acidity (VA) Winemaker's term for the class of chemical substances, principally **acetic acid**, formed in wine by the **oxidation** of **alcohol** and ethyl acetate. VA is present in all wines in trace quantities, but in excess it is a fault, giving the wine an unpleasant acetic taste.

Volnay Red **AC** wine of the **Côte de Beaune** area of **Burgundy**, made from the **Pinot Noir** grape. Most of the wines are quite light in weight, but are intensely perfumed with enticing red fruit **aromas**. The **premier cru** wines generally have more weight, and need more time in bottle to develop their fleshy, complex, violet-scented character.

Vosgros **Premier cru** vineyard of **Chablis**.

Vosne-Romanée Red **AC** wine of the **Côte de Nuits** area of **Burgundy**, made from the **Pinot Noir** grape. The straight AC wine is usually of good quality, perfumed and elegant, and the **premiers crus** can match the quality of some other Burgundy **grands crus**. The *grands crus* of Vosne-Romanée are among the greatest red wines in the world. The very best are **La Tâche**, **Romanée-Conti** and **Richebourg**, followed by La **Romanée** and **Romanée-Saint-Vivant**. The *grands crus* **Echézeaux** and **Grands-Echézeaux** are generally

considered as part of Vosne-Romanée, although
technically they are attached to **Flagey-Echézeaux**.

Vougeot AC wine of the **Côte de Nuits** area of
Burgundy. Most of the wine produced is red, from the
Pinot Noir grape, and at its best is plummy, rich and
quite good value. A small amount of reasonable white
is produced from **Chardonnay**.

The village of Vougeot is most famous for its **grand cru**
red wine, Clos du Vougeot.

Vouvray White **AC** wine of the **Touraine** area of the
Loire. The wines are produced in similar styles to
Montlouis : dry, **demi-sec**, **moelleux** and sparkling
wines, all based on the **Chenin Blanc** grape. The dry
wines are usually quite **austere** and high in acid,
particularly in their youth. *Demi-sec* is the most
consistently successful style, and the Chenin Blanc
grape can develop great complexity with **bottle age**,
with the **aroma** and taste of quince, apples, nuts and
honey. The sweetest, *moelleux* wines are made only in
very good years. The sparkling wines, usually dry and
made by the **méthode traditionnelle**, can be very good
value for money.

VQPRD (vin de qualité produit dans une région
déterminée) French term for **QWPSR**.

W

Wachenheim Important wine-producing village of the **Pfalz** region of **Germany**, producing fine, full-bodied white wines, from the **Riesling** and other grape varieties. The vineyards come within the **Grosslagen** of Mariengarten, Schenkenböhl and Schnepfenflug, and the best **Einzellage** sites include Goldbächel and Gerümpel.

Washington State Wine-producing state of the Pacific northwest of the **United States**. Washington enjoys a warmer climate than its neighbour **Oregon**, producing good-quality **varietal** wines, particularly whites from the **Chardonnay**, **Sémillon** and **Riesling** (unfashionable, but often excellent) grape varieties, and reds from **Cabernet Sauvignon** and **Merlot**. See also **Yakima Valley**.

Wein German for wine.

Weingut German term for a wine-producing estate. If the word *weingut* appears on the label, it implies estate bottling.

Weissburgunder (also called Weisser Burgunder) German name for the **Pinot Blanc** grape variety.

Weissherbst The German term for a pale pink wine, usually – and most successfully – produced from the **Spätburgunder** grape variety.

Welschriesling White grape variety, producing medium-quality wine, not to be confused with the 'true' **Riesling**, (or **Rhine Riesling**). It is grown in **Slovenia** as **Laski Rizling** (or Laskiriesling), in the **Burgenland** region of **Austria** as Welschriesling, in **Hungary** as **Olasz Rizling**, and in northern **Italy** as the **Riesling Italico** (especially in the **Friuli-Venezia Giulia**, **Veneto**, **Oltrepò Pavese**, **Trentino** and **Alto Adige** regions).

Western Australia Important wine-producing state of **Australia**, including the **Margaret River** and Great Southern areas. It produces good-quality **varietal** wines made from the **Cabernet Sauvignon**, **Shiraz**, **Chardonnay** and **Sauvignon Blanc** grape varieties. Margaret River, with its temperate climate, produces high-class Cabernet Sauvignon, and successful **Sémillon**, Chardonnay and **Pinot Noir**. The hot-climate **Swan Valley** produces mainly big white wines, from **Chenin Blanc** and **Verdelho**, and some reds from Shiraz and Cabernet Sauvignon.

White Zinfandel White or, more commonly, off-white (**blush**) wine made from the red **Zinfandel** grape variety.

wine Fermented juice of the grape.

Winkel Small but important wine-producing village of the **Rheingau** region of **Germany**. It produces very good quality, powerful, long-lived white wines from the **Riesling** grape variety. The vineyards come under the **Grosslagen** of Hönigberg and Erntebringer, and the best **Einzellage** sites include Hasensprung, Gutenberg, Jesuitengarten and Schlossberg.

Winzergenossenschaft German term for a wine-producing **co-operative**.

Wonnegau Southernmost of the three **Bereich** subregions of the **Rheinhessen** region, or **Anbaugebiet**, of **Germany**, producing sound, everyday white wine.

wood Tasting term, sometimes used as an alternative to **oak**, to indicate the presence of the flavours that result from **ageing** a wine in wooden barrels.

woody Tasting term used to describe the unpleasant taste of wine that has received excessive **ageing** in old or dirty barrels.

Württemberg One of the 13 **Anbaugebiet** quality wine regions of **Germany**, with vineyards on the banks of the river Neckar and its tributaries. Most of the wine produced is white, from the **Riesling**, **Müller-Thurgau** and **Kerner** grape varieties. Light reds (and **Weissherbst** rosés) are produced from Trollinger, **Spätburgunder**, Limberger and **Portugieser**.

X

Xarel-lo White grape variety of **Spain**, grown throughout Catalonia, particularly in **Penedès**, **Tarragona**, and **Alella**. On its own it produces rather neutral wine, but it contributes body to blends (with **Parellada** and **Macabeo**) in sparkling wines. See **Cava**.

Xérès French name for **Sherry**. The name of the Sherry **DO** is unusual, in that it is trilingual: Jerez-Xérès-Sherry.

Xynomavro Red grape variety of **Greece**, planted particularly in Macedonia in the north, where it produces increasingly good red wine in Naoussa, as well as in Rapsani, Goumenissa, and Amindeo.

Y

Yakima Valley AVA region of **Washington State** in the **United States**. Traditionally **Concord** grapes were grown here, but the valley now produces good-quality **varietal** wines including **Cabernet Sauvignon**, **Merlot**, **Sauvignon Blanc** and **Sémillon**.

Yarra Valley Important wine-producing area within the state of **Victoria** in **Australia**. It enjoys a realtively cool climate and produces excellent red and white **varietal** wines and blends, from grape varieties including **Cabernet Sauvignon**, **Shiraz**, **Merlot**, **Gewürztraminer**, **Riesling**, **Chardonnay**, and perhaps the star of the Yarra, **Pinot Noir**.

yeast Group of bacteria responsible for the enzymes which promote **fermentation** of grape juice, the conversion of grape sugars into **alcohol**, with heat and **carbon dioxide** by-products. Wild yeasts occur naturally on the outside of grape skins, and these will start fermentation soon after the grapes are crushed. Some winemakers prefer to get rid of the natural yeasts using **sulphur dioxide**, and then start the fermentation with cultured yeasts produced in a laboratory. This leads, they believe, to a cleaner fermentation with better expression of **varietal** character.

yeasty Tasting term used to describe the distinctive smell of **yeast**. It is usually indicative of a fault in wine, but yeasty is often confused with 'bready', a desirable characteristic in **Champagne** and some **Chardonnay**-based wines.

Yecla DO wine of **Spain** producing mainly high-**alcohol**, rustic reds from the **Monastrell** and **Garnacha** grape varieties.

yield Measure of how much wine is produced in a vineyard. Low yield is commonly equated with high quality. In Europe **yield** is expressed in volume per unit area (e.g. **hectolitres** per **hectare**) and in the New World in weight per unit area (e.g. tonnes per acre) but these take no acount of differing densities of plantation. A better measure may be weight of grapes per vine.

York Mountain AVA of **San Luis Obispo** county, **California**.

Z

Zell Bereich subregion of the **Mosel-Saar-Ruwer** region of **Germany**, extending from the village of Zell northeast to Koblenz. There is a high proportion of **Riesling** planted, producing good-quality white wines, although lacking the elegance of those from the *Bereich* of **Bernkastel**. Most of the wine is sold under the famous **Grosslage** name of Schwarze Katz (Black Cat), or the *Bereich* name.

Zeltingen-Rachtig Wine-producing village of the **Mosel-Saar-Ruwer** region of **Germany**, producing good, well-balanced white wines, mainly from the **Riesling** grape variety. The vineyards come under the **Grosslage** of Münzlay, and the **Einzellage** sites are Schlossberg and Sonnenuhr (the best two), Deutschherrenberg and Himmelreich.

zestful Tasting term used to describe a fresh, lively wine, with a good balance of crisp fruit and **acidity**.

Zierfändler White grape variety of **Austria**, which along with **Rotgipfler** is used to produce the heady, spicy, rich wine Gumpoldskirchner.

Zinfandel Red grape variety grown almost exclusively in **California** (although it may be related to the **Primitivo** variety of **Italy**), producing a wide variety of styles from 'white' Zinfandel (which is usually, confusingly, pink) to fortified **Port**-like wines. But it is at its best in full-bodied, **tannic** reds, with rich, spicy, concentrated blackberry flavours. It is underrated, and often good value for money.

Zitsa White semi-sparkling or sparkling wine of western **Greece**, produced in high-altitude vineyards around the village of the same name, from the **Debina** grape variety. The wines are light and apple flavoured, of good quality, and getting better as producers install more modern winemaking equipment.

Zweigelt Red grape variety of **Austria**, a **cross** between **Blaufränkisch** and St Laurent.